The Road to Love

The Road to Love

OUR FAMILY'S STORY
1818–1999

Jim McDougall

The Road to Love: Our Family's Story 1818–1999
© 2021 Jim McDougall

ISBN 978-0-578-93714-4 (hardcover)

Book Design by Paul Nylander | Illustrada Design

Front cover: Shown is the author along the Road to Love (C-12). He is standing at the southeast corner of the McFarland farm. Across C-12 (to the south) is the old Nicholson farmstead, with the Moran farm directly east of the Nicholson's. Just beyond the trees (visible north of C-12) is James McDougall's farmstead. *Back cover*: These are the author's grandfathers' farms. The upper picture is James Nelson McDougall with his family in front of their farmhouse. The lower picture is the original house and barn on the William Nicholson property.

Printed in the United States of America

Published by Jim McDougall

This is a work of nonfiction. All names and quotes are accurate to the best of the author's knowledge.

This book is dedicated to:

My forefathers, who are the foundation of this story.

My brothers and sisters and cousins, both here and gone, who are the heart of this story.

My six children and their cousins, who are the continuation of this story.

Contents

Acknowledgements..................................1
To My Family 3

The McDougalls Arrive 9
The Warrens Arrive..............................41
The Morans Arrive 47
The Nicholsons Arrive 65
Why Struble? 107
The McDougalls and the Nicholsons..............119
    James Nelson McDougall and Martha Ann Warren 120
    William Nicholson and Mollie Moran 129
    Chester Nelson McDougall and Edith Rose Nicholson...162
    The Influence of our parents.................. 223
    Cattle.. 242
A Peek at Our Families in the World Today 253
    Kyle and Andrew Swanson 256
    Jack and Jim Nicholson 265
In Closing 281

Appendices
    A visit to the Road to Love 285
    The Timeline 289
    Obituaries.................................... 301
    Attachments................................... 329
Bibliography...................................373

Jackie (McDougall) Seemann and Jim McDougall.

To My Family

In this book you will find a large color photo that includes many of the people that define the McDougall/Nicholson family. I'll bet you can find yourself in there somewhere. I have this same photo hanging on the wall in my hallway, and I often walk past it and look at those smiling faces. As I study those faces, I can't help wondering how many of them know about the brave souls that came before them, the ones that were so instrumental in bringing them not only into this world, but to the greatest place you could possibly live, America.

 I wonder if they are aware that one of their forefathers ran away from home at age 13 and crossed the Atlantic ocean alone to make a new life in North America. I wonder if they know that at age 44, he and his 20-year-old son, signed up to fight for the Union in the Civil War, motivated by the promise of a homestead in northwest Iowa. That after he was granted homesteading rights on C-12 near Struble, his family made the trip in a covered wagon, and were among the very first settlers there.

I wonder if they know that another one of their forefathers lived in a part of England where "the fog was so thick you couldn't see your hand in front of your face." That he lost 3 of his 12 children to the ravages of tuberculosis, rampant in England at that time. That a man named Arthur Gee, living in northwest Iowa, requested a flock of Suffolk sheep be transported to him, giving our forefather the opportunity to get his family out of that country and over to America, where the rest of his children would have a chance of survival.

I wonder if they are aware that their Irish forefathers were Catholic and living under an oppressive government. That the potato famine struck, giving them the choice between starving or leaving Ireland. That they made a rough journey across the ocean to America, and eventually to a farm in northwest Iowa, where they still had challenges, but they had the freedom of ownership and the ability to make a comfortable living.

And lastly, I wonder if they appreciate how very different the circumstances were that brought the final immigrant here, the son of a wealthy Scot, seeking investments. The boy's father had been a successful shipbuilder, speculator and railroad businessman in Scotland. He was looking for land to invest some of the money he had made. He found that good land in northwest Iowa, some of it on C-12 near Struble. Although he, himself, chose not to immigrate here, he saw great potential in America and sent four of his five sons (one being our grandfather) from Scotland to this new land, all set up for success.

To My Family

They all settled on the same road, very near each other, and the children of these brave individuals, met, married and created a life together. It was at this point that C-12 became the Road to Love. Because that road led to all of you.

Four families were drawn to the same area, at the same time in history, and created a path that brought each of you into the family. Following is the story of the steps along that path. A venture through the foundations of the McDougall and Nicholson families.

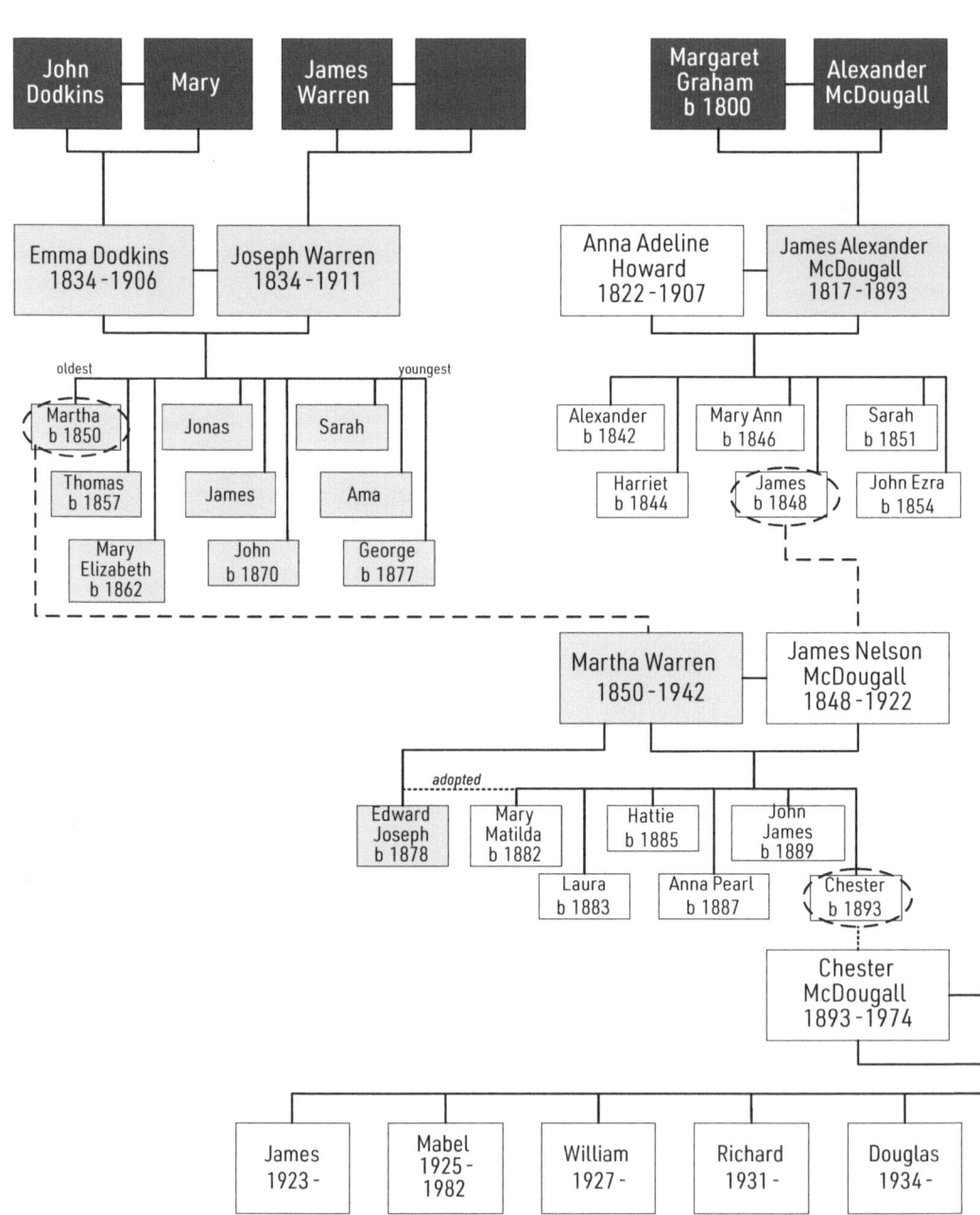

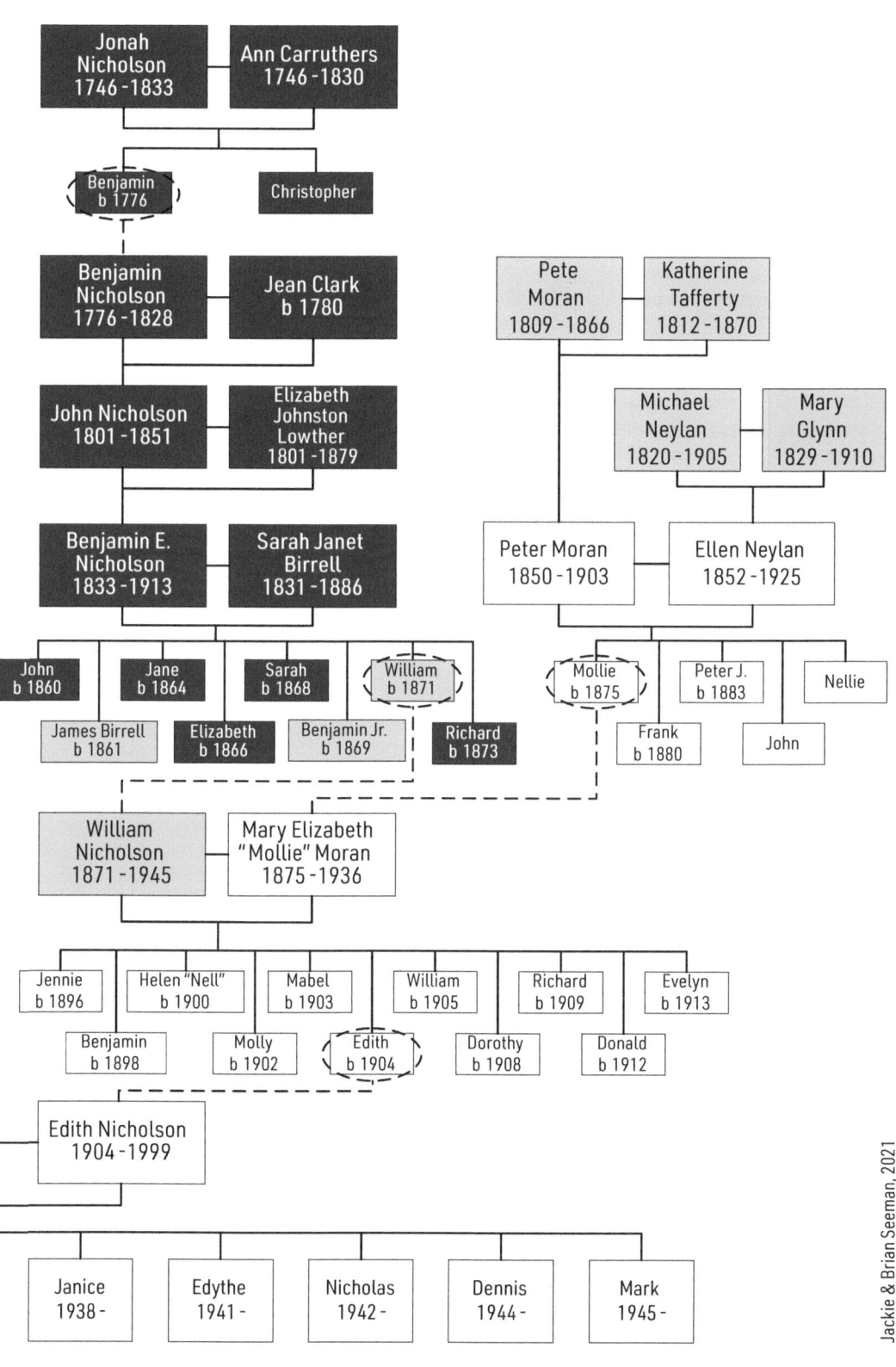

The McDougalls Arrive

Alexander and Margaret (Graham or Gram)
McDougall (paternal great-great grandparents)
James Alexander and Anna Adeline (Howard)
McDougall (paternal great grandparents)
James Nelson McDougall (paternal grandfather)
Chester Nelson McDougall (father)

The beginning of our story takes us back to 1818, the year James Alexander was born to Alexander and Margaret (Graham or Gram) McDougall. The couple was living in the small quiet village of Bowmore, in the county of Argylshire, in Scotland. Bowmore sits in the crook of the Isle of Islay, in the straights between Ireland and Scotland. To the west of Islay (also known as the Queen of the Hebrides) ran an underground river of warm water from the gulf stream, which kept the temperature mostly pleasant. The skies were often sunny, and the land was fertile. The town had been thoughtfully developed into a neatly organized grid pattern, with small fields between the rows of houses. Families had space to grow their own food and keep a milking cow. Most of the yards were home to a couple of chickens or ducks. The town was centered around a unique church, which had been built in 1760, by a gentleman named Daniel of Campbell. At that time, he owned the entire island and wanted a circular church, so there would be "no corners for the devil to hide." There were opportunities for work: farming, fishing, industry, and a distillery that had come into operation as recently as 1816. This town was a beautiful place to live and with a bit of hard work, one could survive quite comfortably.

In this little village, Alexander and Margaret McDougall were running an inn, and caring for their son, James. They loved him, educated him in the public schools and raised him to be a strong confident young man. James loved animals and started asking for a little Billy goat. Because his parents encouraged him to explore his interests, they eventually agreed that he could keep one.

James was often at his father's inn with his goat and some of the guests took an interest in the pair. They helped James teach his pet tricks, a favorite being to run at and butt anything James pointed at.

Now, Margaret was a rather frail lady. Tragically, when James was only twelve, she passed away. It wasn't long before his father remarried. Unfortunately, his new stepmother was very mean to James. She made it clear she would rather not have him around.

One morning, in the early spring of 1831, when James was about 13 years old, he was out in the yard with his goat. His stepmother was hanging clothes on the line. At one point,

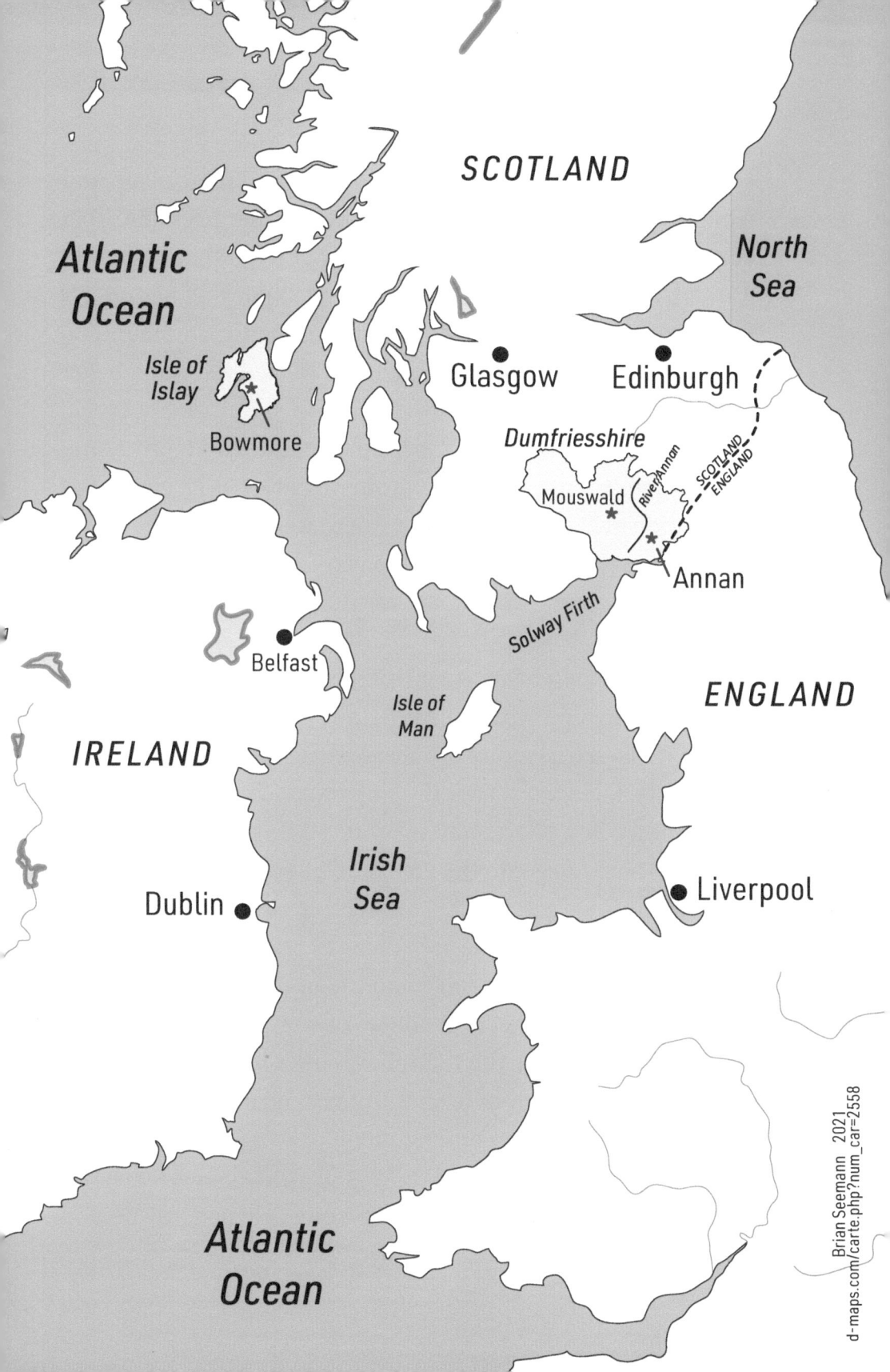

she bent over to get some shirts from the laundry basket, and James, with his eyes on his goat, pointed to her backside. That goat was well trained by now and knew exactly what his owner wanted. He ran at the woman, butted her, knocking her off her feet. James watched with satisfaction, and in that moment, he made the decision to leave. He turned, walked away and never looked back.

James had made up his mind, he would never return home. He was going to get as far away from Bowmore as he could. But James didn't have many options. There were no cars, buses, or trains at that time. There were two ways out of town: by foot or by boat. So, James, without a penny to his name, walked down to the pier.

James had been hearing whisperings about North America and the many opportunities it held for immigrants; but this required a long trip across the ocean. If he should decide to take the trip, he knew no seaworthy ships were able to ferry in and out of the shallow shores of Bowmore. His first challenge would be to find a way to get to the mainland of Scotland, then maybe he could find a way to catch a sailing ship to North America.

Having grown up in the area, James knew of a ferry that regularly transported children to and from the city of Glasgow, Scotland so they could clean houses or work on larger farms to earn extra money for their families. James looked around the dock, located a group of boys waiting to board that ferry, and slipped inconspicuously among them.

It wasn't a long ride to Glasgow, but when James debarked, he felt very alone and very far from home. He had nowhere to go and no money in his pocket. He knew if he was going to survive, he had better make a plan.

Bigger ships were setting sail from the mainland of Scotland to cross the ocean, but James didn't have money for a ticket. He had heard of orphans and runaways working as cabin boys on the big sailing ships crossing the seas and thought that might be a good job for him. It would provide him with a place to sleep, meals to eat, and above all, get him over to North America.

It didn't take long for James to find a ship that would accept him as a cabin boy. The ship happened to be sailing to Nova Scotia, Canada, which James saw as a stroke of luck. He had heard of many people emigrating from Scotland to Canada, referring to it as "the new world." People were headed there to start a new life, which is exactly what James wanted to do. He had faith that Canada might hold some promise for him as well.

The trip across the Atlantic was an exciting but very frightening experience for anyone, much less a 13-year-old, who was on his own. A cabin boy's job was to help the cooks in the galley make meals, (typically oatmeal, biscuits and tea), carry the food to the dozen or so rented cabins, as well as to the officers in their quarters, carry messages back and forth between officers and the crew, stow sails, and occasionally, stand watch at the helm.

James tried to stay busy because when he wasn't working, he was expected to be in his small wooden bunk below deck in the steerage, and the steerage was a miserable place to be. Among the boxes of freight, there were over 200 passengers crowded together. It was extremely uncomfortable: dark, cramped, stuffy, and infested with bugs and rats. There was very little sanitation or water and it smelled terribly. It was a very rough and arduous journey. The 3,000-mile trip took almost two months, and once on land, James was sure he didn't want to do it again. He got off the ship and was happy to take his chances in Canada.

Once again, now in a new world, James was alone and wandering around, trying to come up with a plan. As luck would have it, he became acquainted with a carpenter, who offered him an apprenticeship. Recognizing this as an opportunity to learn a useful skill, James accepted and gladly gained some experience building houses. Although he found he could support himself, he knew himself well enough to know this wasn't his permanent trade. He had a longing to farm, and he had set his young mind on acquiring farmland. This became his primary focus. He was well aware that he would have to work hard and save his money, if he was ever going to see this dream come true. Throughout his time in Canada, James remained on the lookout for any opportunity that would bring him closer to his goal.

Eventually, stories of the railroad expansion across the United States began to catch James' ear. Several years earlier, in 1830, the steam locomotive had made its debut in America, and this young country was racing to connect cities by railroad. James was hearing of untold opportunities for work, and he saw this as a chance to make some good money, save up and get the land he wanted so badly.

In 1837, right after his 19th birthday, James decided to immigrate to the United States. Most of those looking for work on the railroad were making their way to Cincinnati, Ohio; St. Louis, Missouri; or Milwaukee, Wisconsin. James decided to take the route to Cincinnati. Unfortunately, once he got there, the only job he could find was killing hogs in a packing house. He found he didn't have the taste for that, so in the same year, he set out for St. Louis. This was a good move for James, because he found a job working on the railroad and after a time, he met the love of his life, Anna Adeline Howard. She had been born in New York on August 25, 1822.

On June 8, 1840, in La Salle County, Illinois, James married 18-year-old Adeline Howard. James was 22. It was a happy union which ultimately produced six children.

After their marriage, James spent a couple more years working hard on the railroad. He made about $1.25 in cash each day. He saved as much as he could and before long, he had enough money to buy the 80 acres of good arable soil he had found over in Troy Grove, Illinois. Land was going for $9/acre, so he paid $720 for the farm.

When he finally moved onto his own land, he felt his dream was coming true. He was farming. He planted his crops and proudly observed the growing power of the rich black soil.

During their time on this farm, James Alexander and Annie had three children, Willis Alexander (who went by Alexander) was born May 18, 1842, Harriet Matilda was born February 29, 1844, and Mary Ann was born January 24, 1846. As proud as James was with his success at farming, as his family grew, he became increasingly determined to obtain more land and he kept his eye out for bigger and better farms.

Now, James Alexander had a friend from his railroad days who was whispering in his ear about a 160-acre parcel of land that

James Alexander and Adeline Howard McDougall.

was located halfway between Highland and Mineral Point, in Iowa County, Wisconsin. Although it was a bigger piece of land, his friend said he would be willing to trade it for James' smaller 80-acre farm, and James eventually fell for it. James' naïve belief was that the black productive soil he'd been working was the rule, and a bigger farm meant a better farm. He also liked that it was near the progressive business of lead mining at Mineral Point, because he saw that as an opportunity for him and his sons to get some extra work and supplement their income. He finally decided to trade his smaller farm for the bigger acreage in Highland, Wisconsin.

What James didn't realize, was that land in this part of Wisconsin was going for about half of what he had paid in Illinois ($5/acre in Iowa County, Wisconsin vs. $9/acre in LaSalle County, Illinois). This new farmland was nowhere near the quality of James' previous farmland and when he started working the soil, James found it was full of rocks and sand and gravel. He learned the hard way, that a bigger farm is not always better, and he continued to struggle to feed his family.

It was about this same time, on November 29, 1847, that James, at 29, signed the affidavit of "Rejection of Allegiance to the Queen of Great Britain and Ireland and Pledge Allegiance to the United States." James was proud to be granted citizenship. He had developed a deep love and loyalty to the United States, and was thankful for the freedom and opportunities this country offered. He appreciated that with hard work and commitment, he had been able to achieve his dream of owning his own farm.

Throughout the next several years, James and Adeline added

three more children to their brood: James Nelson was born October 30, 1848, Sarah was born June 9, 1851 and John Ezra was born January 21, 1854. As happy as they were, the couple now had six mouths to feed.

It was difficult farming this soil and supporting his family, but James was never one to avoid hard work and took a job at the nearby lead mines at Mineral Point to supplement his income. His sons, Alex and James Nelson, followed suit and made extra money as well. The family continued struggling this way for many years.

Then, when James A was 44, the Civil War broke out. One fateful summer afternoon he received a visit from an army recruiter looking for volunteers to fight for the Union Army. The recruiter asked to talk to both James A and his son Alex, who by now was of military age. The two agreed to talk to him, but they made it clear they wanted no part in fighting a war.

This recruiter, as recruiters go, was probably a leading organizer, and was aware of this family's patriotism and lust for land. He took his time talking with the two men. As they chatted, he could see James and his son were not fools and they both had the ability to recognize a good opportunity when they saw one. The recruiter explained the recent signing of the Congressional Homestead Act of 1862, where citizens of all walks of life, including former slaves, women and immigrants, could become landowners of 80 to 160 acres, if they lived on and improved the land for five years. But the recruiter was also careful to emphasize the additional incentives for Union soldiers: priority in their request for homesteading, access of up to 160 acres (vs 80 acres) of prime northwest Iowa farmland, and up to four years shaved off the five-year occupancy requirement.

All this really peaked James and Alex's interest because, of course, James and Alex were always on the lookout for good land and James thought this sounded like an excellent price. As the little group continued discussing the opportunity, James and his son began warming up to the idea of enlisting. So much so, that as the recruiter ended his visit, and walked down the lane and away from that farm, he had two new recruits to his credit. James and Alex together, enlisted on August 21, 1862, for a three-year term in the Union Army.

James' enlistment papers read:[1]

> *Volunteer Enlistment, State of Wisconsin; Town of Highland, Iowa County—James McDougall born in Scotland aged 44 years and by occupation a carpenter does hereby acknowledge to have volunteered this 21st day of August 1862, to serve as a soldier in the Army of the United States of America for a period of three years, unless sooner discharged by proper authority. I do also agree to accept such bounty, pay, rations, and clothing, as are, or may be established by law for Volunteers. And I, James McDougall do solemnly swear, that I will bear true faith and allegiance to the United States of America, and that I will serve them honestly and faithfully against all their enemies or opposers whomsoever; and that I will*

1—From a paper written by Janice Albert for the NW Iowa Genealogy Fair, August 2011.

> *serve and obey the President of the United States, and the orders of the officers appointed over me, according to the Rules and Articles of War. James McDougall, Sworn and Subscribed to Highland this 21st day of August 1862 Before H.G. Fickmann, Justice of the Peace.*

On October 25, 1862, just two short months after signing up, 44-year-old James, five feet 10 and ¾ inches, with gray hair and blue eyes, along with his 20-year-old son, Alexander, officially mustered into the Federal Army Infantry, Company G, 27th Infantry Regiment of the Wisconsin Volunteers under Commander Colonel Krez. Fortunately, father and son were kept together in the same infantry. They were stationed at Camp Sigel in Milwaukee, Wisconsin.

It wasn't long into their enlistment period, that the pair experienced a critical turning point. On New Year's Day, 1863, a fire broke out in their barracks. We know what happened, because at some point following the incident, James filled out and signed an "Affidavit of Happenings." This is the story in his own words that he signed and submitted:

> *I was home on a furlough and got back to camp on January 1st, 1863 to my comrades. John Downy was on guard that night in Milwaukee so I went to bed alone. About 1 or 2 o'clock, not long after, Sargent Dalen came in and said, "Boys get out, camp is on fire." Or something to that effect. I got up. He said, "McDougall help the rest out." I said, "I want my clothes." He said, "I'll take care of your clothes."*

> *I went back in to try to help. I got my right hand burned and my eye. When I looked for my clothes, (Sargent Dalen had) forgot all about them. I tried to get some clothes, no one had any. It was raining and sleeting, so I had to go to Camp Washburn without cap or coat. I was near frozen when I got to Camp Washburn. I took cold in my head and all over me. I did not do (unreadable word) after that. The doctor said I would never be able to do camp duty again. My ear was very bad, for two years it destroyed my hearing. I am deaf as a post now.*

(Another one of his write-ups, although just a few sentences, stated that as he walked to Camp Washburn, he was barefoot as well.)

James had a difficult time recovering from this event and consequently developed health issues, including "chronic arthritis of the lower back" as a result of his injuries. He was honorably discharged for disability on March 27, 1863.[2]

Alex was also in the fire. He was burned and became sick with a fever and spent three months in the hospital. He furloughed for a time and went home to fully recover. When he was ready to return:

> *He joined up with his regiment at Columbus, Kentucky, where they remained during the siege of Vicksburg and Haines Bluff with heavy fighting on the part of his*

2—Janice Albert

regiment. After the fall of Vicksburg, his regiment was transferred to the seventh Army Corps and then transported by boat to Jenkins Ferry, where a heavy battle was fought, the Union forces suffering a loss of 500 killed and 700 wounded. The members of the corps were then ordered to Little Rock, Arkansas, where they remained for seventeen months. Their next move was to New Orleans where they endured many skirmishes and battles.

The Civil War officially ended on June 2nd, 1865 and finally, on September 1st, 1865, Alex arrived at Madison, Wisconsin and was mustered out of the Army. He went back home to Highland, Wisconsin and returned to farming with his father.

Five years later, in 1870, as promised, both James A and Alex received letters from President Grant informing them that, because of their Civil War service, they were each qualified to homestead 160 acres of land in northwest Iowa.

James and Alex wasted no time making preparations to leave. They claimed their homestead by paying the required filing fees of $10 and received their official patent. Once this process was complete, the family started to plan their move. James was 52 and Alex was 28.

The family had to think of everything they might need to carry them through the beginning phases of establishing a homestead. They had been informed that this part of the state was still a vast wilderness. They did not have the luxury of forgetting something important. I am sure the group made a solid plan of how they were going to approach this immense undertaking.

Monument honoring local Civil War veterans at the Le Mars Memorial Cemetery on 3rd Street SE. James Alexander and Alexander are named on the statue. Photo by Jenna McDougall.

Adeline and her daughters, Harriet Matilda (26), Mary Ann (24), and Sarah (19), immediately got busy scrutinizing every household item. They had to carefully select only what they would need for survival and basic comfort at their new homestead. They packed the necessary dishes and utensils for cooking and eating, the cook stove, medicines, warm clothes and bedding.

Between James and Adeline, there was plenty they couldn't bring along and I envision they had to have a bit of a fire sale. At this time, an auction was the most efficient way of selling extra household items and farming equipment. What didn't sell, James did a good amount of bargaining and bartering with neighbors, which he was pretty good at. A dollar was worth a lot in those days, and he got as much as he could for the things he had to sell. Unfortunately, in the end, the family had to give away some of their more prized, but less useful items.

Meanwhile, James found a buyer for his land and pocketed the cash to fund their trip west. In 1870, land in Iowa County was going for $20 per acre, so he sold his 160-acre farm for $3,200 dollars. In today's dollars, that would be about $63,000. They would have to be very careful with their money.

By the time the family had tied up all the loose ends, packed the wagons with all they could carry, and said their good-byes, it was the middle of September and the worry of cold weather lay ahead. According to a paper written by Janice Albert for the Northwest Iowa Genealogy Fair in August of 2011, there were four travelers in the party: James A, his two sons, Alexander and James Nelson, and his daughter Harriet Matilda, (the paper does not mention Adeline, Mary Ann, Sarah or John Ezra). We aren't sure how and when the others arrived (possibly later by train) but we know they all came at some point because they are mentioned in the Plymouth County Iowa Genealogy and History as settling nearby James Alexander and the family. Harriet was the wife of Stewart Crai, Mary was the wife of Thomas Edwards and lived at Ireton, Iowa and Sarah was the wife of James Andrews and lived in Ogden, Iowa.

The group of travelers is said to have brought two large, covered wagons. I'm sure they were filled to the brim with their firearms, seed corn and seeds, a couple of water barrels, rope, spades, shovels, hammer and nails, wood planks, a sulky plow, pipes, a crude pump for the well, a basic cook stove, some essential household items, lots of warm clothes and bedding, and most likely a milk cow walking behind. James, trained as a carpenter, had a good idea of essential tools they would need when they got to their new land. It is guaranteed those wagons were full, and a full wagon weighed from 1,500 to 2,000 pounds each. There were likely three teams of two horses each, which the men had worked with and trained to haul that heavy load. One team pulled each wagon, allowing the third team to walk behind and rest.

It was mid-September of 1870, when James and his family began their two-wagon journey. They were moving from Highland, Wisconsin, in the southwest part of Wisconsin, to Struble in northwest Iowa. The path the travelers took is not exactly known. We used information about the available river crossings, the topography of Iowa, the roads in existence at the time,

Likely Wagon Path of James A. McDougall

------ Highland, WI to Struble IA, October 1870 ------

Following local roads present in 1870,
many no longer existing

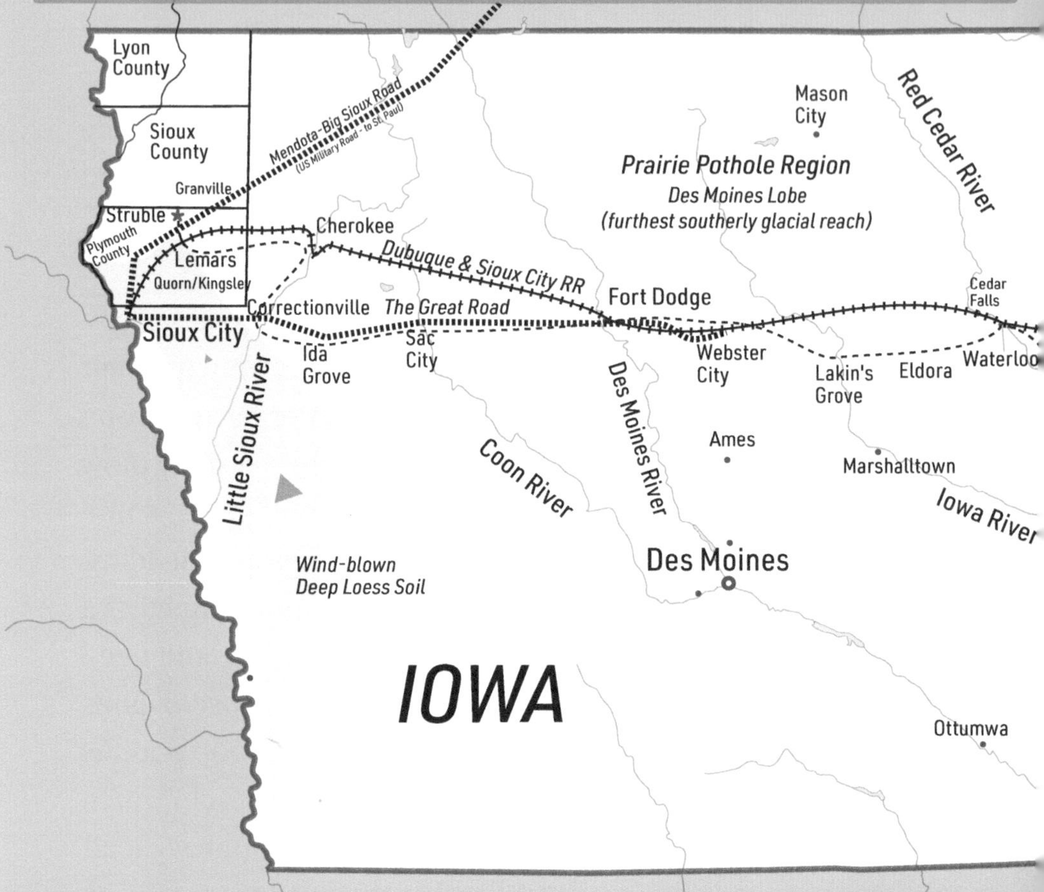

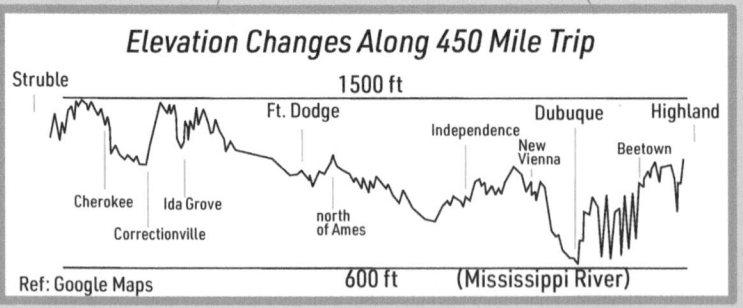

and the progression of the railroad construction, to make some reasonable guesses about their route.

In order to get from Wisconsin to Iowa, the group had to cross the Mighty Mississippi river. To do this safely, they had to take an official ferry. In 1870, there were two available options. They could take a northern route that passed over a road bridge on the Wisconsin River, leading to Prairie du Chien. Once there, they could catch a commercial ferry, taking them across the Mississippi to McGregor, Iowa. After crossing the river, James would have wound through the wooded river bluffs, through Elkader, and onto the Tallgrass Prairie of Iowa. If he had taken this path, he would then travel south to meet the roads along the general path of the recently laid Dubuque & Sioux City Railroad.

But the Prairie du Chien path was somewhat less traveled and relatively rough terrain. More likely, James actually made his way across the Mississippi on the ferry operating in Dubuque. Here, he would have passed through a city much more likely to provide any supplies he needed. And further, it would enable him to travel on paths more directly adjacent to the Dubuque & Sioux City Railroad, which laid from east to west across the middle of Iowa.

In the years from 1836 to 1859, the government land surveys in Iowa began in the southeast corner of the state and proceeded to the northwest corner. This established the one-mile grid system of roads as the land was developed and roads were opened on the section lines. But in 1870, when James made his crossing, many of those section line roads still did not yet exist. So, the

The McDougalls Arrive

existing wagon roads were often paths that meandered across the countryside in somewhat direct routes from town to town. Many of the roads he followed no longer exist today (although they show up on maps from that era). Also, the railroads did not always create adjacent wagon roads, because the railroad was mainly built by bringing in the supplies from behind, on the previously completed rails.

So, James traversed the center of Iowa on roads that generally wandered parallel to the railroad, although often miles away from it. After he got to Webster City (east of Fort Dodge) he would have been able to take what was known as The Great Road toward Sioux City. This was built in 1856 and follows today's US Route 20.

As he got closer to his destination, rather than continuing to Sioux City, James likely turned north at Correctionville, following the Little Sioux River up to Cherokee. Then, continued on an undeveloped wilderness trail to his destination (which was Struble), as it states in his biography in *Genealogy Trails* that "he encountered only a single log cabin between Cherokee and Le Mars."

James was traveling to a part of Iowa that was still a vast wilderness and most of their travel was in isolation, which came with risks and a whole host of worries. They certainly couldn't afford any breakdowns, there would be little hope of help or the needed supplies. There could be heavy rains or an early snowstorm that would mire the wagons into the mud or snow and make survival challenging.

There may even have been the gnawing fear of an Indian attack.

The Road to Love

Their path took them south of the Spirit Lake area, where the tragic Spirit Lake massacre had happened not all that long ago:

On Sunday morning, March 8th, 1857, after a long brutal winter, a Dakota Indian named Chief Inkpaduta, along with eight others, were hungry and on edge. They had been betrayed by the government's "treaty of 1851", guaranteeing them food, and had gotten to the point of desperation. They entered the cabin of Rowland Gardner. The Gardners had fed them the day before, but they returned, demanding more food. When Mr. Gardner, frightened and cooperating, turned to get them flour from the bin, they shot him in the back of the head. He died instantly. Showing no mercy, the men then used pieces of wood and their rifle butts to beat and bludgeon Gardner's wife, son, daughter, and both of his young grandchildren. Gardner's young daughter Abbie (age 13) watched it all in horror and begged them to kill her, too. But they refused and took her and three other women as hostages. All in all, that day the Dakota killed 38 people and took four hostages from that remote little settlement at Spirit Lake.[3]

Following that massacre, Chief Inkpaduta (which means "red end" or "scarlet point") became a legend among settlers, a storybook monster who was often rumored to be somewhere nearby, lurking. And as time went on and relations between the Dakotas and the settlers staggered on, Inkpaduta didn't go away.

3—From *The 1862 Sioux Uprising* by Jeffry D. Wert (www.historynet.com) and *The True Story of the Spirit Lake Massacre* by David L. Bristow.

There had also been a more current uprising a bit further north, in southern Minnesota, on August 17, 1862, again after a brutal winter. This skirmish resulted in the death of 71 Dakota's (Dakota were often referred to as Sioux), 77 soldiers and 800 civilians. Inkpaduta was rumored to be among them. James was aware of these local conflicts and although it had been quiet for many years, the worry still remained.

Despite the risks, James and his travelers lumbered westward. As the miles passed, James began to see some dramatic differences. The eastern areas of Canada and the United States that James was familiar with always had plenty of trees. In fact, the Highland area, where James had been farming, was exceptionally heavily wooded. I'm sure James had taken for granted that there would be plenty of trees wherever he went in this country. But as they moved westward, vast fields of prairie grasses and wildflowers became more and more dominant. Trees became increasingly scarce and as they entered their final days of travel, they found themselves looking over an endless sea of tall prairie grass. There were a few scattered willows and small trees near the streams and lowlands, but other than that, the grasses were so pervasive and never-ending that it became a bit unnerving. The group had to keep an eye on each other and their animals and stay on the rough pathways, because it would be very easy to get lost in the massive prairie. On the other hand, James was also aware that grass had to have rich soil under it in order to grow so full and tall and it gave him promise to what lay ahead.[4]

4—*History of the Counties of Woodbury and Iowa*, A. Warner and Co., Publisher.

Let the reader wander back in thought to 1868 and 1870, when the surface of this section was unbroken by the plowshare; at a period when tall prairie grass, perfumed with dainty wildflowers, made up the landscape scene. Think of the eye of the first settlers peering out over this great sea of grass. The birds which sang were but the wildest, ugliest species, such as love not civilized life. No groves fringed the few scanty water courses and fuel had to be procured from points many miles distant. Indeed, it took hearts, stout and brave to stem that scene, when the wintery winds commenced sweeping down from the cold northwest. It was then that thoughts of old eastern homes thrilled the hearts and not unfrequently bedimmed the eye of a wife and mother.

From the time they crossed the Mississippi river, it is recorded that it took 17 days of travel. It was a 400-mile trip across rough roads and paths. A team pulling a loaded wagon can move about 15–20 miles per day, so they must have worked extremely hard because they made excellent time. It was October 1st, 1870, when the family finally arrived at their homestead on C-12 and were welcomed by some of the richest windblown soil in the country. They would be farming section 2 in Grant township, Plymouth County, Iowa.

The group hardly had time to take in the massive accomplishment of arriving at their new homestead. It was October and they could already feel the days growing colder and shorter. The frigid northwest winter would begin its descent within a few short weeks, and they had to be set up for survival. They were working under a tight timeframe.

I'm sure the lack of access to natural materials was really sinking in. In the east, they would have started cutting trees to build their houses and barns and make stacks of logs for fuel to keep them warm. But here in northwest Iowa, there was hardly a tree to be found. Many settlers in this part of the country built a sod house which would guarantee natural insulation and protection from the winter winds until a more permanent house of wood could be built. In fact, the school that John Ezra would attend was a sod structure.

A sod home was made of sod bricks: big chunks of the top 18" of earth, the twisted roots and dirt still clinging to it.[5]

> *Plowing itself was a new venture on the prairies. So strong and tangled were the tough roots of the grasses and other prairie plants that it took three or four teams of oxen to plow it the first time. They used a huge plowshare with a sharp edge that could cut through the soil and turn over a strip of virgin prairie sod.*

The bricks were cut into two-foot chunks, each weighing over 50 pounds. The bricks were then hauled over to the designated spot and stacked dirt side up, so the roots could settle into the brick above it, creating very strong walls. The chunks had to be stacked before the dirt dried out or they would fall apart and

---
5—The Iowa Experience Iowa, PBS.

not be usable. Building the required 12' x 14' house took about 1,600 bricks.

These houses provided warmth and protection and served to establish the land as theirs. But there were also many drawbacks. They were always damp and dirty, and muddy when it rained. Bugs and snakes would occasionally fall from the walls and ceiling and it was very difficult to keep mice and small rodents out. Getting out of these sod dwellings was obviously a goal of all pioneers because the very last sod house in this area was replaced by wood in 1890, which was the year after the trains to Struble arrived.

Considering the short time frame James and Alex had to build their houses, and the uncertainty of the weather winter would bring, it makes the most sense to me that they would have made a sod house to survive that first winter, and if time allowed, a sod barn to protect their horses. But there are indications that they immediately built a lumber house because James Nelson's obituary states that after arriving here as a pioneer, "His first residence was a cabin twelve by twelve feet in which he lived for some years."

This may well be, because James A had the good fortune of being trained as a carpenter, and equally fortuitous was the very recent completion of the railway that came from Dubuque, Iowa into Le Mars. A nine-mile trek from their properties would bring them to that railway. These trains were bringing lumber in from eastern Iowa.[6] "In 1870 fifty million feet of pine lumber were sold from fifteen Dubuque lumber-yards." In addition, it states that wood from Minnesota and Wisconsin was being shipped down the Mississippi river to Dubuque and put on railcars for delivery to various western towns.

This access to wood and James' capabilities might have allowed the family to complete the two structures before the cold winds and snow arrived. The law required a 12' x 12' house be built on each homestead in order to claim it, so James and Alexander would have to each build a house, on their own property. I'm sure they built them very close together.

As the family was building their shelters, their focus turned to water. At this early point, the family must have been hauling water from the West Branch river which was the closest water

---

6—Palimpsest History of Iowa.

source to their homestead. With winter coming, a continued source of water would become a concern. A well would certainly be a priority. They had to get busy digging.

To locate water underground and find the most efficient place to dig, a water-witch was often used. This required a skill that was passed down within families. If a member of the family didn't know how to use this method, they might have to hire someone to come to their property. This was a very valuable skill in these days, because you didn't want to dig one hundred feet when you only needed to dig twenty. Our dad, Chester, had the ability to work with a water witch and my brother Doug remembers watching him use it.

> DOUG: Dad was walking with this stick and when he went over a shallow spot of water, the stick he was holding started pulling down, you had to see it to believe it. The stick was shaped like a big sling shot. He'd hold the two ends in his hands with the third end sticking straight out in front of him. When he walked over a water source, that stick would pull down. That's the spot we dug the well. We went down about 60 feet and man oh man did we have water. The water came in so fast, it brought up a lot of fine sand with it. When we pumped, we pumped that fine sand so we couldn't use that water in the house, we used it for the livestock. Boy, we had water. And the well is still there, it is still working.
>
> I also saw Dad take two wires about two feet long. They were number nine galvanized wire, the ones we

used to brace fences together. He would point those wires straight out in front of him and then walk along. When he'd come across a pipeline underground, those two wires would just snake across each other. Then we'd know where the pipelines were. If we wanted water someplace and we knew there was a pipeline, we could dig down and hook onto it."

But I know where James dug the well. Right south of the homestead is what we call a draw. A draw is a low swampy spot. A lot of those swampy places are too wet to farm, so they become pastures or a good spot for a garden. There's plenty of water there. They didn't have to dig down very deep, maybe 10 feet and there would be water. So that first well wasn't very deep. It's still there to this day.

Next, they needed a spot for the toilet. They knew this would have to be used during the winter and in cold windy weather. They wanted it dug on the northeast side, so they were protected from the wind. But it also had to be at least 60 feet from the house, and very far away from the water well they had dug. I imagine the well and the outhouse were on the opposite sides of the house.

With the house and well under way, they would then turn their focus to fuel for cooking and heat on those cold days. This would be a difficult task and keeping warm must have been a challenge. They had to find alternatives to the wood they had always depended on in the past. They had to gather sunflower stalks,

James Alexander McDougall.

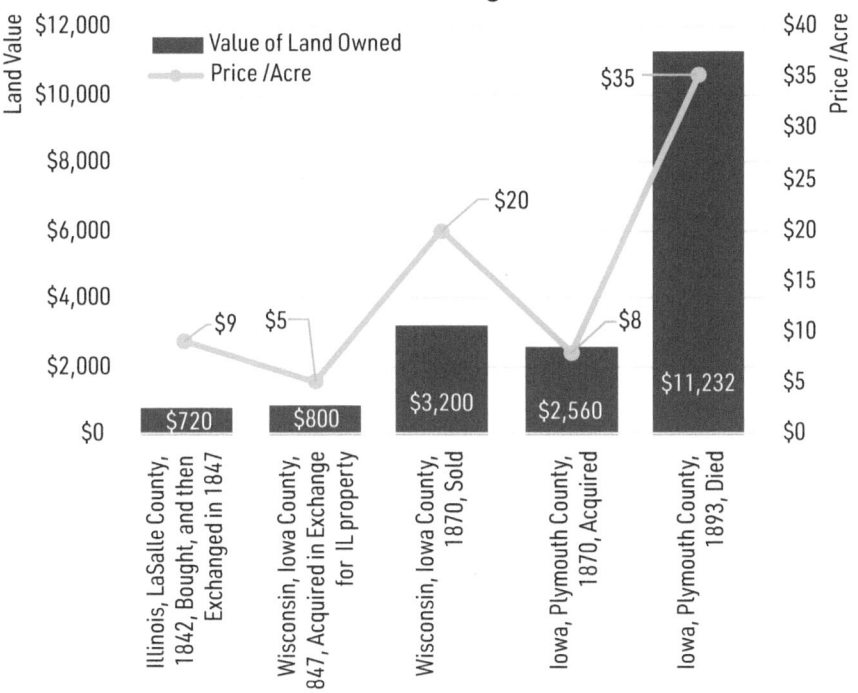

	Price /Acre	Acres	Land Value
Illinois, LaSalle County, 1842, Bought, and then Exchanged in 1847	$9	80	$720
Wisconsin, Iowa County, 1847, Acquired in Exchange for IL property	$5	160	$800
Wisconsin, Iowa County, 1870, Sold	$20	160	$3,200
Iowa, Plymouth County, 1870, Acquired	$8	320	$2,560
Iowa, Plymouth County, 1893, Died	$35	320	$11,232

Value of James A McDougall's Holdings

Four generations: Grandmother McDougall (Adeline Howard McDougall), Alexander McDougall, Annie Nannagie, Grace Nannagie Alberts.

weeds, sticks of any kind, and dried cow chips. (There were very few buffalo remaining.) Eventually they could use corn cobs.

Surviving that first winter was a great accomplishment and required a team effort. As the years passed, they continued to develop the farm. Eventually James replaced that first log cabin with a nicer, roomier house for Adeline and their family.

When James turned 58, he received his official Homestead deed from the Land Office in Sioux City, Iowa. The deed was dated November 16, 1876. He had fulfilled the requirements and the land was officially his. He continued caring for his homestead for the remainder of his life. James Alexander earned a reputation as a well-known and respected farmer of his land and a proud citizen of the town of Struble.

James Alexander died in 1893. He was 75 years old. Adeline died in 1907. She was 85.

The Warrens Arrive

Joseph Warren and Emma (Dodkins) Warren
(paternal great grandparents)
Martha Ann Warren (paternal grandmother)
Chester Nelson McDougall (father)

Down the road from James Alexander and Adeline, was a neighbor named Arthur Gee (also called Captain Gee). He was born in England and had immigrated to the United States. There is no record we could find that tells the story of his journey or why he came, but at one point after arriving in this country, he settled on a farmstead on C-12.

Apparently, he had a particular interest in raising Suffolk sheep and a desire to transfer a flock of those sheep from England to his farm. To accomplish this, he must have contacted one of his friends, or possibly his father, someone that was living in England, to request help in getting a flock of these sheep to him.

This is where our great grandfather Joseph Warren and his

wife Emma (Dodkins) Warren enter the story. Joseph was born in Newsells, Hertfordshire England on April 25, 1834. Emma Dodkins was born that same year in Berkway, Hertfordshire, England. They met and were married in Berkway, Hertfordshire in 1854. At some point, they moved to Cambridgeshire, England and set up housekeeping in the Rochester Hills area. They listed their children as: Martha (August 15, 1850), Thomas (August 1857), Mary Elizabeth (1862), Jonas, James, John (October 1870), Sarah, Ama, George (February 4, 1877), and Edward Joseph (1878). (Edward Joseph is listed here among Joseph and Emma's children, but he is believed to be Martha's son.)

The oldest of this group was our grandmother, Martha, who sounded like quite a spunky youngster. We found a few stories about her youth.[7]

> *Martha played hooky from church one Sunday and her father heard her loud voice. He later asked her, "What was the text of the lesson?" She told him something and he said, "Is that a lie little girl or is it the truth?" She ran upstairs. Her father asked her for weeks if anything she told him, "Was a lie or the truth?" She said she would rather have been spanked.*
>
> *At age 12, Martha went to the city of London as an apprentice in a drugstore and delivered drugs in the city. She stayed for one year (without visiting her house) she was about 20 miles from her home.*

7—This is from a "Family Group Sheet." No name listed as the researcher.

Joseph and Emma were having trouble raising their family in this part of England and sadly, they had lost three children (not listed) to consumption or tuberculosis (TB). The disease was rampant in England and was attributed to the wet, foul weather. Joseph was deeply troubled by his family's situation and was afraid that if they didn't get away from the foggy weather, he would lose their entire family. Joseph was seeking a dryer, healthier place to live.

After the war of 1812 establishing peace between England and the United States, people began immigrating to the United States. I am sure Joseph was hearing stories about the wonderful opportunities in that young country. Joseph was a shepherd, and somehow, he learned of Arthur Gee's request. He had access to the type of sheep Mr. Gee was looking for and seeing this as an opportunity to join the masses and leave England behind, Joseph agreed to sell Capt. Gee the sheep, on the condition that he and his entire family could personally escort the flock to their new owner in Iowa.

The deal was made and passage for both Joseph's family and the sheep was booked on a ship called the US La Mar, which landed in Castle Garden in New York City. This was in 1880, before Ellis Island was open. Once in the United States they all transferred to a freight train and off they went to Le Mars, Iowa.

The Warren family arrived at Arthur Gee's farmstead and transferred the sheep to Mr. Gee. After a short time, they settled on the West Fork at Quorn (which was platted in September of 1880 and was a thriving town by 1882). Joseph worked as chief herdsman of the imported sheep flocks on the Close Brothers ranch near Kingsley, just a mile east of Quorn.

Kinglsey, Iowa's official city website talked about the Close Brothers Ranch:[8]

> *The Close Brothers, wealthy Englishmen, bought up thousands of acres of farmland in this area. They conducted the affairs of the many farms they owned from their land office located in Quorn. English families sent their boys to the Close farms to learn how to farm. Tuition was $600 a year which included board and a horse. They were called "pups" by local community members. These young men were often more carefree and fun-loving rather than serious, and the program only lasted about 2 years.*

Joseph later farmed north of Le Mars and then moved to the vicinity of Westfield.

On November 5, 1881, Joseph Warren and his family filed for citizenship to the United States. They received official citizenship on October 27th, 1890.

8—From the Kingsley, Iowa official city website, Kingsley, Iowa History (www.kingsleyia.com)

The Morans Arrive

> Pete and Katherine Moran (maternal great-great grandparents)
> Michael Neylan and Mary (Glenn) Neylan (maternal great-great grandparents)
> Peter Moran and Ellen (Neylan) Moran (maternal great grandparents)
> Mary Elizabeth Moran (maternal grandmother)
> Edith Nicholson (McDougall) (mother)

Because there are two Peter Moran's in this story, to avoid confusing the two, I will refer to the first-generation immigrant, my great-great grandfather (that came from Ireland) as Pete Moran. I will refer to the second generation immigrant (my great grandfather) as Peter Moran. Peter Moran was born in the United States and settled on C-12.

The Moran story begins in Ireland, where Pete Moran lived with his wife, Katherine Tafferty. They were Catholic; Ireland's major religion, which is an important piece of information, because life at that time was very difficult for the 8 million Catholics in Ireland. The country was still under British rule, and under the Penal Laws of the 16th Century, Irish Catholics had very few rights. They were not allowed to freely worship, vote, own land, horses, guns or even get an education.

During the time our great grandparents (the Moran's, the Glenn's and the Neylan's) lived in Ireland, most of the land was owned by wealthy Protestant Englishmen who lived in London. They invested in these land holdings strictly for monetary gain and had very little interest in visiting their land or making any kind of improvements.

To make managing these distant farms easier, the landowners would rent out large tracts of land with long-term leases to local individuals known as "middlemen." The middlemen were also primarily interested in profit. They subdivided the land into small parcels and rented them out at very high rates to Irish Catholic farmers who were desperate for work. To maximize profits, they would divide the farms into smaller and smaller parcels to the point that the farms became as small as a quarter acre.

The tenant farmers were required to plant the crops needed for export to the wealthy Englishmen. Rent and taxes on the poor farmers land was so high, that once the crops were planted and sold, they hardly had enough left over resources to keep their families alive. It seemed as hard as these farmers worked, they could just barely subsist and hardly, if ever, made a profit.

To make matters worse these families lived under the fear of being evicted at any time, at the will of the middleman or the

The Morans Arrive

landowner. The laws were behind the landowner. Legally if told to leave the land, the the tenant, having no recourse, would have to forfeit any house or barn they had built or improvements they had made. Everything became property of the landowner. Consequently, these farm families endured abhorrent living conditions, often crowding together with another family in a small dirt structure. This system of farming was known as "subsistence farming" and it was the way most Catholics in Ireland existed. It was a difficult and miserable way to live.

These families found solace in the potato, which thrived in Ireland's cool, moist soil. They were versatile, nutritious, easy to grow and harvest, and took up little space. Most importantly, they could be preserved and stored in underground caves through the long winter months. The hungry families soon developed a dependency on them.

The major drawback to the potato was that it only stayed eatable for about nine months and that wasn't quite long enough to last until the next fall's harvest. July and August became known as the "summer hunger" because this is when the stored crop from the previous year would begin to spoil. Some families survived by keeping a pig they could slaughter at this time. Some grew small patches of greens. Other families paid inflated prices for oats or barley meal. The poorest women and children would go hungry or had to beg, while the men would go to England to work in the harvest fields there.

Then came the fateful fall of 1845. Farmers had survived the summer hunger and were eager to harvest their new crop of potatoes. Suddenly, the leaves on their plants started turning black, curling up and rotting. This created a horrible smell through the countryside. Alarmed, the hungry farmers dug into the stinking leaves, still hopeful they could gather their year's supply of food. Tragically, they found the potatoes in that same rotting condition. Even the ones that seemed okay at first, became mushy and inedible within a few days. The blight took out one half to three quarters of the potato harvest throughout Ireland that year.

Unknown to them at this time, but an airborne fungus had been transported in the holds of ships coming from North America to England. Once the blight arrived in England, the fungal spores traveled quickly and easily in the winds over to Ireland where they settled on the leaves of the healthy plants. The spores worked their way to the roots and killed the whole plant within just a few days.

The farmers that managed to get through that first year, found the same thing happened again the next year. Tragically, this blight continued infecting the crops for five consecutive years. By 1850 over 1,000,000 people had died from starvation and resulting diseases, and 2,000,000 had been forced to flee the country.

This was the Great Irish Potato Famine, or the Great Hunger, and it was the reason for the first major influx of Irish Catholics into the United States. It is also most likely the reason Peter and Katherine Moran emigrated out of Ireland. We have the following information on the couple:[9]

9—www.findagrave.com

The Morans Arrive

> *Pete Moran: Birth, 1809. County Leitrim, Ireland. Death, 7 April 1866 (aged 57), Clayton County, Iowa, USA Burial at St. Joseph's Cemetery, Elkader, Clayton County, Iowa, USA.*
>
> *Indications are his wife was Katherine Tafferty: Birth, 1809. Death, 1888. Burial at Saint Mary's Cemetery Maurice, Sioux County, Iowa, USA*

Assuming this is our Pete, we know he was Irish Catholic. We found that the county where he lived, Leitrim, was hit very hard by the famine.[10]

He had married Katherine Tafferty in 1830, so they would have come to the United States together. By 1850, his residence was listed as New Castle township, Schuylkill, Pennsylvania. Pete was a farmer.

All these clues taken together, paint a likely picture that they were a part of that unfortunate scenario of the potato famine and, along with many others from that area, came to America simply to survive, as well as a chance of a better life.

The trip overseas to the United States was a rough ordeal for those Irish immigrants. The 3,000-mile journey on a sailing ship could take from 40 days to three months, depending on the weather and the skill of the captain.

Each ship had hundreds of men, women and children crammed below deck in the steerage. The captain was only required to supply seven pounds of food per week per passenger, which were

---

10—This is told in the book *The Dead Buried by the Dying: The Great Famine of Leitrim* by Gerard MacAtasney.

Ireland, part of the United Kingdom of Great Britain
1801 to 1922

County Leitrim

Galway

Dublin

County Clare

Limerick

Cork

Brian & Shane Seemann 2021
d-maps.com/carte.php?num_car=2294
d-maps.com/m/europa/irland/leitrim/leitrim31.svg
d-maps.com/m/europa/irland/clare/clare09.svg

basically starvation rations. Water typically ran out long before reaching American shores. The passengers were packed together with very little ventilation or sanitary facilities, people had to breath in the stench of vomit and diarrhea. Typhoid, dysentery and malnutrition were rampant, and anyone who died during the sea voyage was dumped overboard, without any religious rites. There are stories of these ships being followed by sharks waiting for the next body to be cast over.

Fortunately, if Pete and Katherine were part of this mass migration, they survived it. Irish immigrants at this time entered America through the Port of New York. Once on American soil, the couple found their way to New Castle township in Pennsylvania, where they chose to settle. After a couple of years, the Morans had their first child Peter, who was born on January 9, 1850.

Also immigrating to the United States about this same time was Michael Neylan (also spelled Neylon) and Mary Glenn (also spelled Glynn). Both the Neylan and the Glenn families were from County Clare, Ireland. This was a very poor part of Ireland that was hit particularly hard by the famine.

Before the famine, the population of Ireland had swelled. People needing to survive were forced onto less and less fertile ground to grow whatever food they could. County Clare was one of these areas. It was located along the Atlantic coast. The soil was extremely poor, but the people had discovered that the potato thrived on seaweed, and they had become highly dependent on them as a source of food.

Life in County Clare was at best a minimal existence. At that time, it had a population of 286,394, with a population density of 91/square mile. The illiteracy rate was 75% and one half of the families lived in 4th class housing, the worst of all housing situations: a small, dark, windowless, one-room sod structure.[11]

When the famine arrived in Ireland, County Clare was hit very hard. Over the next few years, there was a dramatic decrease in the population from starvation, disease and emigration.

Michael Neylan had been born in County Clare in 1820 and was 26 when he immigrated to the United States in 1846. Mary Glenn was also living in County Clare and was about this same age when she emigrated out in 1846. They both settled near each other in Rochester, New York. Michael Neylan and Mary Glenn were married in 1850 and had three children, John, a daughter Ellen, born in New York, on January 29, 1852, and a daughter Jennie.

In 1855, when Ellen was three years old, the Neylans moved from New York to Highland township in Clayton County, near Elkader, Iowa. Michael Neylan bought forty acres of land and began farming. They settled there permanently and raised their children.

Meanwhile, the Moran family was living in Pennsylvania. In 1865, when their son Peter was fifteen years old, they decided to move to Elkader so Pete could farm. The Moran family settled near the Neylan family. It is interesting to note that Pete Moran is listed as dying in 1866, the year after they arrived in Elkader.

11—www.IrelandStory.com

The Morans Arrive

Now living in the same area, Peter Moran and Ellen Neylan eventually met, most likely at church. Pete was a religious man with strong Christian values and considered attending church each week a necessity. It is logical that Peter and Ellen, living near each other and both Irish Catholics, would attend the same church. Peter and Ellen were married in the town of Elkader, Iowa on March 7th, 1875. Peter was 25 and Ellen was 22.

Peter and Ellen were anxious to start a family and later that same year, November of 1875, their first child, (our grandmother) Mary Elizabeth (Mollie) was born.

While Ellen was busy caring for their new daughter, Peter got on his horse and set out for northwest Iowa to scope out the good fertile land he had been hearing about. He wanted to take a look around, see if he might find a place where he could set up his own farm to support his new family.

He located a gentleman who was selling 80 acres after a failed attempt at farming. The plot was on C-12, section seven, of Elgin township. Peter thought it looked like good arable soil, so he paid off the seller. Peter must have had some money in his pocket, because in those days a payment in full was generally required, taking a loan from a bank or paying the seller monthly wasn't common. Once the land was bought, he returned to Elkader.

Through that winter Peter prepared to uproot his family. In the spring, again alone, Peter hooked up his team of horses, loaded up his wagon and trekked the 300 miles east to west, across the state of Iowa. Peter worked on his new farm through that summer of 1877. He most likely wanted to get his planting started and make things as comfortable as he could before his young family arrived. Peter's granddaughter, Mabel Mueller, said he erected "some sort of house," so depending on what condition the previous owner had left that farm, there could have been a sod house that he replaced with a wooden one.

Once things were in order, he arranged for his wife and two-year-old daughter to come by train. Struble was not yet a settlement and the nearest train came into Le Mars. On the day of their arrival, he hooked-up his horse to his spring buggy and rode the nine miles into Le Mars to meet his wife and baby daughter and bring them back to the farm to settle into their little home. Peter, Ellen and little Mary Elizabeth had now settled on C-12, the Road to Love.

Farming for Peter and Ellen wasn't necessarily an easy path, but the couple were hard workers.

> MABEL MUELLER: Farming and daily living during these times was very hard work. Things were primitive and my grandfather and grandmother's successes came the hard way. They did everything on their own. My grandfather broke up his sod with a walking plow. His horses were a very important part of his farming equipment.

There is no question that Peter and Ellen saw some hard times. Soon after Peter settled on his farm, clouds of Rocky Mountain locusts came swarming into northwest Iowa:[12]

12—History of Counties of Woodbury and Plymouth, Iowa

The Morans Arrive

> *... darkening the mid-day sky like a heavy snowstorm, destroying anything and everything in their path; fields of wheat, oats, corn, barley, even the bark off trees.*
>
> *The grasshopper was too great an army for man—with all their ingenuity, strategy and strength, to even begin to cope with—they took the field, destroyed all they found and moved on to greater conquests, undismayed and seldom sacrificing any of their vast winged army. Their work brought gloom, sadness, and poverty upon many Iowa farmers, who fought manfully year after year, hoping that every year would be the last. There are hundreds of young men and women, who in those unfortunate times, went thinly clad during the long severe winters from having their entire crops swept away.*

This was the grasshopper plague of 1873–1879, and Peter wasn't spared in its destruction. The year Peter's daughter, Mary Elizabeth was only a few years old, the locusts ate absolutely everything on the farm, they left no crop at all. Now, it could have been that this one year he got hit particularly hard, or maybe he had endured this devastation for too many consecutive years, but one summer, Peter made the difficult decision to leave his family and travel back to Elkader, where his mother may still have been living, in hopes of finding work. The grasshoppers had not traveled that far east, and there were crops growing there. Peter had to make enough money to feed his family.

MABEL MUELLER: My mother (Mary Elizabeth) was about four or five years old, when her father left and went east to Clayton county. There were good crops there, so he worked in the harvest fields. He worked wherever there was work, and he got some money, and he bought some cows, a team of horses, a wagon and some seed and feed for the horses. He came back home in the fall after the harvest was finished there. Mother said she always remembers that Aunt Jennie, her aunt, had sent a jar of plum sauce with him, a big jar of plum sauce. She had covered it up the best she could with a plate and paper tied over the plate, probably a two- or three-gallon jar. My mother said the best thing she ever had tasted was that plum sauce.

Unfortunately, misfortune hit again. In that same year, 1879, there is a newspaper article in the Elkader Register that told this sad story.

> *The many friends of Peter Moran, formerly of Highland township, will be sorry to hear that he has met with a serious loss by fire at his new home in Plymouth County. The Le Mars Sentinel says, "Peter Moran who lives on the West Branch some nine miles north of town, met with a severe loss last Sunday. He and his wife were visiting about a mile from home, leaving in charge a boy aged 6, and a girl of ten. About 4:00 pm he observed the flames near his home, and hurrying to the scene, found his stable*

and granary and their contents consumed. He lost about 200 bushels of wheat, all his corn, a wagon, his plows, harrows and all his farming implements. It seems the little boy had been playing about the stables, and it is supposed he caused the fire. Loss about $500.

But Peter rebuilt. Time and again, he did what he had to do to survive. He often took on jobs in addition to his many farming chores. According to Mabel Mueller, Peter was a schoolteacher at Mammen, a small settlement about nine miles from his house.

MABEL MUELLER: Grandfather Moran, for several years, taught school in addition to farming. He got $45 a month for teaching. They liked to have him because in the wintertime there were so many big boys going to school. That was about the most education the fellows got in those days as a farm boy. When the work was all done on the farm, then the farmers would let their sons go to school. A lot of the female teachers were just not able to handle these big boys because they got pretty rowdy sometimes. I guess they were afraid of grandpa. My aunt told me that when her father died, one big farmer came to the house. He said, "All I know he taught me," referring to Mr. Moran. This man was from around Mammen. Grandfather Moran had gone out to Mammen two different winters and taught school during the winter terms. He rode horseback. It was nine miles from his house to there. He did his chores, milked the cows, and got on horseback and rode out to Mammen every morning and rode back every night. He had chores to do when he got home. Grandmother said she put newspapers under his jacket because the papers would act as insulation to keep him warm while riding his horse. Riding horseback is a pretty slow process against a strong wind. I'd like to see anybody get out and ride nine miles morning and evening nowadays to teach school in the country. A lot of times the path was pretty well drifted with snow. That was all prairie in those days.

As the Great Northern railroad was making its way to Struble, Peter was improving his farm, and had put up a barn. He and Ellen made extra money boarding railroad workers in their barn. They provided the men with a roof over their heads and Ellen would cook for them. She had the reputation of being a very good cook and after a long grueling day, no doubt the men appreciated those homecooked meals. The couple also occasionally boarded teachers.

Peter and Ellen had 5 children: (our grandmother) Mary Elizabeth (Mollie) (1875), Frank (1880), Peter Joseph (or Petie) (1883), John and Nellie Rose.

> MABEL MUELLER: While raising their children, there were a lot of good times. Mollie loved to ride horses and rode whatever she could find: work horses, riding horses, whatever was around. But there were also some rough times. They saw a lot of hard times—farmers in those

days. My mother used to tell me a lot of stories about her childhood and how primitive it was.

Because of their hard work, Peter and Ellen's farm grew and prospered. Peter was a successful farmer. He continually improved his home and farm. He put up some good barns and buildings. Land acquisition was a major goal of his, and "He gradually increased his land holding until he became the owner of a very large farm of two hundred and forty acres in Plymouth county, as well as a two-hundred-acre farm in Sioux county. Both farms were well stocked with cattle and horses." As Peter acquired land, he was careful to have everything paid for.

An article from the Alton Democrat, dated July 25th, 1891 announced that, "Peter Moran of Stuble has purchased the Owen Dealy farm near Maurice. The old gentleman Dealy and his family, will soon move into town to enjoy their well-earned competency."

Peter wasn't defined solely on his accumulation of wealth and success at farming. As quoted below in his obituary, his community thought of Peter as a "Man with strong convictions, earnest, honest, kindly and thrifty. A man who always made good on his word."

> MABEL MUELLER: My mother's teacher at one time was her own father. He taught (his daughter, Mollie's) school for a while too. He did anything he could to make money. He was also a very religious man, very up righteous and very honest. He had a lot of obstacles to overcome along

the way. He was on the school board. He was constable of the township. In those days it was something like the Justice of the Peace. He used to settle a lot of arguments that they would have in Struble.

In the spring of 1903, Pete died of tuberculosis. He was a fairly young man, only 53. This is a disease that effected several members of our family. It had taken at least three children from the Joseph and Emma Warren's family when they were in England and it hit the Moran family in the United States. It typically affected the lungs and the inflicted would suffer with fatigue, night sweats, weight loss, and breathlessness. It was also called consumption because, over time, it just seemed to cause the body to waste away. It was a mysterious disease, and no one knew much about it, other than that it had a bleak outcome. There was no cure although through trial and error, doctors believed the most effective treatment was good nutrition and rest.

Peter and Ellen's son, Frank, had been suffering from consumption for many years and they did whatever they could to help him through it. Frank had a difficult time breathing. In the winter, Peter would take him to New Mexico or Arizona by train to get some relief. The air was dryer, and Frank found it easier to breath. Peter spent a lot of time with Frank, sleeping in the same bed at night. The belief at that time was that tuberculosis was a genetic rather than a communicable disease. Sadly, as committed as the couple was to their son, and despite all the sacrifice, love and care they gave him, in 1898, at the young age of 18, Frank succumbed to the disease. Not long after that, Peter also

Catholic Church built on Peter and Ellen Moran's donated land.

came down with consumption and after a struggle of his own, died five years later.

Shortly after Peter's death, St. Joseph Church was built on a corner of the Moran farm. They had donated the land.

According to her obituary, after Peter died, "Mrs. Moran made her home some of the time with her children." She moved in with our grandmother Mollie and her family for a time.

The Nicholsons Arrive

> Jonah and Ann (Carruthers) Nicholson (maternal great-great-great-great grandparents)
> Benjamin and Jean (Clark) Nicholson (maternal great-great-great grandparents)
> John Nicholson and Elizabeth (Johnstone Lowther) Nicholson (maternal great-great grandparents)
> Benjamin E Nicholson and Sarah Janet (Birrell or Burriell) Nicholson (maternal great grandparents)
> William Nicholson (maternal grandfather)
> Edith Nicholson (McDougall) (mother)

Before we begin, I want to let you know that in this next chapter, as we move through the generations, there are a number of "Johns" and "Benjamins", but as we studied the culture, we found that similar names, passing from one generation to another, was not unusual in Scottish families. The Scots have a tradition for naming their children in honor of their elders: the firstborn son is named after the paternal grandfather (the baby's father's father), the second-born son is named after the maternal grandfather (the baby's mother's father), the third son is named after the father, the fourth son is named after the father's oldest brother and the fifth son is named after the mother's oldest brother.

This is similar to the girls: the first-born daughter is named after the maternal grandmother (the baby's mother's mother), the second daughter is named after paternal grandmother (the baby's father's mother), the third daughter is named after the baby's mother, the fourth daughter is named after the baby's mother's oldest sister and the fifth daughter is named after the father's oldest sister. Again, this is to honor the elders and in fact, in many families, if a baby dies, they will name their next child the same name as the baby who died, so the relative will still be honored with a namesake. The Nicholson's seemed to follow this tradition.

The oldest Nicholson forefather we've tracked so far, originated out of Mouswald and then moved over to Annan. Both Mouswald and Annan are in the Dumfriesshire area of Scotland. Shires are similar to US counties. Dumfriesshire is located in the area where the southwest border of Scotland meets the northwest border of England. When you locate this area, you will see the Solway Firth, jetting into the land. A firth is a coastal region where the sea water has eroded much of the riverbed, widening it to form an estuary. In an estuary, the tide from the sea mixes with the current of the river, in this case, the Annan river, so that

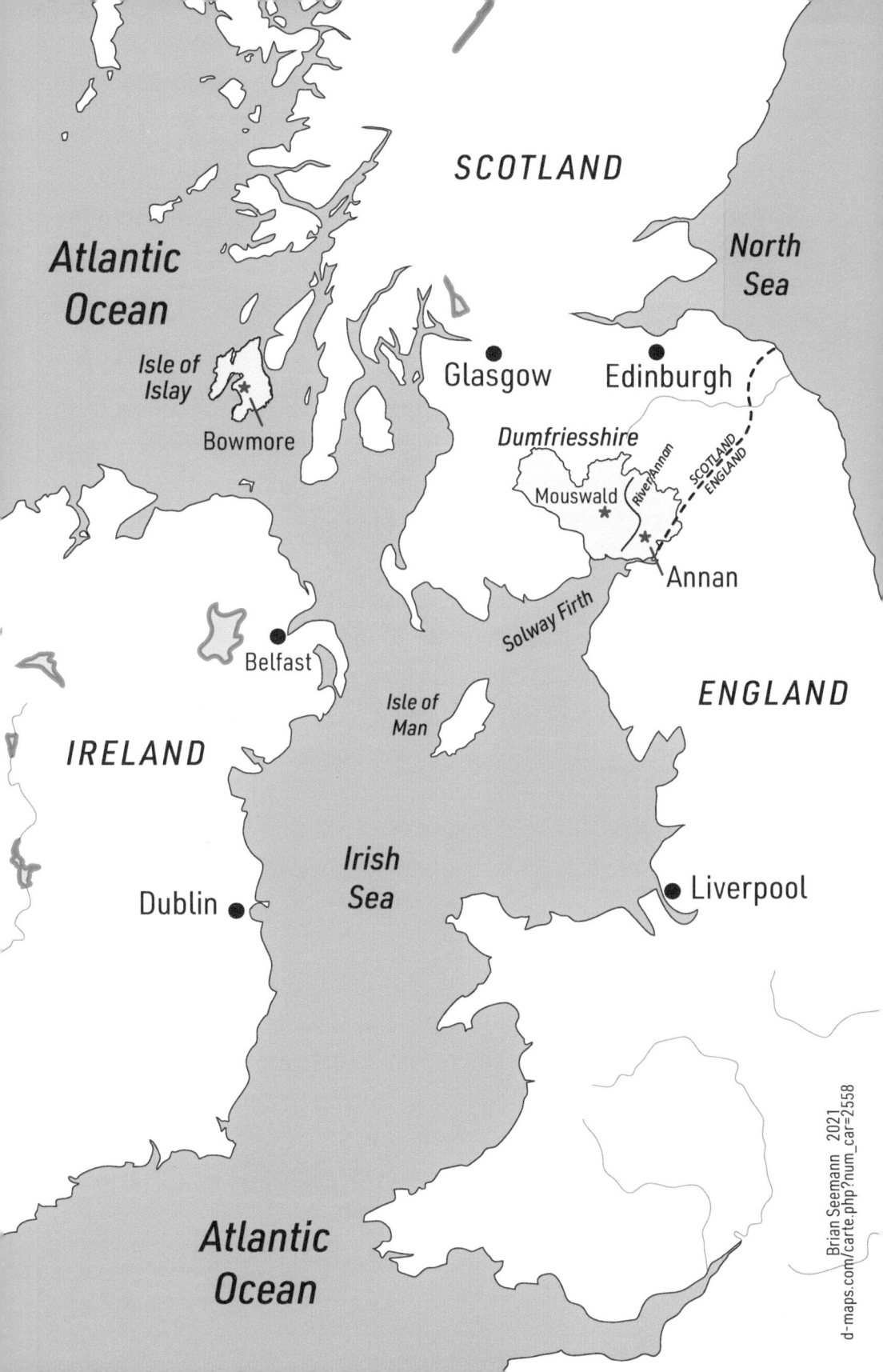

the river current rises and lowers with the tide. This is important because the Nicholson's were launching huge ships into the tide of the Annan river.

If you begin at the mouth of the Annan river, and follow it up about a mile, on the east side, you will come to Annan, a beautiful little market town with all of its buildings uniformly constructed with the dark red sandstone mined nearby. In previous days, if you had gone northwest from Annan a few miles, you would have come to the small rural town of Mouswald. However, in currents days, Mouswald is no longer on the map.

Dumfriesshire has been the home of our Nicholson family for hundreds of years and has been traced back to our great-great-great-great grandfather Jonah Nicholson (May 24, 1746–1833). Both Jonah and his wife, Ann Carruthers (1746–1830) were born in Mouswald. There is strong evidence that Jonah Nicholson's parents were named Benjamin Nicholson and Janet Friend and Ann Carruther's parents were named Joseph Carruther's and Bessy Hardy.

Jonah Nicholson married Ann Carruthers around 1775. Clan Carruthers had been in Mouswald since the 13th century and owned Howthat Farm where Jonah was a farmer. Jonah and Ann had the following children, all born in Mouswald: our great-great-great grandfather Benjamin (1776–1828), James (1778–1847), Christopher (a minister) (1780–1867), Janet (1784–1786) Joseph (1785–) and Jonah (1787–1838).

The Nicholsons Arrive

Sometime around 1800, our great-great-great grandfather, Benjamin married Jean Clark, and within a year or two, they had a son. The baby was born on Christmas eve, 1801 and they named him John (this would be our great-great grandfather). In 1818 Benjamin moved his family over to Annan, at which time Benjamin became Provost of Annan. This is an extremely important position and was similar to a town mayor. No decisions were made, without the Provost's approval. Benjamin also held the title of esquire, which was given only to those with a high social status.

The very same year Benjamin moved his family to Annan, his son John, who was only 17, started building ships. John established what he called his "Welldale" yard and using local timber from the Nithsdale and Annandale estates, began building small sailing vessels under 100 tons in weight. Its quite amazing that at the age of 17, John was already a pioneer of ship building in Annan! Clearly, John was an industrious young man and he worked hard for the next several years, eventually building a company called John Nicholson and Co. By 1825, as John turned 24 , his company had earned an impeccable reputation for quality in the craftsmanship of its ships.

In 1825, John Nicholson sailed to Prince Edward Island with his senior ship carpenter, and within nine months built a 239-ton brig (a sailing vessel with two square-rigged masts). They called this ship the Helen Douglas and sailed her back across the Atlantic filled with virgin timber from the Canadian forests for the Nicholson shipyard in Annan. From *The Heritage of the Solway Firth*: the Helen Douglas continued to sail that same route for the next fifty years.

Interestingly, not only did the Helen Douglas carry timber, but it was involved with cattle as well:[13]

> *The Helen Douglas, in addition to ferrying timber from Canada for half a century, also transported cattle to the Dominion. Many of the great herds of Canada are descended from the best Dumfriesshire beef cattle, and two Canadian farmers made 200 return trips to select the finest from the markets at Annan, Lockerbie and Dumfriesshire.*

Around 1826, Benjamin bought a house called "Cotton Lodge" on Port Street in Annan and became the owner of a cotton factory. Unfortunately, he died only two years later at 52. When Benjamin died, his son John was 27 years old and the following year, October 5th, 1829, John married Elizabeth Johnston Lowther. John and Elizabeth took up residence in Cotton Lodge.

John was a successful businessman and citizen. In addition to the shipbuilding and timber trade, he held many shares in the railway industry and was listed as a slate merchant. John and Elizabeth were good people and significant in many ways to their community. John was known around town for his "amiable disposition, and a gift for friendliness and tolerance." They were devoted Christians, baptized in the Presbyterian church, the national church of Scotland. They had six children and provided them with every comfort. Their first son Benjamin was

---

13—*Annan-Built* written by Andrew Murray

The brig Helen Douglas. Built by John Nicholson in 1825 in Richibuto, New Brunswick Canada.

born on February 6, 1833. This was our great grandfather. The others were William, John, Jane, Elizabeth, and baby Isabella, who sadly passed away shortly after birth.

John and Elizabeth's son, Benjamin was a very bright young man. He spent his early years of education in the Annan school system. Since 1802 the syllabus at Annan Academy included mathematics, physics and natural science, Greek and Latin. Benjamin's parents recognized his intelligence early on and enrolled him in the academy, where he excelled in mathematics and penmanship.[14]

14—Annan.org/UK

As Benjamin matured, he became increasingly interested in his father's shipbuilding trade. After his schooling was finished, his parents decided Benjamin would benefit by going to Liverpool to study under a cousin of Benjamin's father, who was a senior partner in the offices of Nicholson McGill Company, a branch of the Nicholson Company. The Nicholson McGill Company served as a shipping broker handling the cargo and managing the Nicholson ships.

Following this plan, Benjamin went off to Liverpool and studied under his dad's cousin. But the world was much bigger than the British Isles. If Benjamin had crossed the Atlantic Ocean to America, he would have witnessed how rapidly things were progressing in the shipping business. There were dramatic new developments in that young country, and it would soon present a new challenge to England, and the Scottish ship builders.

California had just been purchased from Mexico and was a young developing territory. A man named James W. Marshall was hired to build a water-powered sawmill for a Captain John Sutter on the South Fork of the American River at the base of the Sierra Nevada mountains. It was January 24th, 1848, and as Mr. Marshall was building, he noticed some gold flakes lying in the riverbed where he was working. Although Mr. Marshall tried to keep this a secret, within just a few months, the word was out and "gold fever" hit California, hard. Tens of thousands of prospective gold miners raced by land or by sea, across country, hoping to cash in on the goods. This was the Gold Rush of 1849, when in one year, the population of the California territory swelled from 1,000 to almost 100,000, and with about that many arriving again the next year.

With this huge influx of people, the demand for food and necessities skyrocketed. Towns were popping up all over. But California was in its infancy, and far from able to supply all the food, materials, and resources it now needed. Everything had to be transported in from the more developed east coast cities.

Unfortunately, the far western territory of California was on the wrong side of the Rocky Mountains, and this served as a huge hurdle. The completion of the railroad connecting the Atlantic and Pacific oceans would not be completed until May 10, 1869 at Promontory Point, Utah. Consequently, at this time, the only way to get supplies and people over land was by way of the laboriously slow and expensive covered wagons.

With the mountains presenting such a challenge, attention naturally turned to the water. Ships began transporting people and goods from the east to the west along the coast. The journey would take them south along the eastern edge of North America, past the eastern side of Central America, around South America, then all the way north, to the west coast of California. Although they could move more goods at one time, this mode of transportation was also no easy task, and took between five to eight months.

With such a lack of goods and the need so intense, the laws of supply and demand went to work. Gold seekers were willing to pay extremely high prices for anything they had to have:[15]

15—Some examples were found in an article from the Moffat News and Times, written in February of 1934 regarding previous Gold Rush prices.

> *Salt beef and pork in California was going for $50–$60/barrel, (elsewhere in the country, it would sell for about $9/barrel), spirits in California—$9/quart (elsewhere around $0.11/quart) shoes that cost $11/pair, would be sold in New York for less than $1.00, picks and shovels were close to $4/each, and so on, at proportionate prices for every item. All told, a dollar's worth of items on the east coast would easily bring a minimum of $10 in California.*

The need was great and ships carrying these high demand goods were being paid extravagant rates to bring them to market. A ship in 1850, carrying about 1,200 tons of cargo to California was paid a freight of about $72,000, which was around the cost to build the ship and prepare her for voyage.

Great demand brings great reward, and this certainly aided in the rapid development of a new pioneer in shipping, the American Clipper (synonymous with merchant ship). The clipper ships were wooden sailing ships, built entirely for speed and sacrificing cargo space to do so. Their hull design sliced through the water. The length of the ship was always five times the width, and they had a protruding stem. Each ship had three tall masts, some fifteen to twenty stories, with every inch of those masts covered by a large number of square sails. This unique mast/sail combination enabled the ship to cover over 250 miles per day—far surpassing the previous average shipping speeds of 150 miles per day.

However, the Nicholson's were on the other side of the Atlantic building schooners and brigs, and were very likely unaware of these great advances in shipping. The British Isles were operating under the British Parliament's Navigation Act of 1651, forbidding the entrance of foreign ships into their ports. Anything coming in or out had to be on British built, owned, and operated ships. This allowed the government tight control over imports and exports between England, its colonies, and the rest of the world. British merchants and manufacturers were guaranteed the advantage, so there really wasn't much need for their ships to "keep up with the Jones'" so to speak.

England, without the concern of competition, was not as worried about how quickly a trip could be made and put all their focus on transporting larger quantities of high demand, high return items, the biggest being silk and tea, which were a very big deal in England.

Tea had been made popular a couple of centuries back, in 1662, by the Queen of England, Catherine of Barganza—wife of King Charles II. She was the daughter of the King of Portugal and was a very refined and wealthy young woman. She came to England, bringing with her, a habit of daily tea. The English people have always watched their queen closely and are quick to imitate her. Tea grew increasingly popular in Britain, but because it had to be imported from China, it was hard to get and very expensive. It is said that a pound of tea could cost up to a month's wages of an average worker. So, with the price so high, the more tea they could import, the better. In fact, by the mid 1800's, seven million pounds of tea was leaving Canton, China every year, with over half of it going to England.[16]

The season's finest fresh teas are harvested in the springtime in China, immediately after the winter dormancy period, when the fresh new shoots are at their highest quality. These new leaves had been building up nutrient reserves over the dormancy period, and it is this first harvest that was most sought after, consequently, the highest priced. With the previous years' tea getting old and losing its flavor, the arrival of this fresh tea each year was a highly anticipated event. In fact, the first ship to arrive each spring, is rewarded with higher freight rates, £6–£7 per ton, against the £3–£4 per ton paid to those ships arriving later.

Then, on June 26, 1850, there was a significant event in the world of shipping. The British Parliament repealed the Navigation Act. Foreign ships were now free to enter British ports. Immediately after the act was repealed, those refined new clipper ships from America, raced into the London markets with tea from China. The first American Clipper, the Oriental, arrived in London, just six months following the repeal, on December 3rd, 1850. It's China to London trip had taken just 97 days. That was record time, three times as fast as Britain's old lumbering ships. To say the British merchants were shocked would be an understatement.

The writing was on the wall for the British, the larger, speedier American Tea Clippers were going to take control of their precious tea trade. Britain had always considered themselves the rulers of the sea and they were not happy with this new country

---

16—https://teaepicure.com/tea-harvest-dates/.

infringing on their domain. The ship builders, almost all of them located in Scotland, resolved to build their own clippers to rival the Americans.

This historical event coincided with the tragic death of Benjamin's 49-year-old father John, on June 25, 1851. We don't know why he died, but his son Benjamin was only 18 years old. He suddenly found himself in the position of taking over his father's ship building company. He immediately left Liverpool and returned to Annan, Scotland to become the head of John Nicholson and Company. He eventually renamed the company John Nicholson and Sons.[17]

> *As Benjamin embraced his new responsibilities, he was full of exciting tales of the American clipper ship invasion, known as "the Yankee Clipper." They were the fastest sailing ships ever built up to that time and were making that long journey from America to China, returning with loads of tea; the reward being so high that one trip often paid for the building of the entire ship.*

So, Britain was quick to join America in the race for superior ships and young Benjamin was a big part of it. Inside of two years the Nicholson Welldale yard transitioned away from the brigs and schooners his father had focused on and ushered in a new era of building big clippers. The first of the Nicholson fleet was called the *Annandale*. Following the launch of that ship, the

---

17—Annandale Observer, March 2nd, 1934.

firm turned out nearly one clipper a year. Nicholson, despite his youth, was one of the first Scottish pioneers of these ships.[18]

> In 1851 and 1852 only three British clippers had been built. In 1853, four more were launched, all built for owners of long experience in shipping and backed by large cash resources, and built by such firms as Hall of Aberdeen, Scott of Grennock and Pile of Sunderland, firms again with long traditions and expert skill at their command.
>
> That in the same year of 1853, young Nicholson with no more knowledge or experience than he had gained in a few years at a ship-owner's office should have made his plans and begun to build his first clipper, is clear evidence of an amazing ability to see many years ahead and foretell the coming demand of clipper ships, as well as an extraordinary confidence in himself and in the skill of the workers of the little town of Annan to enter the lists beside the greatest owners and builders of that day, and in contest with the Americans who then stood almost unrivaled in the power and speed of their ships.
>
> So it was, and in that year, Benjamin E Nicholson (a boy of twenty, as we should call him now), thrust himself, the town of Annan, and his Flying Heart clippers in with the first half-dozen pioneers of British clipper owners and builders.

18—Moffat News and Times, February 15, 1934.

> *Benjamin entered the business in 1851 and (soon) the ship building yard (became) an extremely busy place. Records are scarce concerning the day-to-day operation of Annan's shipbuilding empire. We can only imagine now what happened in that busy shipyard. As the high spring tide for a launch approached, the rhythmic thud of the carpenters' mauls wedging the new ship up on the launching-ways must have rung across the harbor. The finished product sailing gracefully away must have been a marvelous sight to anyone on Criffel hill across the estuary. The shipwrights were the main men on the scene, but the blacksmiths, the riggers and the sawyers would be called upon when the big moment grew near. There were 30 carpenters employed by Nicholson on a full-time basis.*

Benjamin's Welldale shipyard was also known to be available to repair a crippled ship if the need arose.[19]

> *If a ship's captain was unfortunate enough to incur damage to his ship coming up the Solway Firth, he could be sure that the firm of John Nicholson and Sons would deal with it to his satisfaction. They would careen his ship, repair her strakes, caulk her and if necessary, haul her up to the Lloyds' requirements for reclassification. The builders were masters of their craft, and the shipwrights they trained and employed were second to none in Scotland.*

19—*Annan Built* by Andrew Murray

Ships built by John Nicholson & Co, Annan

Vessel Name	Year Launched	Sailed Until	Vessel Type (as recorded)	Tonnage	Length	Breadth	Depth
BYRON	1851		2 Masted Brig	190 nrt	92.5 ft	22.8 ft	14.1 ft
BURNS[†]	1852	1897*	3 Masted Barque	363 nrt	123.5 ft	25.8 ft	17.2 ft
ANNANDALE[†]	1854, Aug 10	Stranded Key West Mar 1866	3 Masted Ship	759 grt / 759 nrt	228'6"	32'0"	17'9"
QUEENSBERRY[†]	1856, Feb 8	Stranded 13 Oct 1877	Ship	635 grt / 635 nrt	206.9 ft	28.6 ft	19.2 ft
SHAKSPERE[†]	1857, Feb 25	Stranded 24 Oct 1870	Ship	486 nrt	164.8 ft	27.2 ft	18.0 ft
JOHN NICHOLSON[†]	1859, Jul 2	1891*	3 Masted Ship	685 grt / 685 nrt / 693 bm	177.6 ft	29.4 ft	20.4 ft
MANSFIELD[†]	1861, Mar	Lost 04 Apr 1862	3 Masted Barque	357 grt / 357 nrt	133.2 ft	25.6 ft	
BURNSWARK[†]	1862	Wrecked 14 Dec 1882	3 Masted Barque	253 grt / 253 nrt	122.4 ft	24.4 ft	14.9 ft
ELIZABETH NICHOLSON[†]	1863	1912 storage hulk at Shanghai	Ship	904 grt / 904 nrt	192.5 ft	32.5 ft	22.2 ft
OTWAY	1864		Schooner	100 nrt	78.9 ft	20.1 ft	9.9 ft
SOLWAY QUEEN	1864		2 Masted Brig	216 nrt	104.9 ft	23.4 ft	14.2 ft
SARAH NICHOLSON[†]	1865, Aug 30	1905 hulk in Singapore	Ship	933 grt / 933 nrt	194.7 ft	32.7 ft	22.6 ft
PARTON	1866, Dec 1		Schooner	115 grt / 93 nrt	81.9 ft	20.7 ft	10.6 ft
WILSON	1866		Schooner	110 grt / 82 nrt	81.5 ft	20.2 ft	10.5 ft

†) 3-masted clippers mentioned in story. Information gleaned from historical records.
References: Caledonian Maritime Research Trust, http://www.clydeships.co.uk/
*) *The Heritage of the Solway Firth*, James Irving Hawkins; 2006

Over the next 12 years the yard launched 9 clipper ships. The following names of the ships, spellings, and dates of launching are according to the Caledonian Maritime Research Trust whose aim is to present the vital information and the careers of all vessels built by the shipyards of Scotland.

BURNS 1852
This is a quote from the book *Annan—From Queen Victoria to Queen Elizabeth* by John Thomson:

> In November 1852, a vessel named "The Burns" was launched into the waters of the Solway, from the building yard of Mssrs. Nicholson & Co., Annan. The local newspaper said, "The Burns is 363 tons per register, and is one of the finest vessels ever built in the county." She is the property of Messrs. Nicholson & Co., and is intended for the Eastern trade, under the command of Captain Robert Ewart of Annan.

ANNANDALE 1854
Most certainly named after his father's Annandale brig.[20]

> Her shipbuilder, Benjamin E Nicholson, John's son, had created a minor sensation in shipping circles on both sides of the Atlantic, for the Annandale was the longest ship in the world and young Ben was not yet 21.

20—*Annan-Built* by Andrew Murray

The Annandale is certainly the largest vessel ever built in the south of Scotland, and is supposed, with good reason, to be longer, as compared with her breadth, than any ship ever launched in this country, or of America . . . we trust the Annandale clipper will cut out all competitors as regards to speed, and in every other way realize the expectations of her enterprising builders and proprietors.

Nicholson's work was a source of tremendous pride to the Annan folk, and the launching of a clipper at the Welldale yard was considered such an important event that the school children were given the day off to watch, and carriage loads of the Dumfiresshire elite would rattle down Port Street to be present at the historic occasion. Indeed, people came from all over Scotland and beyond to see the clippers being launched. The crowds were huge—4,000 spectators, for instance gathered on the 10th of August 1854 to see the clipper, the second Annandale take to the tide. The Dumfries Standard of the day recorded the event as follows. "High-tide was about half-past one o'clock and long before that time the immediate vicinity of the shipyard and the adjoining quay were crowded; the opposite bank, too, was lined with a living fringe; and about a hundred yard down the river, we could see a steamer from Maryport and the Annan steam-tug, each with a freight of spectators, and each occasionally puffing and snorting—we are sure not contemptuously—as they waited for the advent of their

> *young but gigantic sister. All the preliminary operations over, the fastenings were knocked gradually away that the ship began to move down the well-prepared plane, her weight giving increased momentum as she proceeded, till, swift as an arrow from the Tartar's bow, she shot easily and gracefully into the tide. There was no great descent, and only about eleven feet of water so that the motion was far from being violent, and as her stern caught the ground slightly, there was no rebound, and the launch was completed under the most favorable auspices.*

The ships were built in the Welldale yard at Annan, but from there, were towed to Liverpool to be fitted with their mast and riggings and sails. This is partly due to an important lesson Benjamin had learned with his first clipper.[21]

> *The Annandale was the first large ship to be launched by Benjamin and after launching, she damaged her hull sheathing while lying on the riverbed while fitting out. After this, when large vessels were launched, they were towed out on the same tide to Liverpool for rigging.*

The Annandale was an exceptionally fast ship and Captain William Crocket who ran her the first four years, wanted that to be known. He wrote a letter to the Sydney Daily Telegraph:[22]

21—*Heritage of Solway Firth.*
22—*Annan—From Queen Victoria to Queen Elizabeth* by John A. Thomson.

According to the *Heritage of the Solway Firth*, "The launch of the Annandale from the Nicholson's Welldale yard in 1854. This contemporary sketch by Joseph Watson of Dumfries shows the timber slipway and building shed. The railway viaduct shown on the left was built in 1848 to carry the railway linking Annan and Dumfries."

I take exception to the statement that the Thermopylae has made the greatest 24 hours run that has ever been made by a craft dependent upon the winds as a motive power. In the ship Annandale, under my command on the passage from Bombay to Liverpool in 1855, we made a distance in one day, from noon to noon, of 381 miles by observation. During the 24 hours, we passed the Island of Rodriques at midnight very close. I am satisfied that during part of this day's run the ship travelled 18 knots an hour. On her passage from Liverpool Melbourne in 1856, the best day's run was 375 miles.

The Nicholsons Arrive

Surely it is time that a plaque should be erected at the Welldale to remind the world that here in Annan the fastest cargo sailing ship that ever sailed the seven seas was built and owned. An amazing feat to average sixteen miles an hour for twenty-four hours.

QUEENSBURY 1856

This is a quote from the Heritage of the Solway Firth by James Irving Hawkins:

The Queensbury of 635 tons. She was built in 1856 by John Nicholson & Co. Built of timber as a fast tea clipper, she sailed from Liverpool to Hong Kong in 97 days on her

The Queensbury, built in 1856 by John Nicholson and Co.

maiden voyage. In 1877 she was wrecked on the island of Palwan in the China Sea.

On her maiden passage she arrived at Hong Kong on 20 July 1857, 97 days out from Liverpool.[23]

Of all the men who know and have spoken of the ships agree that the Queensbury was among the daintiest and the prettiest and fastest of the clippers. The picture I have of the Queensberry most decidedly supports that opinion. It is a print from a painting by a Liverpool artist and now is in the possession of Mr. John Nicholson. It certainly shows one of the sweetest ships I have ever seen.

SHAKSPERE 1857

With dimensions of 164.8 feet x 27.2 feet x 18 .0 feet, she had six beams to her length, tonnage was 565 old and 496 new. Her half-model has survived to show that she was one of the finer-lined hulls designed by Nicholson, but fuller than Annandale or Mansfield. In the autumn of 1870, she was wrecked on the French coast, homeward bound for London from Shanghai.

23—*The Heritage of the Solway Firth* by James Irving Hawkins

JOHN NICHOLSON 1859[24]

Launch at Annan—On Saturday last, a large, handsome vessel, clipper built, was launched from the yard of Messrs John Nicholson and Company, the enterprising ship builders at Annan. Her length is 177 feet, breadth 29 feet 3 inches, depth of hold 29 feet 6 inches, registered builder's measurement 633 tons, customs' measurement 685 tons. The cabin is elegantly fitted up, and altogether the vessel is a model in point of shape and internal arrangements. A large concourse of spectators lined the bank of the river some-time before highwater, while not a few craft floated on the river loaded with onlookers. Shortly after one o' clock the ship which had previously been named the "John Nicholson" by Mrs. Benjamin Nicholson, glided down the slip and entered the water amid a hearty burst of cheering. Unfortunately, the vessel had scarcely passed her own length from the end of the slip when she took the ground. As the tide had still fully one foot to rise, it was hoped she would then float, and the steam tug Senhouse was attached to the vessel, but all attempts to remove her were abortive. The vessel lay in the cut and was got off on Saturday night. She has since been towed to Liverpool to have her rigging fitted up. She is intended to trade to the west coast of South Africa and will be commanded by Captain James Ewart.

24—Dumfries and Galloway Standard, July 6, 1859

MANSFIELD 1861

The barque Mansfield was launched in 1861. After sailing from Liverpool to Shaghai in 115 days, she left Amoy for New York which she reached in 115 days. She then set sail with a load of grain across the Atlantic for the port of Llanelly in South Wales. She never arrived and no trace of her or her crew were ever found.

BURNSWARK 1862
Wrecked on December 14, 1882.

ELISABETH NICHOLSON 1863[25]

Built of wood by John Nicholson and Co. An oil painting of her in the National Maritime Museum shows a vessel with painted ports (rare in the tea trade), square stern, old fashioned bow, full poop with diagonally crossed wire mesh panels, secured to the rail, and no deckhouse. She carries trysails on both fore and main and nothing above royals.

Elisabeth Nicholson was the last recorded large wooden ship constructed in Annan for the tea trade. She was built by John Nicholson & Co. In 1863. Owned by her builders, she enjoyed a surprisingly long life, although had only a relatively short career in the China tea trader for

---

25—Annan's Maritime Connections

Elizabeth Nicholson.

which she had been designed. (It should be noted that the last 3-masted sailing ship built in Annan was the Sarah Nicholson in 1865, but she does not appear to have been involved in the tea trade.) As a clipper, Elisabeth's maiden passage home from Shanghai to Liverpool, in 1864, lasted a disappointingly slow 128 days, under Captain Ewart, who was soon replaced and his successor, Captain Crosbie, did far better, bringing her home from Shanghai to London in the winter of 1866–67 in an excellent 106 days. The following year was even faster and her 92 days, sailing from Foochow to London, was not only the fastest of the season, but also one of the best ever recorded for the run.

SARAH NICHOLSON 1865

The Sarah Nicholson was the largest ship built in Annan. She was not used for the tea trade.[26]

> *An animated and highly interesting scene was witnessed at Annan yesterday—the launch of an immense vessel from the building yard of Messrs John Nicholson and Co., in presence of a large assemblage. She was ushered in the flowing tide at a quarter to twelve o'clock, and whilst gliding gently from (terra hrma) was christened the Sarah Nicholson by Mrs. John Richardson, the name being given, we understand, in compliment to Mrs. Benjamin Nicholson. After being safely launched, amid much cheering, the ship was hauled to a berth prepared for her at the dam-foot; and she will, it is expected, be towed thence today, by a steam tug, to Liverpool. Since Nicholson and Co. commenced operations in the yard in 1851, they have built twelve vessels, the Sarah Nicholson being the largest. Her clipper shape and fine proportions render her extremely handsome.*
>
> *Of the vessels, by far the best known were the three with the Nicholson name and although the others were sold out of the firm after a few years, the John and Elizabeth were retained until well into the 1880's and the Sarah until her hulking. After the passing of tea carrying to the steam*

26—Dumfries and Galloway Standard, Wednesday, September 6, 1865; then the Shipping Gazette

The Nicholsons Arrive

The launch of the Sarah Nicholson of 934 tons at Annan in 1865. She was the last tea clipper to be launched from the Welldale yard of John Nicholson & Co. After her launch the yard's carpenters and apprentices left for employment at a shipyard in Newport, South Wales.

ships, they were put into the Australian (wool) trade and any other where cargo offered. The three were credited with being the greatest and fastest of the fleet. Although there are memories of the fast passages made, no exact record of these appears to have been kept unfortunately.

As you can see, the last of the big clippers built by the Nicholson Company was in 1865 and that year again Benjamin showed an uncanny foresight into the future of those ships as he did when he was first amongst their builders. In 1865, the clipper boom was at its height and the American clippers had been driven out of the competition. The last of the American clippers had come to London in 1859.

It was Benjamin's gift of foresight that brought him into this successful business, and it was this same gift that took him out of it. Benjamin was paying attention to world events and could see what was on the horizon.

Benjamin launched the Sarah Nicholson in 1865 and the following year, 1866, was particularly significant in ending the clipper era. It began with the Great Tea Race of 1866. Tea races are an annual event for the owners of the biggest and best clipper ships. It was an informal opportunity to test their clippers against the others as they hurried back with the year's first long awaited load of tea. The race started from the loading dock at Foochow, China and ended at the West India dock in the Port of London. This was a very exciting event in those days and could be compared to our modern-day anticipation of a big football game.

To begin the race, each ship had to first secure a spot in line and load its shipment of thousands of chests of tea. The lucky captain that secured the first shipment (usually the winner from the previous year's race) had the greatest advantage, the second one in line had the next greatest advantage and so on. The chests of tea were loaded onto the ships as efficiently and as quickly as possible, but each took a day or two or even three to be readied. The last ship in line would have a tough go of things.

Once a ship was loaded and ready to go, they would be tugged out of the port and to the starting point, where they could begin their voyage. Once they took off into the South China sea, it was no easy trip back. They had to go through 14,000 miles of unreliable winds, waves, typhoons, and shoals. But to be the first

The Nicholsons Arrive

one back to the West India Dock, in the Port of London, held a great reward. It was celebrated as "the ship" and "the captain" that stood out from all the others. Sailing a clipper took extraordinary skill. These were very complicated ships to sail, and only those captains with excellent seamanship could handle them, especially in high winds.

Besides fame and recognition, there was the added incentive of a monetary prize. The first shipment of tea to arrive was highly anticipated and could be sold at a much higher price—before the glut of the rest of the tea supply arrived.

Although the race of 1866, was the last year of these races, it was a particularly exciting one. There were sixteen competing clippers. They had all taken their turns loading up their cargos of fresh tea and had left the Foochow Port in China at fairly close intervals, each hoping to be the first ship back to England and win recognition as the fastest ship with the most skilled captain and collect the monetary prize.

But this year there was a "new kid on the block," a steam auxiliary, which had stayed out of the way while the big sailing ships prepared to set out on their voyage. Once those clipper ships had gone, the steamer pulled up to the dock and loaded more tea than any clipper could handle—1,108,100 pounds.

Then on June 5th, many days after the clippers had taken off, her steerage packed full, she pulled out of the China port, well behind all the sailing boats.

Meanwhile, the clippers were racing back, across the South China sea, through the Sunda Staite of Indonesia, across the Indian Ocean, around the Cape of Good Hope of Africa, and up the Atlantic Ocean, into the English Channel. The 14,000-mile trip would take those sailing ships over three months.

This was a particularly exciting competition and is now referred to as the "Great Tea Race," because throughout the trip, four of the clippers—the Fiery Cross, the Ariel, the Taeping and the Serica—remained neck and neck the entire time. Miraculously, after a 14,000-mile trip, the two top contenders, the Taeping and the Ariel, finished within a couple minutes of each other, with the Serica just a few hours behind. The unlucky Fiery Cross came in fourth, but only 36 hours behind Serica. The race was so close between the first two contenders, that a decision was made to split the prize.

However, unknown to the victors, before their big sailing ships had pulled into the dock, London was already celebrating. To everyone's amazement, that steamer, waiting in the shadows at Foochow, had pulled in a full 15 days before the first clippers arrived. It had left a week later and arrived two weeks earlier than the fastest clipper. The trip had taken the steamer only 77 days while the clippers had taken 99!

Benjamin, with his brilliant mind, was most likely already aware of these big steamers and wasn't surprised when it pulled into the dock so far ahead of the clippers. I'm sure he was also well aware of the projected 1869 opening of the Suez Canal, and for the "right ship" (such as the steamers) this would cut a whopping 7,000 miles off the route from China to Europe. He probably also realized that the conditions would not be conducive for a big sailing ship to maneuver through the Suez Canal, or for that matter, the next obstacle, the Red Sea. The Suez Canal was extremely narrow, with unreliable winds and a sailing ship would need a tugboat to get it through the canal. This would be slow and expensive. Clippers would have a difficult time taking advantage of that short cut and would most likely have to continue the old route around Africa.

So, while the steamers were still in their infancy and a full four years before the Suez Canal opened, and while the clipper ship business was still booming, Benjamin jumped out of the ship building business.

Sure enough, Benjamin was correct. Because of the difficulty those clippers had maneuvering through the narrow Suez Canal, the steamers moved in, able to do the job faster and cheaper. The launching of the Cutty Sark in 1869 (built by William Denny at Dumbarton and known as the fastest of them all) officially represented the end of great British clipper ship era.

After the launch of the Sarah Nicholson, Benjamin built a couple more smaller sailing ships and then closed his Welldale yard for good. This date marked the end of the construction of those big sailing ships made of wood in Annan, Scotland. Shipbuilding now entered a new phase with large steamer ships made of iron.

It must have been difficult to say good-bye to the men who had helped build his ships. The building shed was dismantled and rebuilt at a Carlisle yard. John Brown—the foreman carpenter, seven journeymen and six apprentices, needing employment, left to work at a shipyard in Newport, South Wales.[27]

But Benjamin was still young, civic-minded, well connected,

27—*The Heritage of the Solway Firth*

industrious, with an entrepreneurial spirit. He was just getting started in life. He turned his energies to the timber trade, which was very big in Annan at that time, and also began an extensive business as a slate merchant. He found himself an increasingly important and busy individual in Annan.

He was also now married with a family. On January 25, 1859, the same year Nicholson and Co. had launched the John Nicholson, Benjamin married Sarah Janet Birrell (also spelled Burriell), who was born in 1831 and whose family was from Gretna, Scotland. Over the next 13 years, they had five sons and three daughters: John (January 1860), James Birrell (August 12, 1861), Jane (1864), Elizabeth (1866), Sarah (1868), Benjamin Jr. (September 12, 1869), William (April 22, 1871) and Richard (September 1873). All of Benjamin and Sarah's children were very intelligent and the couple made sure their children attended good schools, some of them going to England to study.

As time marched on Benjamin took on many responsibilities. He became involved in the town council from 1861 thru through 1872. He also became involved with the railroads:[28]

> *Ironically Benjamin became director of the Glasgow and Southwestern Railway Company which had been a nail in the coffin of the shipbuilding industry. He devoted great attention to the company and went into the running of the line in great minuteness and knew almost every agent on the line.*

28—*Annan-Built* by Andrew Murray

Benjamin had a forty-year involvement with the Annan Savings Bank as a director, and was a director of Annan gas company, and a charter member of Annan Harbor Trust.

Although Benjamin was clearly a very busy man and had many responsibilities of community, work and family, "He was also a man with unending energy and strived to keep every empty moment filled." Now, a decade after closing his shipping business, he was hearing rumblings about available farmland along the developing railway system over in United States, specifically in Iowa. He was a successful speculator in Scotland, knew the railway business and was confident he could make money with land over in that new country.

Benjamin Nicholson and Janet Birrell Nicholson.

Benjamin took several trips to North America to explore buying opportunities. He traveled north into Canada and as far west as the Pacific Ocean in the United States, but that rich Iowa farmland was what caught his eye. By the early 1880's he became the owner of several sections of untilled, mostly railroad land in Plymouth, Washington and Elgin townships: much of it between Merrill and Le Mars. At one point he owned 9,000 acres, with the intention of selling as the prices rose.

It didn't take long for the U.S. government to get wind of all of this buying and selling by foreign citizens. The goals of the Homestead Act and of the railroad land grants were to aid American expansion into the west. The government didn't like foreign citizens coming in and buying up land they had no intention of living on and improving. They saw this land speculation as a negative thing. They notified Benjamin that he could only keep ownership of his land if he agreed to become a citizen of the country.

Now Benjamin had a choice to make: he could become an American citizen and keep the land or sell the land and return to Scotland. Living permanently in the United States was never part of Benjamin's plan. He had an established and active life in Annan and had no desire to relinquish his allegiance to the Queen and to his home country. He chose the latter and prepared to return to Scotland.

Benjamin sold a portion of the land he had bought, made some good money, but held on to some of this land in Plymouth county because he recognized the great potential of this rich farmland

and all the opportunities America held. When he returned to his family in Scotland, he encouraged his sons to immigrate to the United States and claim the land. His oldest son John chose to remain in Scotland, where I'm sure there was plenty to do to help his dad, but the other four agreed to go. Benjamin gave each of the boys a farm. And they came over to the United States one at a time.

The first to arrive was Benjamin and Sarah's second son, James Birrell, who had been born in 1862. He had gotten an education in Edinburgh and married Georgina Laing from Scotland (in 1882) before immigrating to the United States. The couple settled on the land that Benjamin had set aside for him. James put his energy into breeding short horn cattle and Poland China swine.

The second boy to arrive was Benjamin Jr. (Ben), Benjamin and Sarah's third son. He was born in 1869. We don't have record of the exact date he arrived, but we know he departed Liverpool aboard the Mauretania and arrived in New York, New York, before finding his way to Iowa. He married Minnie Murray on January 1, 1901 at Wave Tree, England, St. Mary's church, Liverpool. He died on January 26, 1939 and was buried in the Le Mars City Cemetery.

William was the third to make the leap. William's mother, Sarah had died in 1886, when he was fifteen and apparently, William was a handful for his father. A scrapbook with notes of affection from William to his daughter, Evelyn, includes a letter from Benjamin to an unknown friend in Iowa. It is dated "Annan, August 28, 1888" and the following is a paragraph from that letter:

James Birrell Nicholson.

Ben Nicholson (son of Benjamin Nicholson from Scotland).

> *Benjamin Nicholson: Your kind and valued favor of the 12th that reached me two days ago, please accept my best thank you for your warm sympathy with me at my bereavement. My family now are pretty well. The oldest with me here is over 26 (John). James is at Hillside, Le Mars 25. Daughters, Jane 22, Lizzie 21, and Sarah 19 are home with me. Ben about 17 is in an office at Liverpool. William, 16 next April (if spared) about the end of next month, we intend to start for Iowa, Richard nearly 13, at school.*

Mabel Mueller said that William's brother, James Birrell, who had been the first to arrive, welcomed William and took him under his wing.

> MABLE MUELLER: Uncle Jim was to teach William to farm, which I guess Uncle Jim did. I imagine it was quite difficult teaching a kid that had never lived anywhere other than a town right beside the sea, to come out here to farm this prairie land. Uncle Jim had been here at this time for eight or nine years. He was married and had two or three children by the time William came out here in 1888.
>
> EDITH: My dad came from Scotland when he was quite a young man. I think he went to some kind of college (Morningside College in Edinburgh). I don't think they had a regular high school in those days. As soon as he got done with his schooling Grandpa (Benjamin) sent him out here. I think my dad was about 21, he was quite young when he came here. You see his mother died when

The Nicholsons Arrive

he was real young and I think he was kind of wild and I think grandpa sent him out here because he was kind of a handful for him. He farmed for a while with his brother James, south of Le Mars. James was supposed to teach him and Uncle Dick how to farm, but that didn't go very well with my dad. They didn't care for Aunt Georgie (Georgina), so it didn't really work out.

After farming south of Le Mars for five years, William moved up to Section 7 of Elgin township and began improving his 320-acre farm. William had now taken his place on C-12, right next to Peter Moran.

William was naturalized on October 20, 1900.

The last of the bunch to arrive was 22-year-old Richard. He had first attended Morningside College in Edinburgh and then worked a couple of years as an engineer at Kilmarnock before immigrating to Iowa in 1895. We have record that he departed Liverpool aboard the Britannic, and arrived in the Port of Arrival, in New York, New York. Benjamin had bought for him, a quarter section (160 acres) from the Adden family.

Apparently, life in Iowa was not Richard's cup of tea. After three years of farming alongside his brothers, he handed his farm over to his brother William to manage. William referred to this place as the Adden Place. Richard went to Scarboro Bluffs, Ontario, Canada, before moving permanently to Seaton, Devon, England where he lived until his death on Sept 22, 1943.[29]

29—Annandale Observer.

Standing William Nicholson, seated Ben Nicholson. This picture was taken in 1883 (according to scrapbook compiled for Evelyn Nicholson).

Richard Nicholson 1887 age 14 (According to the scrapbook compiled for Evelyn Nicholson).

Why Struble?

What brought our forefathers—James Alexander McDougall, Peter Moran, Joseph Warren and Benjamin Nicholson—thousands of miles from where they were born, to end up in this particular spot, barely a mile from each other? Was it just a coincidence? Personally, I don't think so. I believe there was a common magnetism; and I think it had a lot to do with that rich windblown northwest Iowa soil. The soil here was of a very high quality, created by the way the dirt was brought into the area. It blew in on the Kansas and Nebraska winds, picked up because of its particle size and carried into Iowa. As the winds died down those particles dropped, and over many years, this process would accumulate up to 20 feet, in some areas, of rich windblown soil. I believe these individuals could see the excellence of this area, and the great potential this part of the country held.

James Alexander, I believe, recognized his lust for farming earlier and more vividly than the others. "Sometimes farming is just in someone's blood, it's just a part of who they are." James went from a smaller acreage with arable soil in Illinois, to a larger acreage with poor soil in Highland, Wisconsin. He experienced, the hard way, how the earth can bring about different results, and the value of good rich soil.

He experienced the difference between quality and quantity of farmland. He may have heard about the quality farmsteads in northwest Iowa and when that military recruiter tempted him with the promise of all that good land available to veterans for homesteading after serving in the Civil war, he joined the military and volunteered to fight for his country. He was 44, and that was quite a sacrifice. But that was a way to achieve his dream of finally owning a sizable farm with good arable soil at a price he could afford.

The actions that brought Joseph Warren to Iowa were totally different. He didn't come necessarily for the land, but the land was an underlying factor. He and his family were escaping a disease that had already taken several people from their family. In the process, they were also helping supply the new world with livestock that, at that time, could probably only be acquired from England. Once off the ship, Joseph's family transported the livestock via the country's newly developed rail system to a spot where grazing land for the sheep was plentiful.

As a Catholic living in Ireland, Peter's father had most likely grown-up living on practically nothing, and if he stayed in this country, he would never have had the hope of owning land or farming for anything other than shear survival. I believe that had it not been for the potato famine and the threat of starvation, he may never have come to the United States. But because of his circumstances and the choices Pete made, his son Peter grew up in a completely different world. Peter didn't have to cow down to what others, such as the British landlords demanded. In the United States, he had the freedom to pursue his dreams. One way or the other, the elder Pete ended up farming in Elkader, Iowa, and his son Peter, fully aware of the way his life could have gone, appreciated that he could move forward in his life. He could own his own farm and with hard work, improve his situation. We don't really know what was happening in Elkader, but after the younger Peter got married and had a child, he ventured out to take a look around and ultimately found an excellent farm of his own near Struble, on C-12. This was fortunate because he brought along our grandmother Mary Elizabeth and it was especially good for our grandfather William, because in Mary Elizabeth, he found a mate that would share his dreams.

Benjamin's situation was very different from the other three. He was well-educated and had money behind him. He was moving fast, investing in land, using the knowledge he gained by working with the slate and timber merchants, and the rail lines in Scotland. Benjamin was a brilliant speculator. He came to America because he knew there was money to be made with their railroad land. He traveled around the country looking for the right place to buy good land. He went all the way to Canada and as far west as the ocean, but in the end, he came back and bought land on C-12. He bought that rich Iowa soil along the railroad. He knew the importance of being in the right place at the right time. He knew he wouldn't have any trouble selling it at a higher price. Then when he had to make a choice, between staying or leaving, he chose to leave. He had a full life to return to, but he recognized the great potential of the land and this country and encouraged his sons to immigrate and establish themselves in that promising area.

Straight east of James, Peter and William's farms was the small thriving town of Struble, Iowa. This was their community. But we might wonder: how much did these families have to do with the development and betterment of their growing town?

James and his son Alexander had secured their land under the Congressional Act of 1862, and at the time they arrived, this part of Iowa was desolate and unsettled:[30]

> *Here the Struble area, as in many other parts of Plymouth and Sioux County, the first settlement was affected by homesteaders who secured their land under the Congressional Act of 1862, by which any American Citizen was entitled to a quarter section of land, if he had been a soldier; and eighty acres if he had not been, providing he would live on the same five years and properly improved the same. It should not be forgotten that these years were fraught with many a trial and hardship. Away from markets and without bridges and good roads; a great scarcity of timber, the settlers far distant*

30—Struble Iowa Centennial 1890–1990

> *from schools and churches, all made life anything but comfortable. Yet these brave hearts—women as well as men—struggled on in hope of the brighter days, which did finally come and were greatly appreciated by those who had the courage to remain; but many left the county in disgust and went to other locations only to fare worse.*

James Alexander and his family are recorded among the very first to arrive in the township.[31] The first ever settler recorded was Geo Dailey. He was followed by a Welshman named Davis (who came along with a few other Welsh families—the Littles and the Jones'), next was James and Joel Andrews, Henry Taylor, William Benton, Scholers, J Kinks, George W. Stillman, Jacob Oler, Amvou Wood, Mathias Wood, S Lane, Sylvester Bradford, William Van Clevo and then came James Alexander McDougall and family. Now, to James Alexander's credit, it should be noted that not all the named newcomers remained here. Some couldn't endure the hardships.

However, James and his family, despite the difficulties, made Struble their home, and today, they are remembered as an important part of the area's development and improvement.[32]

> *Coming to the county, as he did, in the early days, when the unbroken prairie was for the most part one stretch of unbroken grass, with no houses or groves to mar the view,*

31—The book *History of Counties of Woodbury and Plymouth*, lists those first arrivals.
32—From Iowa Genealogy Trails, Plymouth County.

> *Mr. McDougall has seen the transition of this unbroken waste to well-developed farms, improved with the best building, surrounded by fields of golden grain and protected by well-established groves of the finest of trees.*
>
> *Today, where then there was only the prairie trail to guide the weary traveler, we find well-built roads, over which the residents travel in their automobiles instead of making their weary journey to market with the slow plodding oxen or horse. At that time there were few, if any, schools and churches, but today we find modern schools and beautiful churches, where the children can receive an education equal to that in the cities and the people can worship in beautiful structures, dedicated to the Great God of the universe. These great advances have only been made possible by the sacrifices and hardships of such men as Mr. McDougall, who have devoted their lives to the development and improvement of the district in which they have lived for so many years. It is to them that the world owes a debt of gratitude that can never be repaid.*

When James and Adeline arrived, the children attended school in a sod structure.[33]

> *In the winter of 1870–1871, (the year James and his family arrived) what few children were then old enough,*

33—*History of Counties of Woodbury and Plymouth.*

> *gathered together at the sod claim-shanty of Uncle "Geo" Daily, and there, in that little tucked up and dirty place, the first lessons were taught by Mr. Daily, who received whatever the parents felt like donating in the way of fuel, provisions etc.*

The children's school environment quickly improved:[34]

> *In the summer of 1872 or 1873, Sally Parsons, wife of Alfred Parsons, taught school, at public expense, in a frame house on section four. She had but seven pupils, but she made a good and faithful instruction. What is now No 9 schoolhouse was originally built on the southwest quarter of section twenty-nine in 1872 and was the pioneer school building of Grant township.*

Could James with his carpentry skills have something to do with that new school? It appears so because it is written that:[35]

> *James and Adeline had much to do with the establishment of the early schools and the organizations of the first churches. They were very much interested in the educational problems of the district and through their efforts schools and churches were established.*

34—*History of Counties of Woodbury and Plymouth.*

35—This is from the *History of Plymouth County, Iowa*, W.S. Freemann, Editor, published by B.F. Bowen and Co.. (Indianapolis), 1917 submitted by Mary Kay Krogman.

Seven years after James and his family arrived, Peter and Ellen Moran along with little Mary Elizabeth, took their place right next to the little town. The Moran's were invested in the development of the Catholic church in Struble.

MABEL MUELLER: The Durband's and the Moran's were both Catholic people.

Peter was "a very religious man, very honest and up righteous." It was important to him that his family attended church every Sunday. But there was no Catholic church in Struble. The family went to the schoolhouse at nearby Maurice, where Father John A. O'Reilly of Sheldon periodically visited to offer the Holy Sacrifice of Mass. Finally, on November 10, 1884, St. Mary's church in Maurice was completed, and the parish transitioned out of the schoolhouse.

It was important to Peter that Struble have its own church. When he died, he donated land so Struble could build St. Joseph's church. The church was completed in 1903, the same year he died.

Peter influenced the community in other positive ways as well:

MABEL MUELLER: Grandfather Moran was on the school board. He was constable of the township. In those days that was something like a Justice of the Peace. He used to settle a lot of arguments that they would have in Struble.

Why Struble?

By 1885 Struble was a thriving town:[36]

> *Struble was one of the last villages platted in the county, in the fall of 1889. When the Sioux City and Northern railroad was built, this became a station on section five (of Elgin township). It was also made a post office about March 1, 1890. The only business found was a general stock, kept by Eldredge and Land, who embarked in merchandising and grain shipping in February 1890, a hardware and implement store by Ritter Bros, livestock shippers, Isaac Speer and Peacock and Sons, a blacksmith shop completes the list to June 1890.*

When Benjamin Nicholson settled his son William into this area in 1888, the railway was just coming into Struble. In fact, Struble would be platted the next year. They had a country school for the younger kids, but they didn't have a high school or a

---
36—From *Plymouth County History Book*

consolidated school (a public-school serving pupils from several adjacent, often rural districts).

> EDITH: My dad tried hard to get a consolidate school in Struble, those schools were really good in those days, they went out with buses and brought the kids in and I'm sure if there had been one in Struble we would have all gone.
>
> MABEL MUELLER: When we were young children going to school, we went to Struble school. There were always quite a number of us in school. It was too far for us to walk. We were a mile and a half from town. We used to drive a horse and buggy or a team and sleigh in the winter. We had one old horse whose name was Sam. When we went to school in Struble, it was quite a town. We had two or three grocery stores, a doctor, two saloons, barber shop, newspaper, and a harness shop. It was an up-and-coming little town. They also had a butcher shop. After school, at night, we girls would walk up to Kaiser's store. The boys would get the horse from Geysee's barn, drive it around and stop out in front of the store for us to load up. Old Kate Kaiser would always see to it that we had our mittens on, and our scarves tied around our neck and were ready for the trip home in the wintertime. She told my mother that old Sam always looked around to see if we were all in the buggy before he started. Poor old Sam was a very faithful old horse.

Why Struble?

Putting all the pieces of our families' influence in the town, is made more difficult because of two unfortunate circumstances. The records of the development of Struble are few, because most burned in the big Struble fire in January of 1930, which wiped out half a block of the business district, including the city hall where the records were kept. In addition, by admission, village records were poorly kept:[37] "Since the records of the village have been carelessly kept no information is at hand concerning the early municipal organization of the town."

But there are people within the family that know much more about the development of Struble than I do, or could find, in the time I had. And most certainly there is a bigger story to be told. My hope is that someday this will all be laid out so you can look with pride at the money, time and energy invested in the improvement of this small American community they chose for their children.

37—*Plymouth County History Book.*

The McDougalls and the Nicholsons

I am now entering the next generation of this story. In the previous chapters I referred to interviews and recordings of my mother, her sister Mabel, and my brother Doug, to help tell the story of that generation. Now, as we move forward, I will be adding perspectives from the rest of my brothers and sisters who can help paint the picture of the next generations. I'm fortunate that they have been willing to share their memories and experience growing up within this family. I'd now like to share authorship not only with my mother and her sister, but also with my brothers Bill, Dick, Doug, Nick, Denny, and Mark, and my sisters Janice and Edythe.

Two particularly significant events for our family happened in Struble in the late 1800s. First, in 1881, James Nelson McDougall married Martha Ann Warren, which was the beginning of our McDougall Clan. Then in 1894, William Nicholson married Mary Elizabeth Moran, which was the beginning of our Nicholson Clan. We don't have many details on these two unions, so we made a few guesses as to how these couples might have come together.

JAMES NELSON MCDOUGALL AND MARTHA ANN WARREN

(paternal grandfather and grandmother)

James Nelson was thirty-two, single, and farming with his dad, when that nice-looking Martha arrived in the little settlement of Struble. When the local folks discovered she was 30, and also single, they must have jumped all over James Nelson. I bet he heard a lot about her fairly quickly. They were both Methodist and I imagine the church played a role in their meeting. They were also both getting up there in age and no doubt ready to find a partner and begin a family of their own. Once they met, it didn't take long for the two to start thinking about getting married, because one year after Martha arrived, the two were wed in Struble, Iowa and the year after that, their first daughter Mary was born. In all they had 6 children: Mary Matilda (Aunt Mary) (January 2, 1882), Laura Isabell (December 11, 1883), Hattie Mae (September 22, 1885), Anna Pearl (August 6,

James Nelson McDougall and Ann (Warren) McDougall.

1887), John James (Jack) (June 27, 1889), and Chester Nelson (October 7, 1893).

They lost a baby girl in late August or early September of 1896. This is according to "Ireton News" recorded by Le Mars Semi-Weekly Sentinel, September 7, 1896:

> *The little girl of Mr. And Mrs. James McDougall living southeast of town died Thursday. The funeral was held from the M.E. Church Sunday afternoon, Rev. F.S. McChaffree preaching the funeral sermon. The parents have the sympathy of a host of friends.*

After they were married, they moved onto James Alexander's farmstead. James Nelson continued to work with his dad until James Alexander died in 1893, at which point James Nelson officially took over responsibility of the farm. He continued his dad's work of caring for his precious soil, raising hogs and cattle, and expanding his acreage. In 1908 James Nelson replaced the cabin with a very nice house for his family.[38]

> *James Nelson was well-known as a successful farmer and stockman of Grant township, increasing the 160-acre homestead to 240 acres, planting one hundred acres of corn and one hundred twenty acres of small grain. Each year he turns into the markets 100 head of good hogs and two carloads of the finest cattle.*

38—History of Plymouth County, Iowa

The McDougalls and the Nicholsons

(Upper) James Nelson McDougall in the center. (Lower) James Nelson riding behind the tractor.

Standing (left to right) Chester, Mary, Pearl, Roy, Laura, Hattie. Sitting on chairs (in front) James Nelson, Martha with Mertyl Edwards on her lap. John (Jack) in buggy. Taken in front of James Nelson's house.

James Nelson and Martha raised six children on their homestead, two boys and four girls. Of James Nelson's two sons, Jack, was most consistently interested in farming and spent his life helping his dad on the homestead. Jack married a woman named Agnes Werth and they had one boy, who they named Jack, but called Jackie. Agnes worked for the newspaper. She stayed on top of the social events that were happening in town and reported anything of special interest in the local paper. She might let everyone know a new baby had been born or an out-of-town family had "motored" down for a reunion.

James Nelson McDougall with Laura Edwards on his lap.

While Jack was helping his dad, James Nelson's other son, (our father) Chester, ventured off for a while. Central High School had been built in 1905, when Chester was 12, but I don't believe Chester ever attended high school, which wasn't unusual in those days.[39]

> *In 1900, only 11 percent of all children between ages fourteen and seventeen were enrolled in high school, and even fewer graduated. Those figures had improved only slightly by 1910. At the decade's end, the average number of school years completed by Americans over the age of twenty-five was only slightly more than eight.*

It does appear, however, that Chester took some classes at Western Union College (known later as Westmar College) but mainly he tried his hand in business, selling cars.

In 1920, James Nelson left his farmstead to Jack, and bought a big, beautiful house from the Mullen family, on the 400 block of North Central Avenue in the town of Le Mars. It was right across the street from the light plant. There was a short article in an issue of the Le Mars semi-weekly Sentinel, with the announcement, "James McDougall moved into his commodious new residence Friday." James had also put some money into purchasing a bank building on Central Avenue. I think he was sort of taken up by the bankers and the big players in town and enjoyed hob knobbing with them. He seemed to have some illusions of grandeur.

39—enidia.com 1900 education overview.

(Upper) Martha McDougall is sitting with her five children. From left to right, Jack, Pearl, Hattie, Mary, Chester. This is taken at Martha's 47th birthday celebration on June 27, 1936. (Lower) Chester and Martha.

The house James Nelson McDougall bought in 1920, when he retired from the farm.

EDITH: But they claim that the times started to get bad. He was supposed to have all this corn. That was when corn went to two or three dollars a bushel, but then everything dropped, and corn went down, and he couldn't pay for the house. I think that is about the time my dad (William) started going broke too. They talk about the Great Depression in the east, but I think it kind of came out here first.

BILL: He had a big crop of corn and it was worth about $2.50 a bushel, but he was going for $3.00, you know, you always want a little more . . . but I think he ended up getting $0.15 or $0.20 a bushel, that put him out of business.

Two years after moving into the Mullen house, James Nelson died. He was 74 years old. This same year his son Chester married

Edith Rose Nicholson. Chester and Edith moved into the Mullen house, with Chester's mother Martha and sister Mary, for a short time. Not long after they moved out, Martha and Mary gave up that big house and moved to a smaller house at 125 Second Avenue SW, owned by the Collins family. The Collins family also operated the Gus Pech foundry (kitty corner from their house).

WILLIAM NICHOLSON AND MOLLIE MORAN
(maternal grandfather and grandmother)

When 21-year-old William Nicholson arrived on C-12, he settled next to the Moran farm. Mary Elizabeth (Mollie) Moran

William Nicholson and Mary Elizabeth (Mollie) Moran Nicholson.

Mollie and William's wedding picture. Best man, William's older brother, Benjamin Nicholson, bridesmaid Ella Deegan, groom William Nicholson and the lovely bride Mary Elizabeth (Mollie) Moran.

was 17, and I'll bet that pretty Mary Elizabeth caught William's eye as she occasionally drove by his farm in her spring buggy. William's farm was right next to the Moran farm, so I imagine William eventually found the opportunity to talk to Mary Elizabeth "over the back fence."

Two years later, on December 12, 1894, William married Mary Elizabeth and another piece of the family story fell into place. Mary Elizabeth was 19 and William was 23. They had a nice Scot Irish wedding at the Moran farm. The price was right, and the place fit very well with the cost. Ellen cooked up one of her outstanding dinners and then the little group went off to Struble to get a wedding picture taken to send back to William's folks in Scotland. Mary Elizabeth moved that same

Original house on the William Nicholson farm. Picture taken 1902.

day into William's farmhouse and that was where she lived until she died in 1936.

William and Mary Elizabeth (who was called Mollie by everyone but William) raised eleven children: Jenny (January 11, 1896), Benjamin (Buzz) (April 28, 1898), Nell (March 17, 1900), Molly (March 6, 1902), Mabel (April 2, 1903), Edith (August 6, 1904), William (Buck) (September 20, 1905), Dorothy (January 4, 1908), Richard (Dick) (October 31, 1909), Don (June 2, 1912), Evelyn (August 18, 1913).

Mary Elizabeth (whom I will call Mollie from now on) gave birth to all her children at home and in the later years this caused her kids a few problems.

> EDITH: I wasn't baptized as a kid and when Dad and I went to go to Europe and wanted to get our passports, I wasn't registered at all. You see, we never went to church, so I hadn't even been baptized. Our mother was Catholic and our dad I think was brought up Presbyterian and there was a Methodist Church in Struble. Our dad wouldn't let us go to the Catholic church, but he didn't take us to the other church either, so we never went to church. I was born at home and I don't know why I wasn't registered. When I went to get my passport to visit Edythe and Gene, there was no record of me. I said here I had ten kids and I wasn't even there. I had to get my school records to get a birth certificate to get a passport. My sister Mabel signed a paper that said I was born because she was older than I was. I think some of the rest of

The McDougalls and the Nicholsons

(Upper) Mollie Moran and children. (Lower) Later image of Molllie with children in front of house. Back row: Buzz, Molly, Jennie, Nell, Mabel. In front: Evelyn, Edith, Don, Dick and Dorothy with Mollie Moran.

my brothers and sisters probably had that problem too. When kids were born in the hospital, they kept a record of them, but we were all born out in the country. All of Jenny and Mabel's kids were born at home too. People didn't go to the hospital then like they did later. But mine were born in the hospital.

Mollie gave birth to her fifth child, Mabel on April 2, 1903, the very same day her father was buried.

> MABEL MUELLER: My mother told me that on the morning I was born, she drove from our farm on the west side of section 7 over to the Moran farm. The dashboard broke on the buggy and the whip hit the horse and the horse ran away with her over the rough road. She said it had been thawing and then it froze. It was a very rough road. She did not go to the funeral because the funeral was in Maurice, and she had had a good rough ride that morning. So probably that made my birth come earlier.

Our mother Edith was born the year after Mabel. When her dad William saw her, he gave her the nickname Bitty.

> EDITH: They always said my dad looked at me when I was born and said, "She's a regular little bitty, an Irish bitty." I think Bridgett is an Irish name with the nickname Bitty. I always said I don't know why they didn't call me Bridgett. But I was named after some friend of my mother's. I was

really called Rose Edith, but I didn't like Rose, when I went to school, I was Edith, I changed it.

In 1906, shortly after their seventh child, Buck, had been born, William built his family a beautiful house, especially for those times. Now typically, houses built in this era had first started as a 12' x 12' or 12' x 14' structure (which is what the homesteading laws required). As the family grew and needed more space and bedrooms, the homeowner expanded the main structure with an addition or two. This was the practical and low-cost way of doing things. In these days very few homes had indoor plumbing, electricity or many luxuries.

William's house was different. This house was designed and built to be a big, high quality home from the ground up. I believe he wanted to build one of the nicest houses in the area, and he succeeded. *The History of Plymouth County, Iowa* by Freeman says it was "One of the most pleasant and substantial country homes in the county." A man named Zack Eyres from Le Mars constructed it for him.

The house was very large, it had five bedrooms upstairs and a bedroom downstairs. There was also what they called a "storeroom" that went out to a balcony and in it was a single bed where someone could sleep. This was on the northwest corner of the house, so it was pretty cold in the wintertime and couldn't be used the whole year. On the main floor were a couple of sitting rooms, one had a bay window. They were nicely furnished, one had an overstuffed davenport, and there was a couch, and a couple of nice chairs and a piano. There was a dining room, and a hall that went to the upstairs and a door that lead to the outside. Mollie had a pantry in the kitchen, where she could store dishes, food and some canning. There was a basement, and from the basement you could access a deeper cave, where it stayed colder. Mollie could store most of her canning jars of meat, fruits, vegetables, and potatoes—things to eat through the winter. There was a dumb waiter that went from the cellar up to the kitchen for transporting those big jars and heavy sacks of potatoes for the big meals she cooked up for her family. The dumb waiter also went upstairs to the bedrooms so laundry could be sent up and down for washing.

But I think one of the most amazing things was that this house had indoor plumbing. It had a unique type of toilet. There was a big tank in the attic that held water. The water was pumped up into the tank by a windmill. When the toilet was flushed gravity took over. The water would flow down from the tank, through the toilet, and out to the outdoor sewage system. The water from the tank also went into sinks and to the basement where Mollie washed clothes. Downstairs she had a big oval shaped cast iron sink that she could build a fire underneath. Water from the tank in the attic would run into this sink and then they would start the fire to make the water hot. She would wash clothes with that nice hot water, ring the clothes through the ringer and then hang them on the line outside or occasionally in the basement to dry. We didn't drink the water that came from the tank. Next to the kitchen sink was a big three or four-gallon pail of fresh cold water from the well. It had a dipper in it, and that's the water we would

North view of William Nicholson's new house.

drink. Mollie also had a reservoir on the stove that would heat water for washing the dishes.

This house also had power. It came from a generator in the basement where there was an engine that powered the electrical system throughout the house. In the evening when we needed lights someone would go down and start up the generator and the lights would go on. Luxuries like indoor plumbing, electricity and a dumb waiter were unusual for that time.

It was a very comfortable house, a nice place for the family to gather and play the games our family enjoyed: checkers, bridge and pitch. I have pleasant memories of gathering in the two sitting rooms with the Saturday Evening Post to look at the pictures. There were some nice little knickknacks, lamps and painted portraits that reminded me I was in Grandma's living room.

The house was spacious enough that William had his own room upstairs. His room always smelled like flavored pipe tobacco and there were always pipes laying on the bureau.

After Grandfather Moran died, Grandmother Ellen Moran moved in with them and she had her own room as well.

> EDITH: Grandmother Moran was a big woman, nice looking, snow white hair and big brown eyes and could she ever roll those eyes. She was always with us kids. I really remember some things about her more than my mother. She would come out and help us pick chickens and help us do dishes. Oh, she was a fast worker. She could make her hands go. She was kind of like Aunt Mary, but she didn't do that much work. She was Catholic and some of us always had to take her to church on Sundays. That was the only church we attended.

There was also a second little house on the property. It was a modest two-story house with a couple of bedrooms, a kitchen, and a room for sitting. Sometimes Grandma and Grandpa would put up the hired help there. Or they might use it to help people out when they needed a place to stay, maybe a family was

The McDougalls and the Nicholsons

between houses or their house had burned down. Uncle Don and Aunt Helen Nicholson stayed for a bit when their son Jack was first born. I remember visiting newborn Jack at that house. Everyone was amazed at how long that baby was.

There were several other buildings on the property as well, one of them was a big barn with stalls for ten or twelve horses.

EDITH: My dad thought a lot of his horses. They had a lot of horses. The barn held ten or twelve head and that would be full. They did all the work with horses. There weren't any tractors.

Soon after William had built that house, the family experience a big fire.[40]

The large barn of William Nicholson burned to the ground Monday night. The barn contained nearly all of this year's crop being filled with hay, 500 bushels wheat and double the bushels of oats. There was fortunately but one horse in the barn at the time, it being a pony which the children drove to school for years. A very faithful animal much thought of by everyone the animal came into contact with. Winnie as she was called. The fire was first discovered by Mrs. Nicholson who was awakened by an unusual light in the hall. She phoned at once to Struble which is, but 1.5 miles and a bucket brigade was formed

---

40—Le Mars Sentinel dated Friday, October 25, 1907.

> *and rushed out, but were too late to do anything with the barn, as it was all in. They, however, gave valuable assistance by keeping the adjoining building from catching on fire. If it had been a windy night, all buildings on the place would have burned up. Mr. Nicholson considers the loss at about $2,500, which is covered by about $1,200 insurance.*

For the most part however, Mollie and William's children enjoyed a comfortable environment:[41]

> *The home life of the Nicholson's is ideal, and they are held in the highest regard by their many friends throughout the county. William Nicholson's home is noted for its hospitality.*

Like all the women in this story, Mollie stayed busy doing all the things her big family needed. She fixed lunches for the farm help and big meals for her brood, kept her house tidy, gardened, did laundry for all those kids, canned for the winter months, and the millions of other things a mother needs to do to take care of 11 children. Mollie did have some help:

> EDITH: When we were kids in school, my mother always had help, that is if she could get it. Old Alice Tierman, she worked for us for years. She lived with us.

41—*The History of the Counties, Woodbury and Plymouth, Iowa*

I'm sure there was always plenty going on. Edith remembers getting ready for school in the mornings.

> EDITH: When we got ready to go to school, we would always wear dresses, with long underwear and cotton stockings. We never wore any kind of pants in those days. We all had our hair in braids and that was quite a deal to get all that hair braided. Our dad would say he was going to cut it off and our mother would say, "If you do, I'll go cut your horses tails off." Then we would pack our lunch and if we didn't have a lunch, we would walk to the store and buy something at noon.
>
> We went a mile and a half to school, but we didn't walk. For a long time, we went in a surrey pulled by a horse and then our dad went to town one time and bought something with two long seats facing each other in the back with a horse pulling it. It was kind of enclosed, it had curtains on it. We needed a big buggy because there were always about five or six of us going to school. Dad never wanted us to go to school on a real cold day because when we got to school the schoolhouse wouldn't be warm. They had a furnace that never worked right and an old guy that didn't know much about it took care of it. Somedays the room would be full of smoke instead of heat. We never wanted to miss, we always wanted to go, but Dad didn't want us there if it was too cold. One day he and Uncle Dick went down to Hot Springs and bought a thermometer and if it was below a certain temperature,

William and Mollie family. Back Mabel, Nell, Dorothy. Middle Dick, Buck, William, Don, Buzz. Front Jennie, Evelyn, Molly, Mollie, Edith.

we weren't to go to school and if we didn't eat breakfast, we weren't to go to school because he said if his horses didn't eat their oats in the morning, he wouldn't work them that day.

MABEL MUELLER: We had a lot of fun when we were kids growing up on the farm. On Sundays we would play ball in our own backyard. The McFarland kids would come down. There were six McFarland kids: Ralph, Grace, Dan, and Stel were the older ones, but Les and Jean were the ones that used to come down and play ball with us. Kids from Struble, probably Norma and Allen Becker and our own little brood would be out there playing ball

The McDougalls and the Nicholsons

Captioned by Mabel or Edith; "Out on the farm, our Sunday p.m. baseball team in spring of 1916 (I think). From left: Vern Keough (holding Ralph Becker) Don Nicholson, Len McFarland (back of Ben), Dorothy Nicholson, Mabel Nicholson, Edith Nicholson, Norma Becker, Alwin Becker, Buck Nicholson (leaning on bat) Gene McFarland, Dick Nicholson (standing in front of girls). Molly Nicholson took the picture, I'm sure, because she had a camera."

on Sunday afternoon. There were enough of us that we would always make our own fun. We had a lot of fun. We had ponies to ride, some of them were too foxy for me though. I wasn't such a good rider. I never enjoyed it too much, but a lot of times it was ride the horse or we didn't go so maybe two of us would get on a horse and go around and see some of the neighbor girls and some of the neighbor boys.

EDITH: The Beckers used to come down to the farm pretty near every Sunday, they had an old horse they rode, they called him Old Colonel, and we'd play games outside.

The McFarland kids lived up the road a half mile and maybe they'd come down too, so we'd have a good gang. We'd play baseball and hide-and-seek. The girls and boys would all play together.

EDITH: My best friend was Margaret Durband, that was until I went ahead of her in school. Then we weren't very friendly after that. Margaret, Bob Edwards and I were in a grade together. One day the teacher said I should come up and read with the next grade, and I went up and read with them and she said well, you can stay in there. So, I really went two grades in one year and Margaret stayed behind, and she never liked me after that. Well, I think it was because Mabel, Molly and I were all stuck in one room at home, when we would go to bed at night, they'd tell me everything they learned that day. They were ahead of me in school.

I suspect my mother's best friends were her sisters. Mom was always close to her sisters, especially her older sister Mabel.

EDITH: Mabel and I shared everything, and we always got along. Mabel, Molly and I shared a room, and we never had a fight, and Jenny was always easy to get along with. Mabel and I never ever had a fight. Never to her dying day did we ever have any words.

Mollie enjoyed shopping in Sioux City and Edith talked about those trips downtown, and how they'd always take the train.

Molly standing behind Edith and Mabel.

(From back of photo) "Buildings south side of Struble. Mrs. Nick Schlesser's horse and buggy. Girls are Edith Nicholson and Ida Sayer. 1916.

EDITH: Our mother used to go to Sioux City to shop and one of us always went with her. There was a train down in the morning and another one back at night. That train didn't go through Le Mars; it went west of Le Mars, it was called Dalton in those days (now it's called West Le Mars) and its still there. It goes from Sioux City to Struble. It doesn't come through Le Mars. The Illinois Central and the Great Northern, the long pull train that goes through Le Mars, that one doesn't go through Struble, that goes up through Seney and up that way to Minneapolis. But we had a train that went to Sioux City in the morning and came back at night.

William Nicholson and Mollie (Moran) Nicholson.

My mother generally bought furniture from Sioux City. My dad would always be mad when she got it—she bought a new davenport one time and he about threw a fit, but it wasn't long before he was laying on it all the time.

My father was a pretty well-off man, but we never knew it. We always had plenty to eat, a warm house and clothes to wear, but we never took trips or anything like that. One time when I was 14, they rented a place at Lake Okoboji and we all went up there, but that was about it. That is where I learned to swim. My dad had some friend who had a place up there, so my mother and Buzz and

The Road to Love

Mollie Nicholson with her children on their trip to Okoboji (Edith is standing in the center).

some of us kids went to the place. Well, there were weeds higher than us kids' heads and my mother said, "We're not staying here." There was a Detloff, who was married to Hugh Daley, and we went to see her. They owned a house and beside their house was a house they rented out, so we rented that house for a month, for $100. Mom stayed there for the entire month and us kids took turns going up. Before the month was up everyone had had their turn. But they never did anything like that again. That was 1918.

I went to high school the fall of that year. World War I was going on, I remember that. I came down to Le Mars and stayed with Norma Becker. Norma, Allen and I were all starting high school and what a jolt that was, to go from a country school to a high school. I'd never even been in a high school before. I was sure scared. I was green, dumb. Well, I wasn't so dumb, but you know, everything was different, I'll tell you that.

But I didn't get homesick. I was staying with Norma and I knew her really well, because after Jennie got married, we got very well acquainted. They were part of the gang that came down to our farm pretty near every Sunday for games. And then Mabel joined me about a month later. That was when we went to stay with Elsie Cane. She was a cousin of ours. In those days nobody wanted to keep anybody in their house, but she was going to keep us. We had a room there and we'd have breakfast, and she'd fix us a nice evening meal. Well, she had just had a baby, she kept us maybe a month and then she said she just couldn't do it anymore. So, we moved across the street from Norma Becker to a bungalow. We'd eat our supper and our breakfast there and go to a restaurant for our dinner, our noon meal. We did that through our freshman year, but I didn't want to go back the next year. Mabel went back another year, but I didn't go past my freshman year.

When I went home, my mother wasn't really well, so there was plenty to do. Molly and I were home, but Jenny and Nell were gone.

Mom described our grandfather William, as quite a stern man. He had eleven children to support, and I imagine that most of the time he was concentrating on making a living.

William spent a lot of time on his farm making hay. This was quite an ordeal and required knowledge, management, and several different types of machines. William had people doing the physical work. He mainly managed the farm hands. He had a hired man name Chet Long that helped him out a lot. The hired man would run the farm implements, put up hay (cut it, cure it and stack it into haystacks) and help feed the hogs and cattle. These are all things my dad would do himself on his farm, but William preferred to have help on his. This may be partly because William did more than run a farm. He was a premier of his time, but he was also a creative entrepreneur. He lived during a time when our nation was developing its railroad system and with that growth came the opportunity to develop its agricultural system as well. William found a way to tap into these developments and generate wealth.

Most of the homesteaders in northwest Iowa were diversified livestock producers, by necessity. They raised a variety of animals to feed their family and generate a small income. Their stock of animals generally included a number of chickens for meat and eggs, pigs to provide bacon, sausage and ham, and cattle for beef and milk. When their cows had calves, they kept a number of females for milking and males for beef, but there was a limit to the number of livestock their land could support, especially when one considers the crude farm implements of the times.

Then came the completion of the railway into Struble in 1889, and this paved the way for diversified farming to take a step toward commercial farming.

William had a very good friend named Ed Durband, who was also his business partner. Ed was the owner of quite a bit of land around Struble and lived very near William. After the railroad connected Sioux City to Struble, William Nicholson and Ed Durband, jumped into a new business. They began what my mother called "scalping." The two would get in their horse and buggy and go off to visit the nearby farms. William was a husky guy, very friendly and he smiled a lot. The two knew the farmers in the area, and they loved talking about cattle. They would take their horse and buggy around, visiting the farmers, and chatting with them about their cattle. If the farmer had some to sell, the pair would go out into the field and take a look at them. A farmer might have seven or eight head which was hardly enough to justify all the logistics involved in loading them on a train and sending them to the cattle yards. William and Ed would buy up these cattle. They had a pretty good sense of what they could get for them in the stockyards.

In the afternoons, when they returned home, if they had bought any cattle, they would talk to Buzz and Buck, two of William's sons, and let them know what farm they were at. The two boys would get on their horses and ride out to that farm, round up those cattle and drive them to the railyard in Struble.

William and Ed rented a pen nearby, where they would keep them until they bought enough to load into a livestock car and send them down to the cattle market in Sioux City or Chicago.

This picture was taken at Tom McFarland's farm sale—the McFarland's were our neighbors ½ mile north on the corner from our farm—their children and us kids were good friends. They had four boys and two girls—the two youngest boys were about the ages of Nell and me the rest were all older. Buzz wrote the names of these fellows on the back of this picture—you can certainly see what a big guy Grandpa was. He was really in his "Hey Day" at this time. Please notice the "horse blanket pins" in his sheep skin coat. This was the great coat that he always wore to sales.

This type of cattle-buying William and Ed were doing was called "country buying" (buying from the individual farmer).

William or Ed could ride in the caboose for free if they had "freight." So, they would ride down with the cattle to the stockyards, but they would have to pay a fare to return.

Once at the cattle market, companies like Armour, Cudahy and Swift would send buyers to the yard and the buyers would go through the same process as William and Ed went through when they visited the farmers: the buyers would go from pen to pen looking for cattle they thought looked good, selecting the ones they wanted to send to the packing house. Outside cattle buyers might come through as well, to select the younger calves to fatten up to be sold later. The buying that was done in these stock yards was referred to as "city buying."

> MABEL MUELLER: William and Ed really made most of their money dealing in cattle. They bought them from the farmers and shipped them to Chicago to the city markets. They didn't ship by truck. They would ship several railroad carloads at one time.

William also increased the number of hogs and cattle he raised.

> EDITH: He always had a lot of hogs and he fed cattle. If he had a hundred head that would be a lot of cattle in those days. And they raised quite a few hogs. Buzz was a good hog man, he used to do the hogs. They would drive them to Struble and load them on the train.

William and Ed were good at what they did and as time went on, they had a pretty good business going. William also began speculating in land. This was something he had seen his father do and he saw the price of land in Iowa rising.

MABEL MUELLER: Dad went out and speculated in high priced land after World War I ended in 1918. He bought a lot of land and paid $375 per acre for it. Then when the land started dropping in price, he started mortgaging the 1,000 acres that he owned. He lost that and the other land that he and Ed Durband had bought, a big tract of land up around Granville. Dad had paid $375 an acre for it, which was a lot of money. There was some land, at that time, that sold for $500 an acre. That was the limit. They did not buy it really to keep. They were going to speculate on it, sell it as the prices rose. But the prices dropped very quickly. They were stuck with that $375/acre land. The people they bought from lived in Chicago and didn't want the land back. They wanted their money. Eventually, both Ed Durband and our dad lost pretty much everything they had. It was really sad because they thought they were doing the right thing to speculate. They had done some speculating and done very well on it, which gave them the idea to keep on with it.

DOUG: At one point William had 1,600 acres. He had 11 kids and he had close to a quarter section for each kid.

It was right after William bought some land in Granville that things started to go downhill.

BILL: Mom said her mother (Mollie) was up all night trying to talk William out of buying that section of ground up at Granville. But he was determined to buy it, and after he did, things turned a somersault.

It is easy to see why William thought this would be a good place for his money. This article explains fairly succinctly what was going on in Iowa in William's time.[42]

> *Farm owners had hard sledding in the 1920's and early 1930's. The low point in farm values came in 1933 at $69 an acre as the average value for farmland in Iowa. Every year from 1920 to 1933 farm values dropped—a total decline of $186 an acre in 13 years or an average of $14 an acre a year.*
>
> *The contrast between the situation before and after 1920 was striking. From the beginning of the state's history to 1920 there was no record of any decline in farm values for the state as a whole. All of the Federal Census values, reported to 1900, show increases, and all the annual values, reported from 1900 to 1920, show an increase, (with the exception of 1904, when values remained stationary). The farm family in 1920 which looked back could*

42—State History Society of Iowa—the Palimpsest.

see nothing but rising farm values for three generations back to the original settlers in the 1840's and 1850's. On the other hand, this same family in 1933 could look back 13 years and see nothing but declining values with each year bringing a new low to the value of its farm.

William and Mollie went on to experience some very tough times. They were losing everything they had worked so hard to build. Then tragically, in 1934 they also lost their daughter

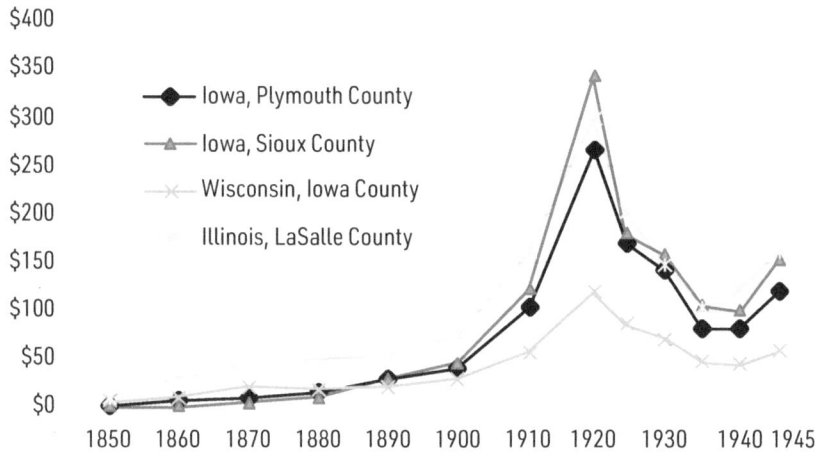

Farm Real Estate Values in the United States by Counties, 1850-1982; Charles H. Barnard & John Jones. Public Domain, Google digitized, www.hathitrust.org.

Place	1850	1860	1870	1880	1890
Iowa, Plymouth County	-	$6	$8	$13	$27
Iowa, Sioux County	-	-	$4	$10	$28
Wisconsin, Iowa County	$5	$10	$20	$18	$21
Illinois, LaSalle County	$9	$30	$42	$49	$54

Dorothy. She was married to Lorenz Bertram and had five children: Jean (9), Charles (7), Joyce (5), Lawrence (3½), Allen (2).

The night of August 10, 1934, there had a been a storm. Early the next morning, 26-year-old Dorothy got up and went into the bathroom. This is a brief summary of a long article in the Thursday August 16, 1934, Hawarden Independent:

> *Early Friday morning while Mr. Bertram and the hired help were downstairs getting ready to do chores, they were suddenly startled by what seemed to them a scream, followed by a fall upstairs. They rushed up and found Mrs. Bertram lying in the bathroom where she had gone after rising and in making her toilet had reached to light the electric bulb.*
>
> *From indications Mrs. Bertram had washed her hands and leaned against some of the fixtures when she reached for the bulb to put on the light, it caused a complete circuit, and the electricity went through her body, causing almost instant death.*

It was only a year later that Mollie died. According to Mom's interview, she had been sick for a long time before she died.

1900	1910	1920	1925	1930	1935	1940	1945
$40	$103	$265	$170	$142	$80	$80	$120
$45	$121	$342	$179	$157	$105	$99	$152
$29	$56	$118	$86	$70	$47	$44	$58
$74	$160	$298	$201	$148	$102	$122	$160

She had tuberculosis of the kidney. They had removed one of her kidneys and then later, in 1935, the other one wore out. It became infected, she lost functioning of it and it killed her. Death Records Plymouth County, Iowa, book 1 page 277 lists her cause of death as Uremia.

My memory of my grandmother Moran was that she was very stern. She didn't like crying. I remember once when I was whining about something, she was nearby and she said, "Shut that kid up" and let me tell you, I shut right up. When I mentioned to my mom one time, that Grandma sure didn't seem to be very happy, Mom said, "Maybe she didn't have much to be happy about."

After his wife died, William Nicholson remained on the farm until 1940, and then he moved into town with Mabel Mueller on 125 First Street NE. In his older years he was having trouble with his hearing. He had, for the times, a type of hearing aid. It was a long flexible tube with an earpiece on one end and a talking piece on the other. When we were around, he liked to have his earpiece available, so we could talk into it. He seemed to appreciate communicating that way, rather than having us holler at him.

> JANICE: My grandpa used to make me feel special, I thought I was his favorite. I remember playing with the other kids and he would say, "You all go now, but she can stay." Then we would sit together, and I would talk into his earpiece.

Grandpa Nicholson also smoked a pipe and I remember watching him light it with his wooden matches. He had a unique

William Nicholson with his "hearing aid."

William standing by house.

way of holding his pipe because he had cut a tendon in his left wrist in what I believe was a farming accident and could no longer bend his index finger on that hand. He'd hold his corncob pipe in his left hand, and his stiff finger would stick straight out. He'd strike the match with his right hand and hold the flame to the flavored tobacco, then he'd give some loud puffs, as he drew in the air.

I think our grandpa might have imbibed a bit. In his later years, when he was living with Mabel, he would walk down the couple blocks to the bar each day and meet up with his buddies to have some beers. When I was working for the dry cleaner one of my jobs was to take the men's hats to the post office to send to Mike Means' dad in Yankton, because he wanted to wash the hats down there. I would put them in a hat box and as I was running them down to the post office, it was a common occurrence to bump into Grandpa and his friends walking to or from the bar. The last few years he developed heart trouble, although it didn't weigh him down, and he was able to remain active. Pneumonia got him in the end. *Death Records Plymouth County, Iowa Book 3*, page 334 lists his cause of death as acute cardiac decompensation to arterio sclerotic cardiovascular disease.

There was a nice write-up about William after he died. They thought very highly of him around the area.

> *William Nicholson was widely known in Plymouth and Sioux Counties and was popular in a wide circle of friends. Mr. Nicholson was interested in community affairs and a liberal contributor to any project for the benefit of the*

people. He held various offices in the township and was active in affairs. He was affiliated with the republican party in politics. He was a member of the Order of the Elks, and for many years a member of the world known Prairie club of Le Mars. Mr. Nicholson, while living on the farm engaged in buying cattle and stock and was for a number of years, a notable figure in the cattle buying business and his compeers rated him as a sensible and competent judge of stock. Mr. Nicholson built a fine home on the farm near Struble. The Nicholson place was noted for its hospitality and was always open to the friends of its generous and free hearted owner. Mr. Nicholson was a man of fine address, well educated, of courtly bearing, and a pleasing conversationalist, although handicapped in recent years by deafness.

CHESTER NELSON MCDOUGALL AND EDITH ROSE NICHOLSON

DOUG: I heard the story that Dad was selling cars and he went to sell William Nicholson a car. He asked Mr. Nicholson if it was okay if he had a date with one of his daughters. As the story goes, it didn't particularly matter if it was Edith or Mabel.

Apparently, William gave his permission, and we know who he chose.

(Upper) Chester between Mabel (left) and Edith (right). (Lower) Chester and Edith.

EDITH: He used to come out to our place and Buzz kind of ran around with him. I never had anything to do with him, but then one time there was a parade in town, and he had his car all fixed up and he called me and asked if I'd ride in the parade with him. I think I was about 16 then. After that we dated off and on. But I don't think it was "love at first sight", I never had a lot of steady guys.

Then one day Chester asked Edith to attend a celebration at Remsen. That was the day Chester and Edith decided to get married. They didn't have a fancy wedding; they just went to Sioux City and got married. Chester's sister Pearl, and a friend Pearl worked with, stood up for them.[43]

43—November 28, 1922 Le Mars Sentinel newspaper. Le Mars Globe Post November 29, 1922.

Chester and Edith

Popular Young Couple Wed
Well Known Residents of Struble Vicinity

Miss Edith Nicholson and Chester McDougall, well known young people living in the neighborhood of Struble, surprised their friends last Wednesday when they went quietly to Sioux City and were married at the First Presbyterian church in that city, Rev. Wallace Hamilton officiating. Mrs. Barkel, a sister of the bridegroom, was one of the witnesses to the ceremony. The bride is a daughter of Mr. and Mrs. William Nicholson, of Struble. She is a very popular young woman in that community. The groom is a son of Mrs. J.N. McDougall of this city and was engaged in the automobile business here for a time. Of late he has been engaged in farming on the McDougall place in Grant township. They will make their home in Le Mars for the present.

Chester McDougall of Le Mars and Miss Edith Nicholson were married Thursday in Sioux City. Both young people are well and favorably known and popular among a large circle of friends who join in wishing them happiness in their wedded life.

Now married and raising a family, Chester didn't feel the car business was going particularly well and he decided he'd like to get back into farming. When James Nelson retired, he had handed his farm over to his older son Jack, so Chester had to explore other options.

His new father-in-law, William Nicholson, was managing the Adden Place for his brother Richard, and he offered to rent it to Chester. William was willing to take share rent for the place, rather than cash rent. This opened the door for Chester to get back into farming. This is really where he got his start. He had a good relationship with the First National Bank in Le Mars, and he took out a loan for $10,000 to buy horses and the necessary machines and basic tools to get a good start because he was basically starting from scratch. After living a short time with Martha and Mary, the couple moved over to the Adden farm. The house Edith moved into wasn't particularly nice.

> EDITH: My uncle Dick had lived there for a long time. When he went back to Scotland, he just left the house the way it was. He married some woman there and he never came back. Then all his friends and everyone from Le Mars came out and took anything that was any good from the house, so it was just junk left when we moved out there. There were some beds upstairs we could use, but we had to refurnish the downstairs. My mother and I bought a dining room set and a living room set, and I had bought some dressers before from some woman that was selling them in town. Dad (Chester) had a bed, so we had the downstairs furnished nice. But the house wasn't modern at all. It had a heating stove and an outhouse. But it did have a bathtub in it, a great big bathtub. It had a pump, and you could pump soft water into the bathtub,

and I guess Uncle Dick used to pump that water into it every morning and get in there and take a bath in that cold water. It was in a little room off the dining room. The house had a summer kitchen and believe me, it was a summer kitchen. It didn't have a foundation under it, and it wasn't plastered. It was okay in the summertime, but we couldn't use it in the wintertime, so we moved that bathtub out into that summer kitchen and then we used that little bathroom for a kind of a kitchen. It wasn't very handy.

We stayed on the Adden farm for seven years. When they moved out there, I was two, and my sister Mabel was born a month later. Then two years after Mabel, in the summer of '27, Bill came along and four years after that came Dick (1931).

Of all Edith's children, only Bill was born at home. She had all the others in the hospital.

Sacred Heart Hospital opened on May 11, 1923. My dad was counting on me being the first baby born there because they had a "special" going. The first delivery would be free of charge and of course my dad liked that idea. Unfortunately, we missed it, Mark Meis was the first baby born, I was the second.

> BILL: Jim and Mabel were born in that hospital, but I was born at home. Dr. Lamb delivered me in the house by the foundry, the Collins house, where Martha and Mary were living at the time. When Dick was born, I remember

mom wasn't feeling good that day and Dad and I went to Amel Mueller's brother's funeral, I was four. Dad got home and then he took Mom to Sacred Heart hospital in Le Mars. From then on, all the other kids were born in the hospital.

These were very simple times and as we grew up, my parents were never much for toys, so we didn't have many. We did have a coaster wagon and we had a lot of fun with that wagon. We'd get into it on one knee and propel it with our other foot. We'd steer it with the handle and coast along. We'd take turns pulling each other and driving it on pretend roads that we had carved in the dirt. From as early as I can remember Bill had an imaginary livestock business and he'd pull that wagon around "buying livestock."

As for the adults, wine and beer was a treat they would enjoy before dinner and Dad liked to have a cold beer at thrashing time. He also liked to give the thrashing crew a bottle of cold home brew with their noon meal.

This was during the prohibition (1920–1933). Our Uncle Buzz bottled homemade wine at his house and he and my dad made beer at the Adden place. I think they made it at our place because we had an ice box you could enter from either side but also, I don't think Buzz liked the mess it left. I remember watching them with fascination. It was quite a complicated procedure. They made the brew in a big crock, mixing together malt and yeast etc. with water. After letting it sit for a certain number of days, it would be time to bottle it up. This process entailed gravity and

The McDougalls and the Nicholsons

suction. First, in order to get the beer out of the crock and into individual bottles, they would use a long rubber hose as a syphon. One end of the hose went inside the crock (which they had elevated). Then they would suck the lower end of the hose and as it started flowing, they'd put the hose in the bottle below and fill it up. As they'd move the hose from bottle to bottle, in order not to lose suction, they would stick the hose in their mouth. So, they were taking a drink of beer every time they went from one bottle to the other. The next step was capping the full bottle. They had a capper with a handle on it. They set a cap on the bottle and then pulled the handle down. It would mash the cap on the bottle, and it would stick there. When they were finished, they laid the bottles on their side in the big ice box. They laid a lot of beer down in that icebox.

One night us kids were in bed and drifting off to sleep. We heard a sudden, very loud BAM! It was an explosion from the ice box! Then we heard another "BAM" then . . . BAM . . . BAM, BAM, BAM!" First thing in the morning, we ran out to the ice box to see what had happened and boy did we find a mess! Yeast was part of the beer making process and when that hose went from Buzz and Dad's mouth into the bottles, it picked up bacteria. Some of the beer "worked" and produced a gas and caused the bottles to explode.

My grandpa and his friends used to share some bootleg as well. I recall a time on the Nicholson homestead while I was visiting there with my mom. I was about seven or eight years old. An old friend of my grandpa's, named Frank Smit, came to visit him and brought a gallon jug of some sort of homemade hard liquor. They sat down on the ground on the shady side of the toolshed and talked and passed that yellow jug back and forth while I sat and watched wide-eyed.

In March of 1932, Mom and Dad moved over to the McFarland farm. I don't know the reason for this, but I'm fairly sure it was for financial reasons. I was now nine, Mabel was seven, Bill was five and Dick having been born in August of 1931 was just a baby. I remember that move very well because a few years earlier, Dad had bought our mom a Copper Clad cookstove, the Cadillac of cookstoves, and it was really heavy. They got it up onto the wagon along with a couple other pieces of furniture. Dad still didn't have a tractor, so it was the horses' job to pull that heavy wagon. To lighten the load for the animals, Dad made the decision to cut across the field, shortening the path from 1½ miles by road to ½ mile through the field. Unfortunately, that spring the fields were muddier than my dad realized, and those poor horses kept getting stuck in the mud and it turned out to be a very tough trip for them.

Fortunately for Mom, the McFarland farm had a much nicer house than the Adden place. It was a big house and was modern for the time. There was an indoor bathroom, although they had to haul hot water upstairs to take a bath. There were at least four big bedrooms upstairs and one bedroom downstairs for my parents. There was a big kitchen, a big living room and a big dining room. The ceilings were very tall, a couple feet taller than you'd see in a normal house and it made the rooms look very big.

By this time, the depression had really set in and money was tight. Martha and Mary had moved from the big house on Central Avenue over to the Collins house, but when Chester and Edith moved into this bigger house, it was decided that Martha and Mary should come and live with them. The house was big enough that Martha and Mary each had their own room upstairs.

In her youth, Grandma was very attractive. She was slim and short, just over five feet but she was feisty. She wasn't mean, but boy was she opinionated. She was proud of her age and origin and she had a nice English accent. She pronounced "eighty" as "eye-dee." She'd say, "I came over to this county in eye-dee, got married in eye-dee-one and Mary was born in eye-dee-two."

I couldn't count how many times she told the story of how she had come over with a flock of sheep on a ship called the Lamar and when a sheep would die along the way, the men would just throw the carcass over the side. She saw the sharks following the ship, staying nearby and when the animal was thrown overboard, they would eat it up. She told that story many, many times. Mary got tired of hearing it and always rolled her eyes.

Although both our grandmother Martha and our aunt Mary loved us kids and were very good to us, there was quite a contrast between the two.

> BILL: Mary never said much, but boy ol' Martha would tell you what she thought. I used to give her a hard time, try to get a laugh out of her. I'd pick her up sometimes, there was nothing to her, she only weighed 72 pounds. She'd

Grandmother Martha with the kids.

say, "Put me down ol' boy! You be sorry some day!" She had a sense of humor.

BILL: One time I went to a sale with Dad, and I came home and got a little twine to put around my dogs, Captain and Rover. I named them that because those were the names of the dogs Martha had over in England, the ones she brought over with the sheep. I took them out on the porch to auction them off. Martha was always saying, "Don't be talking to yourself or you'll be going to hell." Well, I was out on the porch, talking to my dogs and myself and all of a sudden, a pitcher of water comes flying out the window. Oh boy, she had her ways!

DICK: Grandma liked to take a nap every day. She'd take me up with her. We'd go lay in her bed for an hour or so. She was a good grandma, but she was pretty feisty.

BILL: Martha was set in her ways and was never afraid to express her opinion, but she was a good grandma. She loved us kids and was very kind to us. Our mom and grandma got along. Martha wasn't too bossy with Mom. Martha and Mary were a lot of help to Mom with us kids.

As feisty and opinionated as Martha was, Mary was the opposite. She was quiet and empathetic. She was a saint and made life easier and more enjoyable for all of us. She had blue eyes and as long as I knew her, she had white hair. I think my aunt Mary was about as close to an angel as you could find. She was a wonderful remarkable woman and all of us kids were very lucky to have her as part of our family.

Aunt Mary.

BILL: She was an awful good aunt, she was the best soul you ever met, so good to all us kids. She loved Edith and Edith loved her. She was never married; she just took care of her mother and dad and then she took care of us kids. Most of her life she just took care of people.

Mary was always a lot of help to my mom on the farm, whether she was living with Mom and Dad on the McFarland farm, or living in town and spending days with Mom, she would keep an eye on us kids and help out with the all the countless chores Mom needed to do to sustain her big family. She'd gather eggs, take care of the poultry and livestock, and can food. Mary did all the things other people didn't like to do. She would look for potato bugs in the big garden she kept. She'd pick those bugs off the plants and put them in a can of kerosene, that went a long way to control the potato bug population. That garden also went a long way in feeding our big family.

EDITH: I remember how we used to get dinner. She'd be working with me getting dinner and we'd sit down to eat and Mary'd be gone. Out in the cattle barn or someplace chasing after eggs. She'd never sit down and eat a meal with us. OH!! And an old hen would be sitting on those eggs for a week, and she'd pick them up and bring them in. She'd milk the cows, and no one ever wanted to touch those cows.

Grandmother and Mary lived with us (at the McFarland farm) and I think it would have been a lot harder if they hadn't been there. Mary used to raise this great big garden in the summer and that sure helped out a lot. We always had enough to eat. Nobody had any money, so it wasn't so bad to be without money. But our kids will never remember a day they went to bed hungry. Jim will tell you that. There was always something to eat. We always had three meals a day. But that house was pretty cold. Dad would always cut a lot of firewood and in the real cold weather we'd sometimes burn coal at night. We didn't have money to buy coal so we couldn't buy very much but it was possible to go to Struble and buy coal.

As far as paying the rent, it was hard scraping. We had 240 acres and we paid that rent in shares. But we also had the 80 acres with the house and buildings on it and we had to pay cash rent of six dollars an acre, for that part. We paid $480 for 80 acres. We'd make it in two payments. We never had a good crop down there as long as we lived there. It always dried out or hailed out or something. We never really started raising a crop till we came over to this (Doug's) farm.

BILL: Dad farmed by milking the good milkers and the hard milkers would have a couple of calves on each cow to live on that milk until they got big enough to eat. He'd raise those calves and feed them out, sell them and pay the taxes and if they had land payments, they'd pay that. The hogs were the mortgage lifters, the main go. They wouldn't have the original cost to pay on the hogs because they'd come from his sows.

The thirties were tough years for farmers, not only because of the depression, but nature brought in its share of challenges as well. Through the mid 30's there were several summers of severe drought, and the winter of 1936 is described in the history books as "one long terrible blizzard." Huge drifts of snow jammed the trains. Important supplies, like coal, ran low. When the spring finally came, farmers hoped it would break the previous cycles of drought, but no such luck, what corn did begin to grow, ultimately withered in the fields. Summer after summer the plants died, leaving nothing to hold the soil in place. When the southwestern winds blew in, they picked up that loose dirt, and blew it around in dark swirling clouds, blocking out the light. These years are remembered as "the dirty thirties." Next came the grasshoppers that thrived in dry hot weather. Millions of them invaded the farms, devouring anything that grew. We were out there, helping our dad as he desperately tried to get ahead of the army, spreading hopper bait, a mixture of sawdust, poison and oil, hoping to fend them off. But as tough as those times were, we were always taken care of.

> BILL: Our dad was a good manager, a good farmer, and a good provider. We always had plenty to eat, a warm place to sleep and we had clothes to wear. In the thirties lots of people didn't have that.

With Martha and Mary's help, Edith kept the house neat, and the kitchen and storage stocked. Mary grew her big garden and Martha helped wherever she could. I remember one year Martha

Blizzard in the winter of 1936. From left Dick is under Edith's arm, Jim is above Bill, Mabel is to the right.

Edith and Chester McDougall.

Blizzard 1936 on Highway 75. From left, Bill (on top of snowbank), Jim is standing by Chester. Mabel and Dick are on top of the car.

raised a turkey for our Thanksgiving meal. She called him Old Tom. When Old Tom was out, the yard was "his," and he ruled it accordingly. If a little one ventured into the barnyard, he'd chase them back to the gate by the house. When November came around, no one was happy about killing Tom, especially Martha. But like it or not, he was a good tasting bird.

While we were at the McFarland farm, Mabel, Bill and I went to country school, a one room schoolhouse. We usually walked the mile to and from school, but occasionally Dad would take us in his Model T sedan. I remember that car having three doors, two on the passenger's side and one on the driver's side. It had a passenger seat in the front and a bench seat in the back. On really cold snowy days, Dad would want to drive us to school, but there were very few snowplows, so the snow would be left on those dirt roads for a long time. Those were the times Dad would harness up old Bert to the cutter, which was a one-horse sleigh. He'd wrap a horse hide robe around us and we'd stay nice and warm. Dad had bells on the horse's harness, and they would jingle as Bert trotted along. I really enjoyed that.

I loved horses, and Grandpa Nicholson spent a lot of time talking to us kids about them. He thought a lot of his horses. He had a barn with ten or twelve stalls, all full. To me, my grandpa was the absolute authority on horses. We grew up with an English-bred, called Happy Go Lucky. We called him "Hap" or "Happy." He was a cross between a standard bred riding horse and a racing horse. My grandpa used to tell me he was a "gentleman's pony" not a rough neck pony like several of the others that belonged to my cousins. We also had a Welch pony named Flash. When my cousin Jackie was younger, his dad bought him a Shetland pony, but he turned out to be too much for Jackie, so we took her on and settled her down. Her name was Bubbles.

One day when I was about 10 years old, my grandpa and Uncle Buck were working on Grandpa's farm, putting up hay on Struble hill. They needed someone to drive the hay stacker cart and since this was a simple job, my dad told me to go over and help.

This hay stacking cart was actually a broken old corn planter that had been in a couple runaways and was now just a seat on a couple of wheels. Uncle Buck and I took the horses out of the barn and were working together to harness them up to the cart. Well, I thought Buck snapped the reins onto the bit, and Buck thought I had, and as a result, neither of us had.

When I got onto the cart, the horses took right off, because they knew Grandpa was working on Struble hill. As we trotted

Out for a buggy ride with Flash.

along, I had the reins and I thought I had control. From the barn, to get to Struble hill, you have to cross a wooden bridge, pass through a gate and then head up to the right.

As we got closer to the bridge, I wanted to slow the horses down because I knew the noise of their hooves on the wooden planks would spook them. But when I pulled back on the reins, nothing happened. The horses were moving too fast when they hit the bridge and just as I feared, they got spooked and really took off. Now there was nothing I could do to keep from flying off the seat but hang on! As the horses headed through the gate, I was just barely holding on. When they made that turn to head up the hill, the cart started tumbling and I flew into the ditch. My grandpa was on the hill raking and he saw the whole thing

The McDougalls and the Nicholsons

happen. He grabbed his team and ran with them in front of my horses to stop the cart. But I was no longer there. I had flown into the ditch. When I jumped up to try to catch my runaway team, Buck said he'd never been so happy to see a kid get on his feet as he was when he saw me. He thought for sure I'd been hurt.

Before the advent of tractors all the machinery was pulled by horses. My dad had a couple teams, Mabel and Bill was one. They were always together. He had another team of grays that he bought from Amel Mueller. One of those horses was named Mabel too, Mabel and Bess. A farmer needs at least two teams, because some of the machinery, like the cultivators, require the power of four horses. Mabel and Bill stayed in a double stall and the other two would stay in a double stall if we had it. If we didn't, we'd put them in two single stalls near each other. Our horses had a manger for hay, with a box on either side for oats.

Our family also had racehorses. Our uncle Jack had a horse name Chadwick, our uncle Vern Keough had a horse named White Rose, and our dad had a horse named Tony. They would take them to the Orange County fair in Orange City to race them. Chadwick and White Rose were two of the fastest horses that raced up there.

My dad's sister Pearl and her husband Henry both worked in department stores in Sioux City. Each year they took a two-week vacation to Lake Okoboji. They would bring me up with them. One year they rented a cabin right across the street from where the Spirit Lake massacre had happened. I could look right out the door and see the monument that had been erected there.

Dick: My Uncle Henry had bought a new Model T Ford. Uncle Henry, Aunt Pearl, Mom, Dad, Doug and I drove that car from Le Mars to Lake Okoboji. Some of those roads were still gravel. We drove it up and parked it at the Queen dock, and Doug and I got into the water. I don't recall where we stayed at night. But it was a big trip, and a lot of fun.

After five years on the McFarland farm, Mom and Dad started considering a move. When the landlord came around to collect the rent, they mentioned it to him and the landlord goes right into town, and just like that, finds someone else to rent the farm. So, the first of March (farmers always moved in March) Mom and Dad have to move. They managed to find a house to rent in town. It was owned by the Gallagher's. The address was 120 12th Street, which is directly across the street from Doug and Vonice's current house. We all moved in there, our family, Mary and Martha.

Now, we had a house in town, but Dad still needed a place to work and put his equipment. He rented Uncle Buck's farm, straight across from William and Mollie's farmstead. This was by no means an ideal situation. Buck's farm was small and in disrepair. It had a broken-down house and a broken-down barn. But it did have a well, a windmill and enough of a kitchen that, if needed, Dad could cook his meals in the evenings and stay overnight.

Bill: Dad lived in that house at Buck's place. He farmed there one year. It wasn't much for buildings, but he got

The McDougalls and the Nicholsons

by. He had some hogs there and a few cows in the pasture. Those were tough times.

EDITH: That summer of '37, we lived in Le Mars; Grandma, Mary, and us. We lived in that house on the hill, we moved in there because we had given up the farm we were living on and then we didn't find another farm to live on. Dad put his stuff over across from my folks where Buck had a farm, while we lived in town.

Then that summer they had this contest in the shoe store, they were giving away a bicycle for the one that brought in the most old magazines and old pairs of shoes and Bill entered (and won) the contest. Well, Dad wasn't real busy, he just had that land to farm and he kind of got into the contest too. Bill and I went all over getting shoes and magazines. We went into Seney one day, where Grace Alberts and her sister Annie Nanagie were living. They were Dad's cousins, Alex McDougall's daughters. Grace told us about this farm. She said, "The Utechs are losing that farm and the loan company owns it and they're going to move off of it." So, Dad got busy and asked the loan company about it and they started considering us for renters for it. We had to drive down to their office in Ida Grove, but they did rent the farm to us. The man who made the decision was Glen Denning. He was a nice fellow and Dad really liked him.

Mr. Denning thought highly of Chester and he liked his farming practices. He recommended that Chester rent the farm. This was a prize farm. It had a very nice house, a big cattle barn, a horse barn with stalls for six horses and a hay loft, a corn-crib, a hog barn and a hog house just south of the horse barn. Metropolitan Life held the title and had gone in and patched up the things that needed fixing and painted the buildings. They put new roofs on the barns.

This was certainly a stroke of luck for our parents, this was a big improvement over the situation they were currently in. They now had a nice house, buildings and 250 acres for farming.

In March of 1938, Mom, Dad, Bill, Dick and Doug, moved to the Utech farm. Mom was pregnant with Janice. I was 15 and Mabel was 13 and we were going to school in town, so we remained in the Gallagher house with Martha and Mary. Eventually we started working. During our high school years, I worked for Elster Link at the Royal movie theater and for Mike Means at the Vallet Cleaner. Mabel was at the Co-op. Within a couple of years, Bill started working at Meis's grocery store and then started over at the packing house.

After Bill, Dick and Doug moved over to the farm, they started out at country school, Elgin number 8. Mom was the director of that school; she hired the teachers and oversaw the running of it. But that was only for three years, because as it happened, there was a big family, the Nip's, and they had a lot of kids going to that school. The Nip's moved away in March of 1941 and without that family, there weren't enough kids to keep the school open. In the fall of 1941, it was permanently closed. Bill, Dick and Doug transferred to school in town, and from

The McDougalls and the Nicholsons

Originally bought by Chester and Edith from the Utechs. This is what we now call "Doug's Farm." (Lower) An overhead photo of Doug's farm.

that point on, the rest of them went there as well. Chester and Edith drove them in every day. The younger four never went to country school.

Then came that fateful day: December 7, 1941, the day Japan attacked our country and World War II broke out. I was 19 and I made the decision to join the Iowa State Guard and get some military training because I could see what was coming.

> DICK: I was in fourth or fifth grade when the war broke out. I went down to Central that morning. Everyone was talking about it. That's all they were talking about. I had no idea what was going on. Now that I know what was

Elgin No. 8, Elizabeth "Betty" Schlesser, teacher (standing in doorway). Back row: Bernard Nipp, Bob Nipp, Bill McDougall, Dick McDougall. Middle row: Joyce Schilling, Delores Schilling, Don Nipp, John Nipp. Front row: Ray Nipp, Doug McDougall.

happening over there in Germany and what they had to put up with over there . . . we just don't know how lucky we are.

Early in 1942, while I was in Guard training, Martha and Mary moved straight north from the Gallagher house, over to Edith Prest's house on 36 2nd Ave SW.

> JANICE: Mary rented the house from Mrs. Prest across the street, who I always thought had a lot of money, because when I went to pay Mary's rent, she would give me a chocolate. I thought she was really wealthy.
>
> It was a nice little house. It didn't have a great kitchen and the bathroom was an add-on to the back and was always cold, unless Mary ran the heater. But there were four bedrooms upstairs and Mary's bedroom was downstairs right off the kitchen.

After guard training, I enlisted in the Navy. As I was preparing to leave for training, that October of 1942, my grandma made it very clear that she was not happy about my choice. She hated war. She had grown up in England and England had always been at war. She had come to detest it. My grandma and I had always been close and she was very worried when I went off to fight. She died the same month I left. She would get sick every fall and although she always managed to recover, the year 1942 was too much for her, she was 92 and she just couldn't make it through. It was a day four-year-old Janice would never forget.

JANICE: I was the one that went to wake her up. She had been walking around that day and had gone up to her bedroom at the top of the steps to take a nap. Aunt Mary sent me up to see if Grandma was ready to get up. I came back down and said, "Aunt Mary, I can't make her wake her up." My dad went up to check and I remember him coming down the stairs kind of clutching the banister. He was crying, and you know you don't often see your parents cry. I knew something had happened.

I always felt bad that my grandma never knew I made it back from the war and I guess it was for the best that she didn't know how many of her grandsons would ultimately serve in the military.

JIM'S MILITARY EXPERIENCE: After finishing State Guard training at Camp Dodge, Iowa, I joined the Navy. I was accepted by the Navy Air Corps and trained in Memphis for ordinance duty, then went to Hollywood Florida for gunnery training. In September of 1943, I went to fight as an aerial gunner/bombardier on a PBY-5 Catalina in the South Pacific. I flew with patrol bombing squadron, VPB-52. I started out as Second Ordnance man where my battle station was behind a machine gun in the port waste blister of the PBY. I was then promoted to First Ordnance man where my battle station was behind a machine gun in the turret of the open bow in front of the pilots. I fought in the South Pacific from September

James Robert McDougall, United States Navy.

1943 until December of 1944. After I returned to the United States, I was transferred to Memphis Tennessee, Naval Air Station, where we built a four-unit gunnery range and trained new Cadets how to fire at moving targets. I mustered out in January 1946 and returned home to the farm.

BILL'S MILITARY EXPERIENCE: I graduated from high school on a Friday in May of 1945 and was on a train to Minneapolis that next Monday. I had decided to join the Merchant Marines, some of my friends had joined and they seemed to think it was alright. It seemed better than being drafted into the Army. I spent most of my time on a freighter and a tanker in the South Pacific. I was in many of the same areas as my brother Jim had been: Leyte, Lindenou, Australia and for a time in New Zealand. I served for 18 months and mustered out on December 1, 1946.

DICK'S MILITARY EXPERIENCE: I enlisted in the United States Army in 1954. When I filled out my application for the Army, I told them I could type 35 words per minute, which alerted them I could be used for a desk job. I did four months of basic training at Fort Bliss in El Paso, Texas and then two months of special training at Fort Benjamin Harrison in Indianapolis, Indiana on how to take care of military records. Once I graduated from Fort Benjamin Harrison I was sent to Chicago and that's where I spent the rest of my time in the Army.

In Chicago there were four artillery units or batteries:

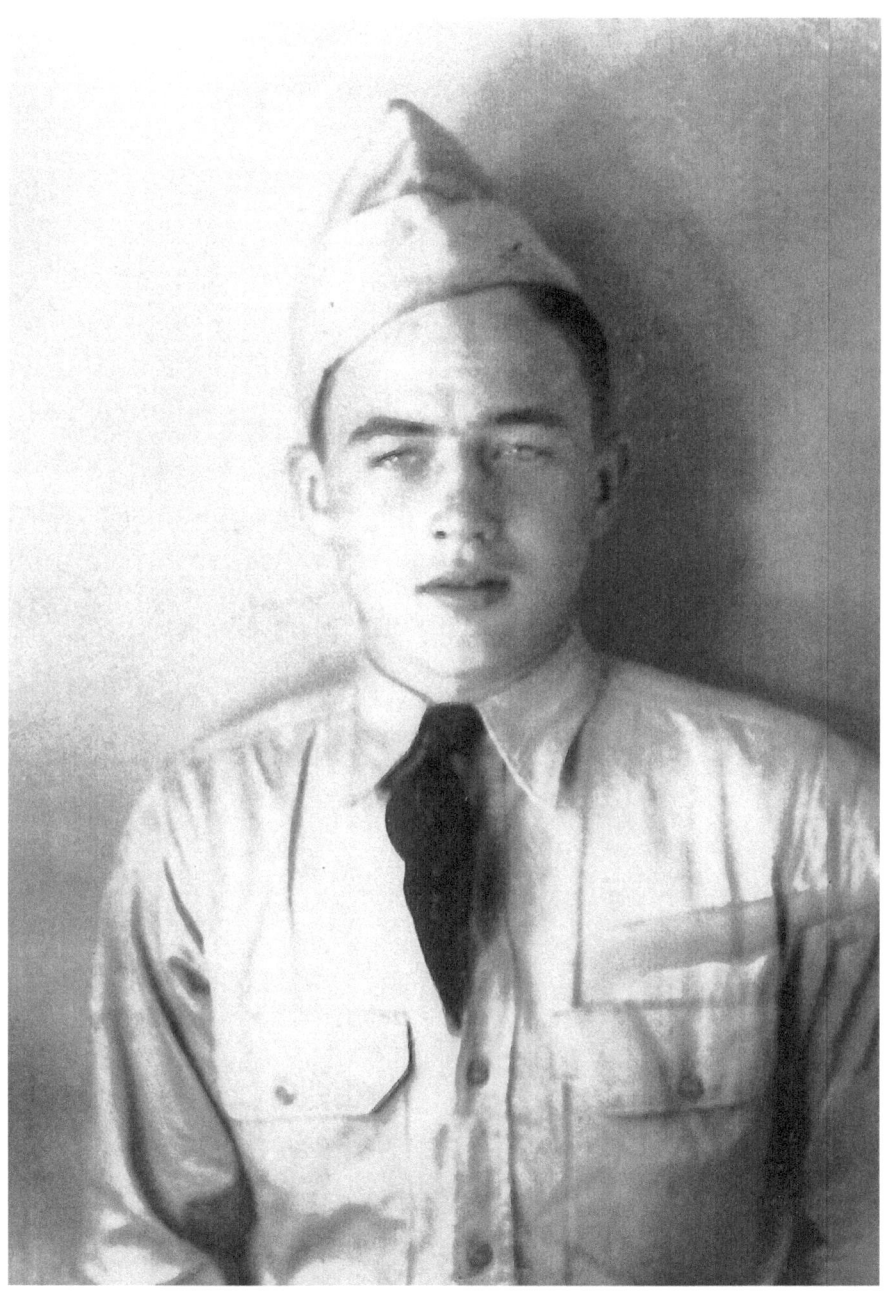

William McDougall, Merchant Marines.

A, B, C and D. Artillery Unit D was down on Navy Pier, which was the group I processed records for—especially the new recruits.

These guys were taking care of big 120mm artillery guns! They had these batteries of guns and gunners in different locations around Chicago because they thought if the enemy came into bomb the US, they would attack Chicago and we would be there with the big guns. Those 120s could definitely shoot them down! I was discharged from the United States Army in 1956.

DOUG'S MILITARY EXPERIENCE: Sept 1956, I volunteered for the draft and went into the Army. At that time in the Army, they gave you a choice of about three areas. I said medics and they put me right in. They trained me very well. I first went to Fort Chaffey, Arkansas and was there two months, then I went to San Antonio, Texas for two more months. Now it is Christmas time, so I got to go home, then I went back for more training at San Antonio in January and bango we went right to Korea. From San Antonio, I went to Fort Louis, Washington where I got on a ship and went to Okinawa and then to an area near Soul, and I got off the ship in Korea.

We weren't very busy with combat. When I got there, it was 1956 and there was no fighting at that time. There was a new hospital in Puson so a bunch of us got sent down there. I trained with a civilian x-ray tech that was there in the daytime hours. I trained with her and then took x-rays in the evening/nighttime hours. I was in

Richard McDougall, United States Army.

Douglas McDougall, United States Army.

Korea about 14 months. I got out a bit early to help my dad with the crops.

MARK'S MILITARY EXPERIENCE: I graduated from high school in 1964. At this time the Vietnam war was hot and heavy. Now if you went to college, you could get a student deferment, so I went to Westmar from 1964–1968. I knew after graduating I would be doing some sort of service and I was looking at a choice between enlisting and going off to war for a couple years or serving in the reserves for six years. Mom and Dad helped me make that decision. I joined the US Army reserves, which was very similar to the National Guard, except it was under the direction of the Federal government, rather than the state of Iowa.

About a year before graduating from Westmar, I started my time with the US Army reserves and served from 1967–73. I went to a four-month basic training; two months at Fort Leonard Wood, Missouri, and the rest at Fort Sill, Oklahoma. From there I was assigned to Cherokee, Iowa where I reported once a month for the next four years.

My military operational specialty (MOS) was in "Fire Direction Control" for the 105 Howitzer. How this played into the war is that during a skirmish, Fire Direction Control would figure out how big a charge should be used, and what kind of projectile should be used, to be most effective. I didn't like sitting in a truck figuring out where to shoot the guns, I wanted to see where those shots were going, so after a while they made me a

Forward Observer. I would watch an area for a "target" and call in the directions to the control. It was a good job, but you sure didn't want to do it in war. The enemy wanted to get rid of those guys right away, because they could cause them a lot of damage. Fortunately, I never got called up. All in all, I think it was a very good experience.

The United States was involved in World War II until 1945 and these were busy years, not only for our country, but also for our family. Farming during the war became a very important and patriotic thing. Most of the young men who normally helped on the farm were off serving. There were fewer resources to draw from, but at the same time, our country was demanding more from our farmers. They needed those farms because it was important to feed the men that were out fighting and keep their bodies fueled. Dick was in his early teens and really stepped up.

> DICK: I worked the farm as it was impossible to hire help. Everyone was off fighting in the war. Dad and I worked together out on the farm. We didn't have all the big machinery to get things done in a hurry. We had a Ford tractor; it was a two row. I'd cultivate the beans two rows at a time. We went across as well as lengthwise. Then, we'd do the corn. We worked that way until Doug got big enough to run the other tractor, then he and I would do it together. I really enjoyed being outside working with my dad. Mom was an excellent cook, and always had good meals for me. She made sure I had a clean

The McDougalls and the Nicholsons

Mark McDougall, United States Army Reserves.

bed and clean clothes, and that's all I ever wanted for my work on the farm.

It was also during the war, in 1942, that Mom and Dad decided to purchase the farm they were renting.

EDITH: Now this farm (that we were living on) was for sale, the loan company didn't want the farms, they wanted to sell them, they said that wasn't their business. So different people were coming out to look at it, you know, we'd have to show them the house and that.

Evelyn wanted us to buy the farm, but we didn't have enough money to buy it. We had to have three thousand dollars to pay down on it. Evelyn told us she'd loan us $1,000.

"Well," we said, "Why don't you buy it with us." But no, she didn't want to do that. She said she'd loan us $1,000 and she said we could pay back $500 when we could, and she didn't care if she ever got the other $500.

So, I always say, if it hadn't been for Evelyn, we wouldn't be where we are today.

Now Dad said he'd buy it, but he wouldn't buy it from anybody but this Glen Denning. And so, they sent Mr. Denning out to see us one day. Nick was a baby, and it was corn picking time and Dad was out picking corn. He came in at noon and he set in the other room and they talked about it. Dad was just fussing to get back

Evelyn Nicholson.

out there and pick more corn. He was anxious to take that team and wagon out and pick another load.

Glen Denning said, "Chester, just take it easy, this may be the most important day of your life!" And he was right!

So anyway, we agreed to buy it, but see, we didn't do this until the fall; if we'd done it in the spring, then when we'd get the crop that year, we wouldn't have had to pay rent. But we didn't do it do it that way, so . . .

It was '42, when he made the deal with New York Metropolitan Life to buy it. And if we hadn't bought it then, it would have been sold, someone else would have bought it and I don't know what we'd have done. I don't think we would have gotten another farm and Dad didn't know much of anything else, besides farming. Well he did work as a mechanic. That's probably what he would have done, gone to town and worked by the day. It just seems like things were supposed to work out this way, doesn't it?

Dad was always afraid he was going to lose the farm. Dad put it on the market one time to sell it. Land agents were bringing people out to see it. But then he took it off the market, and after that it seemed that things started picking up a little bit.

Finally, the year 1945 arrived. That was the year "crops were planted in war and harvested in peace." That was also the year Mom had her last baby. She now had 10 kids (she'd actually had 12, but between Doug and Janice, she miscarried twin girls).

Mom always said, "I had my twin girls (Janice and Edythe) they just came in separate years." Her last four, Edythe, Nick, Denny and Mark had all been born during World War II. Edythe in February of '41, Nick in May of '42, Denny in March of '44 and Mark in October of '45.

I was mustered out in January of 1946 and I returned that winter to turbulent times for farmers. During the war, the government had anticipated wild price fluctuations on livestock and other farm goods. In order to stabilize the market, they had frozen the price of livestock and assured the farmers they would receive at least $17.75/hundred weight for their cattle, up until the controls were removed.

It had been announced that the controls were to be removed the first of March. Shortly before that day, my dad and I went down to the Sioux City stockyards. We were on the walkway that took us through the middle of all the pens. We looked out toward the road and there were trucks lined up as far as we could see. The farmers wanted to be sure to get that government subsidy of $17.75/100 weight. Some made it just under the wire.

The next day we picked up the market paper and cattle had gone up to the limit for the day. The next day they went up the limit again and they kept going up each day. After about four or five days of this Dad said, "I wonder what those guys are feeling like that were rushing in to get that $17.75."

Now, my dad was under the impression that hogs would continue to rise as well, so he decided to take advantage of these prices by breeding additional gilts. He always farrowed out 16 sows and raised the piglets for market, but this year he decided

Jim returns from World War II, getting acquainted with his brothers and sisters, Janice, Nick, Eydie and Denny.

to breed an extra 24, with the intention of selling the bred gilts as the prices came up, to make some extra money.

So now, my dad's in the market to sell gilts. He took them down to the sale barn, but they didn't bring what he thought they should, so he brought them home. He ran an ad in the paper that said, "Bred Sows for Sale." The market price at that time was around $90–95, but my dad hadn't put in a price, he just said they were for sale.

I remember Doug and I were in the yard getting ready to do some mowing. A car drove up with four farmers in it. They had Sioux county license plates. One of them got out of the car and my Dad walked over. The farmer said, "I understand you have bred sows for sale." My Dad said, "Yes I do." The farmer said, "What are you asking for them?"

My dad was a lot better at buying than he was at selling, and he said, "$125." Bear in mind that you could buy sows at this time for about $90–95 each. But Dad liked to bargain, he always started high because he wanted to get the most a man would pay.

Well, this guy never gave my dad a chance. He just turned around, got back in the car, slammed the door, drove out and that was that. We didn't have any other takers on the ad.

Dad was anxious about having all these pigs, so a few days later, he called his brother Jack, who had a stock truck, and asked him to come down and help him take the bred sows back to the sale barn.

> EDITH: Jim was home from the service. He was going to go to school in the fall, but he was at home. And we had

all these sows coming in . . . oh, they were just coming in all over the place and Dad thought he had more than he could handle so he was going to sell some. He called Jack to come with his stock truck to take them to the sale barn. Well, it had been raining, and it was muddy when he came. And he got the truck backed in there and got the hogs into the truck and after they got all these hogs in, they couldn't get out of the yard, it was muddy, and they just couldn't get out. So, they had to unload the hogs.

BILL: Jack came over one day, and I suppose his truck held 20 of those sows and they were going to take them to the sale barn.

Once in a while, the tank used to run over and there was a mud hole there. Jack had a truck and he backed up to the barn and loaded the sows into the truck, then he got stuck coming out of there. Well, Dad hooked on with a tractor and about every time Dad was trying to pull, Jack was backing up because he had a few drinks in him and Dad got mad and said, "Let 'em out, open the end gate and let 'em out." Jim was in on that one, because he helped that winter, he was at the farm.

So, we've still got all those sows, and they're getting ready to farrow. We've got more than twice the number we normally have. In those days, each sow had to have her own pen to farrow her piglets. Our hog barn had 16 pens, and we could put a few more in the alley way, but that was it, somehow, we had to come up with 24 more pens.

Bill was in the Merchant Marines, so Dick, Doug and I really had to get busy making pens for those pigs. We made pens in the horse barn. We made pens in the cattle barn. We made pens any place we could make pens. I don't know how, but we did find places for all those sows. But that wasn't the end of it, our next problem was that we didn't have water near some of those new pens, so all spring and summer, we had to haul water in five-gallon buckets. We would haul two 5-gallon buckets at a time, that's about 80 pounds of water. We'd water the hogs, and then start up again, doing the same thing with their feed.

That year was really a struggle, finding spots for all those pigs, keeping them fed, watered and farrowing them out. We wound up with a lot more hogs than Dad ever anticipated having.

But luck was with my parents, because through that summer the price of hogs went up. Dad decided to hold onto them, and we fed them out to 300–400 pounds each.

> EDITH: The next spring, Bill came home from the Merchant Marines and he wanted this stock truck so he could do some trucking. Dad bought him the truck and they started hauling those hogs to town and then the hogs went up to a good price. It was just luck that we kept them, and we had all these hogs the next spring and that's what we paid the mortgage on the farm off with.
>
> BILL: Dad had pigs and he just had the best luck there is. He kept them all. Things really started up after the war. He paid for the farm with those inflated prices. That's really easy. But don't try it the other way because Grandpa

Nicholson tried it the other way, and it didn't work, it's a matter of timing.

EDITH: When we first bought that farm my dad and my uncle said we'd never get it paid for, but we paid it off in about 6 or 7 years. I think it was like $32,250.00 or something we paid for the whole farm. In town these days they pay that much for one lot to build a house on.

I always said instead of paying it off we should have paid down on another one, but we had never had anything, and we wanted one farm paid for.

After the war, things improved for our country and our family. We were out of the depression and we had turned the corner on the farm, but with my Mom and Dad, things stayed pretty much the same.

MARK: Dad lived like the depression might start again tomorrow.

NICK: My parents stayed pretty frugal all the time, they'd lived through that depression and they weren't going to get living too high and lose everything.

My parents had ten kids in 22 years. They really had two groups of kids. Mom used to refer to them as "the older bunch"—James Robert or Jim (May 12, 1923), Mabel (April 23, 1925–Aug. 15, 1982), William or Bill (Aug. 4, 1927), Richard or Dick (Aug. 11, 1931) and Douglas or Doug (Jan. 26, 1934)—and "the younger bunch"—Janice (Dec. 21, 1938), Edythe or Eydie

The McDougalls and the Nicholsons

Janice, Eydie, Nick, Denny and Mark standing with their dog Rex in front of their dad's 1947 Chevrolet.

(Feb. 16, 1941), Nick (May 13, 1942), Dennis or Denny (March 18, 1944) and Mark (Oct. 20, 1945).

> JANICE: Doug was the youngest of the older bunch and I was the oldest of the younger bunch.

It was about the end of the war that we older kids started moving on with our lives. In June of 1946, I married Yvonne Welch and we moved to Yankton for college on the GI bill. That same year, Mabel married Bud Scholer and moved in with Aunt Mary for a while.

> JANICE: Mabel stayed with Mary for a while before she got married, and then, after she married Bud, they rented two of her rooms, one they used as a bedroom and one they used as a living room. That was until they moved to California.

In 1947 after Meg was born, they left for California, so Bud could go to photography school. They stayed about 18 months. While they were out there, the family took a trip to visit.

> DOUG: Mom and Dad, Janice, Edythe, Dick and I drove out to California in August of '48 to visit Bud and Mabel before they returned that fall. That was a big deal, that was our first big trip!

Then Bill married Erlene Plueger and went off to try life in California for a while.

NICK: Jim, Mabel and Bill were off. They were old enough that I never really lived with them. In my younger years, Dick and Doug were doing most of the work on the farm, but we did have our chores.

MARK: They would tempt us with time at the pool. We didn't have air conditioning and we couldn't wait to get into that water. The whole bunch of us could go swimming all summer long at the municipal pool with lifeguards, for a $15 season pass. And boy would we pester Mom to take us swimming. Mom's answer was usually, "Go ask your dad." But generally, if we'd get our chores done, we could go swimming.

Bud and Mabel Scholer with Chester.

And in our bunch, I'll tell you, there was someone who was always trying to wiggle out of doing something. Nick liked to "figure things out," so he's over there figuring things out and Denny and I are doing the work.

I remember one day, Dad said, "Now I've had enough, you boys get over there and walk those beans."

Well, Nick takes a step or two away from Dad and says, "I don't have to do that." Dad looks down at him and says, "Oh, really Nickie? Why is that?" and Nick says, "Cuz you can't catch me." Dad just turns his back to Nick and looks at me and Denny for just a second, but it was long enough for Nick to let his guard down, and in that moment, Dad takes a couple quick steps back and just like that, had Nick by the arm and was holding him there. He gave him a couple kicks in the butt and said, "Now Nick, you get over there and get to work." Nick was pretty amazed at how fast Dad was.

NICK: I'd had enough, and I said to my dad, "I'm not gonna do this anymore, and you can't catch me." I knew I was pretty fast. But right after I said that, Dad ran me down in about four steps. I'd never seen my dad move fast in my whole life! Dad always walked! I didn't know he could run! I was so astonished I couldn't think straight for a day. I'm guessing I got a little belt action that time.

DENNY: Nick used to like to climb up to the very top of the windmill. It had a little 1 x 8 board around the top if it needed some work. He used to climb up and crawl all the way around it and come back down. He was a little monkey daredevil, if there was anything you weren't supposed to be doing, he'd love doing it.

NICK: I can still hear that belt going through the loops, when I heard that sound it wasn't good. When I'd get in trouble, I used to run up and hide under the bed, where Dad couldn't get at me. He'd come from one side and I'd just get over to the other side. One time Jim was down visiting, I think it was 1952. Denny was in on this one. I was about 10 years old and Denny was 8. I don't remember what we'd done, we were always doing something, but we were under the bed and Dad was trying to get at us. Well Jim walks up to the foot of the bed, lifts it up and there we were like a couple of exposed rats and I thought "Jim! You traitor!" We never dreamed that bed could get picked up like that. We were always doing something!

I was never too keen on Jim's crew visiting. I knew Mom would be busier fixing food and waiting on them and she wouldn't have as much time for her little Nickie, I was always glad to see them go!

MARK: All ten of us kids will remember our reward coming on Saturday. This was the day we always went to town. Mom would trade in the cream and the eggs. She would have about 20 or 30 dozen eggs, which would bring in about nine or ten dollars, that would be the grocery money and she would do the shopping. We each got 15 cents every Saturday. Now I grew up in the fifties and, well, Jim grew up in the thirties, and I was still getting that same fifteen cents! But really, I think we got about what it took to go to see the show at the Pix or the Royal and buy a treat. That was our big entertainment.

NICK: If Dad had played cards on Saturday and made some money we'd stop at Miller's lunch for a malted milk and a hamburger, that would be the thrill for the week.

JANICE: Some of us could talk Mom and Dad into more than others. Nick was pretty good at it, especially with Mom. But with Dad, it was Bill. Sometimes our dad would go into town on Wednesday and the rule was, you could go into town once a week, which meant, if you went to town on Saturday, you don't go on Wednesday. Well, Bill always went on Saturday, but then, come Wednesday, when Dad was shaving and getting ready to go, Bill would be sitting in the bathroom watching Dad with his blue eyes. He'd follow Dad everywhere he went, looking at him with this long face. Finally, Dad would say, "Oh, get your clothes on." And of course, this was what Bill was hoping for, he'd get to spend that extra time in town with Dad.

NICK: On Saturdays Mom and Dad would take us to town, Mom would do the shopping, we'd go to the movies, and Dad would look at machinery or go have a beer. We'd meet at Aunt Mary's later that night, maybe nine or ten. We hung out at Mary's a lot. We would stop by after school and have something to eat. We'd spend our evenings there.

JANICE: I would beg to stay at Aunt Mary's, my friends lived nearby. We were always at Aunt Mary's after school, and sometimes we ate lunch there. We had to be driven into town every day, so after school, we'd meet Mom at Aunt Mary's. There wasn't a school bus until I was in about sixth grade.

DICK: I was a left-hander; we'd sit at the table and Mary would put my left hand down and make me eat with my right hand. She wouldn't let me use my left hand. When I went to school, I used my right hand. But when I shoot a gun, I shoot left-handed and when I shoot pool, I use my left hand. So, I guess I'm ambidextrous.

EYDIE: I stayed at Aunt Mary's all the time. We called it "staying in." I'd always ask if I could "stay in." My mom had four kids in five years, so there were a lot of kids at home, and I liked to be at Aunt Mary's. I remember crying when it was time to go home. I liked to play in the neighborhood, there was a little girl about my age that lived nearby. I stayed almost every Saturday night. On Sunday morning, Mary would help me get all dressed up, my hair curled, and we would walk to the Methodist church for Sunday school.

DENNY: I got to stay with Mary every Tuesday night. I'd always go to the movies. I'd just walk up to the Royal on main street by myself. After the movie, I'd come back and go to my bed at the top of the stairs. When I'd get in bed, there was always a hot water bottle in there, warming up the bed.

Mary'd always want to know whose was the better cook, her or our mom. Of course, we'd always say, "Oh Mary you're the best cook." Then she'd say, "Oh you're just saying that." But she really was a good cook. She had a stove that burned corn cobs. After my Dad shelled corn out at the farm, we would help him drop a truck load of corn cobs off in the shed that was in the alley in the back of her house.

While Mary lived at the Prest house, she started taking in renters to help with finances. There wasn't social security at that time, and she always struggled to make ends meet. She had inherited some land from her dad and rented that out. Sometimes she'd get her rent money, but sometimes they couldn't pay her. It was the same with her renters.

> EDITH: She had a two-story house, her bedroom was downstairs, then she rented out some of the rooms upstairs. Mr. Britt was the best roomer she had. He paid his rent every week. But there were others she'd get so friendly with, and they'd be so nice to her, and then they'd say, "Well, I'm short this week," and she'd say, "Oh, that's alright." Then the next week they'd be shorter, and the bill was bigger. She wound up with the short stick every time. Sometimes I would get mad at Mary because she never took anything for herself.
>
> DENNY: Mary didn't have much money, but she sure made things special for us. At Christmastime she would make her special pudding and she'd put dimes in it. As we were eating the pudding, we might get a dime. That was a big deal.

EYDIE: I remember watching Mary take sugar out of the sack and put it into the sugar bin and she would take all the seams apart to get every last grain of sugar.

DENNY: There was a grocery store just a block away called Council Oak and Mary would go shopping over there and she'd buy all the dented cans because they'd give her a one or two penny discount.

    She was the queen of making Oleo, margarine. It was one of her rituals. I think it started in the wartime. When she got done it looked like a little haystack, then she'd add a little packet of orange powder, to make it look a little more like butter. And oh, by the way, she loved to keep a bottle of castor oil in her refrigerator, if you weren't hitting the pot right, she'd get out that castor oil and that was some nasty stuff.

NICK: Then Dick married Pat Schilmoeller, and started raising a family of his own, and after that Doug joined the military. With those two gone, and Dad getting older, the three of us really had to get to work. For a while, Denny, Mark and I got a pretty good work out on the farm. None of us were carrying much fat, and we hardly rested all day, so we really needed that food Mom would bring out. She'd drive the car out to the field with sandwiches and drinks and maybe a cake for dessert.

EYDIE: I remember driving their lunches out in the car. All we had to do was go down the lane cross over the road, drive a little way into the field and they would come over to the lunch. Now, my dad's cars were right on par with his kids in terms of love—make no mistake about that! And this one day I was bringing them lunch, so I'm driving Dad's car, thinking I was really cool. I drove across the road, into the field and went right into a patch of hay or wheat that had been cut. Well, fairly soon, I start hearing this funny noise. I stopped the car and got under it and there were all these weeds sticking out of this big round thing on the underside of his car, hundreds of them! I took the car right home. When things like that happened, our goal was always to get that car back in the drive, so the next time we got in it, if something was wrong with it, we could say it was Dad's fault, not ours.

DENNY: When the older boys were gone and Doug was in the service, we weren't very good to our dad. We weren't very willing workers, and he'd get discouraged with us. You know how they say, "These young kids nowadays are worthless?" Well, we were those "young kids" back then. Then when Doug came back, he started up with the field work again.

NICK: We worked hard sometimes and after we finished on those hot days, we'd lay on the cool floor in the basement for a while. We didn't have air conditioning, but we did have a little fan, a round hassock fan and we would all gather around like a bunch of kittens. We all wanted a place at that fan.

DENNY: Our sister Mabel's husband, Bud, was the one in charge of the fun. When Bud came around there was going to be some entertainment. He'd do things like bring out a gun, the .22 for us to shoot, or he'd bring out these things we called torpedoes, little balls of silver that would explode when we threw them at the garage door. Well one summer, I was at church camp, Bud brought out a go-cart and this go-cart was pretty fast. They were driving it up and down the lane. Bud's boy Steve was small, but they decided to let him drive it. They put him in the cart and after Steve took off, they could immediately see that he was on a course to run right into the blades on the sileage chopper. So, Nick took off running as fast as he could. When he caught up to the go-cart, the only thing he could grab onto was the red-hot muffler. Nick grabbed it and held on until it couldn't run anymore, and the power shut off. I got home from church camp and he had a pretty bad burn on his hand.

NICK: Really I think I had a storybook childhood. Never a dull day, we'd have a fight or two each day and argued about one not pulling their weight, but really it was a fairy tale childhood, good parents, good area, good period of time. Jim, Mabel and Bill, they lived in the days of the depression, they didn't have an extra peanut butter sandwich in their time, but then comes the war and we really came of age in a golden era, after the war, we had pretty nice going. We were very lucky.

It was during these later years, while Mom and Dad were on the farm, that Aunt Mary started having trouble.

EDITH: She had this stroke early in the spring. I think it was '55 because it was when Jim's were still living in Kingsley and they were moving to Minneapolis. Dad had worked out this deal, he would give Mabel so much a month to keep her. She had just moved into that big house and we thought it was all going to work out. But they got up one morning and she was gone, and they got up another morning and she was trying to fix breakfast and she burned her hand quite bad. And then she got sick, she had another kind of stroke and we took her to the hospital, and she was in the hospital about a week.

When she got out of the hospital, I said she should come live with us. I thought she'd be satisfied at the farm with me because Mary and I always got along so well. But every time a car drove in the yard, she'd say, "I gotta go." She always thought she was taking up someone's bed. I heard her coming down the steps real early one morning and she had her bag and her purse, and she was going to leave. She would just wander off.

Then when we went out of town, Mary went to Hattie's and she got away from Hattie. That was when Hattie said we should put her in a home. She went to the Plymouth County home, and that's where she was living when she died. She had high blood pressure and they claimed they could never get it down. She finally had a last stroke and was in the hospital four or five days. She died in the hospital.

DOUG: I returned from the military in May of 1958 and moved in with the folks and started farming again. After I got married in November of 1959, Vonice and I lived in town. But Dad had retired in 1958, because in 1954 they had started social security for farmers, and Dad was eligible. Mom and Dad decided if anyone was going to live in town it should be them, so they bought the house at 901 2nd Ave SW and Vonice and I moved out to the farm.

On January 1st, 1960, 67-year-old Chester and 56-year-old Edith, along with Nick (18), Denny (16) and Mark (14) moved to town. Edythe had gone off to a 36 month nursing program,

Doug and Chester McDougall.

but she would visit sometimes and they kept a room for her in the house. This house had just been built in 1959 by Don Paulin. Nick remembers Second Avenue still being a dirt road. The kids thought moving to town was a nice break from all that farm work and their school was practically in Chester and Edith's back yard. Mark was busy with football and he played in every varsity game from his freshman year to his senior year (except for one week when he broke his hand).

> DENNY: By the time I was 14, I was done with the farm. I went to town and got a job carrying out groceries. I'd work as much as I could, I wanted to get my hands on some money, Chet didn't pay very well. I was elated when we moved off the farm. I wanted to get to town where my buddies were. I didn't have a car, and now I could walk over to my friends' house.
>
> DOUG: Dad still came out to the farm for years after that. He helped me a lot. He liked to pick corn and pull the loads in. I think what Dad really liked was that new tractor I bought in January of 1968. It had a cab on it, and it pulled a six-bottom plow. He always wanted to plow with that tractor. He'd run the tractor when we cut sileage. He really enjoyed it. When Mabel and Bud bought the Western Auto store in 1966, Dad was there, helping out too. He'd put stuff together, like bicycles, and if someone was having trouble with their bike, he'd fix it. He'd put the things together that needed assembling.

Chester and Edith never really retired. When they moved off the farm to town, they were still raising their younger ones. It hadn't been long after they had their last son, Mark (October 1945) that they had their first two granddaughters. Our daughter Dana was born in March of 1947, and Mabel and Bud Scholer's daughter Meg was born in September of 1947. They just moved seamlessly from parenting to grandparenting.

THE INFLUENCE OF OUR PARENTS

The ten of us watched our parents live the life of a hard-working couple with the responsibility of managing a farm and feeding and supporting a very large family through some very tough times. However, while we were watching them work hard, we were also watching them do what they loved.

As we were out working with our dad, he was passing along to us kids, his love of farming, planting crops and raising animals. Janice wrote a eulogy to read at Dad's funeral and she did a wonderful job of describing him:

> *Long forceful steps leading across the barnyard, a broad, erect figure seated behind a team of horses or on a tractor, a lift of the hat and running of fingers through the hair; these are among the first recollections for many of us of this grand fellow who was our dad. For more than three-quarters of his life we think of him always in connection with his ambitions, his dreams and his land. Surely his vision of success for himself and his family lay in the*

soil, and it became his challenge and his reward. We all know what strength and fortitude this challenge took; we saw this strength demonstrated many times down through the years.

The glimpses of our dad in those years tended to be more of the rougher side of the diamond, a stern discipline to his work, with little time for fun or play. With so much responsibility and so many dependent on him we don't but wonder why he was not less cheerful but cheer he did have and cheer he gave to us, many, many times. We cannot bring our thoughts to our dad in a cheerful, happy mood and not think of Christmas, for this was most certainly his favorite season of the years. So many times, over and over, we were to see his love and generosity given so freely, with "no strings attached," to those of us he loved. Especially we felt this spirit at Christmas. We cannot say or think enough of our dad's wonderful generosity, for we all knew it in great measure at one time or another in our lives; whether it was the gift of our education, furniture to begin married life, or the down payment on a house.

As are birds to the spring and water to the rivers, so was the correlation between our dad and unbounding energy. From the moment his feet touched the floor in the morning, we saw this tireless energy in every movement, be it lifting a bale of hay or building a doll chest. We watched this force sustain him through long, arduous tasks about the farm and through the tortures of his last illness. It was always there almost seeming to make him leap at any task. We just had to say, "Fix my bike, plant this tree, put up a shelf," and he was there, tool in hand.

Our dad had the expectation that we would help out around the farm. We didn't expect to be paid, we just knew if there was something that needed to be done, we should do it. His boys were out there hauling grain, feeding the hogs and cattle, putting up hay, helping with the harvest, fixing fences . . . Dad was busy and there was always plenty to do.

DOUG: One day Dad was harvesting. He had bought a combine and was very busy and we were pestering mom to take us swimming. Mom asks Dad, "Should I take them swimming?" and Dad said, "No! Don't take them swimming. If they drown down there I ain't got time to stop and bury one of those kids. Just leave them home." We didn't get to go swimming that day. But that was just one day. There were plenty of times Mom would take us down to the pit so we could swim.

EYDIE: While our dad was outside working hard, our Mom was our refuge. She always softened the way to our dad, be it shopping twice a year in Sioux City, or going for daily fun at the municipal pool in the summer or sometimes handing us a little extra money. These things were not important to my dad, but mom always understood they were to us.

EYDIE: She was always there for all of us! We never came home from school when she wasn't there, waiting with an afternoon snack or preparing a big dinner.

NICK: Mom didn't do much outside work, she mostly hung clothes and gardened, because she had her hands full inside.

DICK: Mom didn't go anywhere or do anything but stay home and take care of us kids. She'd cook for anybody who came in the house to eat at noon, or supper or dinner. She worked every day of the week. Every morning she made my bed and there always clean clothes in my drawer.

EYDIE: She knew how to make delicious meals and she would present them so beautifully. She'd set her table with a white damask tablecloth and white damask napkins.

DICK: One of my favorites was her fried chicken, but that was among other things. Mom made a great leg of lamb. That was a special treat, because she made mint sauce to go with it. It was just a different taste. I loved her liver and onions. After we butchered a hog or a cow, we'd have pork or beef liver. We ate a lot of beef, roast beef . . . she was just an excellent cook.

EYDIE: Every Sunday we had a big dinner. The preparation actually started on Saturday morning. Dick or one of the men would cut the heads off three or four chickens. Mom would carry tea kettles of boiling water up the hill to dip the chickens in while we picked off their feathers. She would call Janice and me to help, but we'd pretend we didn't hear her. By the second call, we knew she meant business. One time when I was 12 or 13, I was picking chickens and I said to Dick, Mom and Janice, "When I grow up and get married, I am going to tell my husband I don't know how to do this!" Dick grabbed my chicken and said, "And by god, Eydie, you won't be lying!"

NICK: Our mom knew how to process chickens. She was a great "chicken plucker." She'd pick three or four chickens to our one. None of us kids were any good with the chickens.

Every Sunday morning, we got up and put on our best clothes for church. We'd already had our baths on Saturday night. Dad would let us know when it was time to leave because he knew exactly how long it took to get to town. He would drop us off at the First Methodist church, and we would all go to our separate rooms for Sunday school. While Dad was waiting for us to finish, he would go down, buy a Sunday paper and then go over to Wells Dairy to the locker he rented and pick out some frozen meat for the week. Mom was not a part of this, she was home getting dinner ready.

After Sunday school, Dad would pick us up and we would follow our noses into the house. We'd walk in the door and Mom would have the table all set, the house would smell so good, and we could hardly wait to sit down for that big Sunday dinner.

EYDIE: On Sunday mornings, Mom would get up and get us ready for Sunday school. Then she'd set about preparing that big dinner for an untold number of people. We'd have chicken, mashed potatoes and gravy with all the fixings. The yard would line up with family cars, and in would come our brothers and sisters and all their little kids, more and more as our family grew. Eventually we had to have two seating's, first for the children and then for the adults. Think of how much work that was for her, but these were some of our best memories.

DICK: Mom would have a sit-down dinner every Sunday at noon. She'd cook the meal in a cook stove. Mom would stay in the kitchen while we ate. Dad would cut the meat and she'd be in the kitchen getting things ready, making sure everything was as it should be.

DENNY: My mom's weekends were "full of rewards" starting with Saturday mornings, after the chickens' heads came off and they bled out, she'd pluck them, clean them, then she'd take them to the house and pour alcohol in a coffee can lid, start it on fire and singe the little pin feathers off. Then for doing that so nicely, she got her "next reward" which was to fry up a big chicken dinner on Sunday. Everyone would show up to enjoy it. After dessert, they'd get the kitchen cleaned up. But there were more rewards coming to Mom because Monday morning was wash day and she got to go down to the basement and fill up the washing machine with water, do all the washing, then haul it up and hang it on the line. She just had one reward after another!

Every Monday was wash day. All the bedding would

The McDougalls and the Nicholsons

Edith served many meals at the farm; she was usually busy serving until everyone was eating. Clockwise, starting with Dad at the head of the table, Mom, Mark, Nick, Barb, Steve, Bud, Mabel and Denny.

Clockwise from Edith, Chester, Pat and Dick, Jim, Edythe, Nick, and Von.

come off the bed and Mom would gather up all the clothes and put them in piles in the basement. She worked every day of the week, winter, or summer. I was amazed at how much work she could accomplish and how quickly she could do it.

She worked around the house each and every day of her life. She was an excellent cook and very efficient around the kitchen. There was no wasted motion with her. She liked to have her kitchen clean, and the dishes washed and put away. The rooms were picked up and the beds were always made. She canned and stored up the fruits and vegetables she and Mary grew in that big garden.

The way she kept her house and fixed those big family dinners showed how much she loved what she was doing. At that time, they didn't have all the conveniences people take for granted today. Mom raised 10 kids, most of the time without a dishwasher or a washer and dryer, and for a long time she didn't even have hot water. But Dad did take care of Mom and tried to see that she had what she needed for the family, like freezer space for meat. Dad rented a freezer in town from Wells, until about 1955 when he bought a freezer for the farm.

> NICK: Everyone liked to visit with mom, she paid attention, she remembered a lot of stuff and she didn't embellish like we often did, she just told it like it was and we loved that honesty and that great recall. If we had a question, we knew where to go, our kids have Google, we had mom.

MARK: Mom was a warm compassionate person who had a keen curiosity and interest in every one of her kids and grandkids. When you told her something, she paid attention and you knew it, because often the next time you saw her, she would mention it. She truly loved all of us and we all knew it. She made every one of us feel like we were her favorite. She was very careful with her consistency and love with all her kids.

Our mom had more "looks" than anybody I know. She had more ways of wrinkling her nose, pursing her lips, or rolling her eyes, and she could say paragraph after paragraph just with those looks. She was great at that. And boy, when you got "the look" you knew you got "the look."

This way of communicating also went on between Mom and Dad. I don't ever remember my mother and dad getting into an argument. When she didn't like something, she wouldn't nag or yell, she'd just look at him, and Dad was very sensitive to those looks and he would pay attention. I remember one time Dad had sold some cattle and bought a tractor. All of a sudden that tractor shows up at the farm, and here's Dad with this proud look on his face. Mom is out there too. I'm watching Dad and he's all excited, telling her why he needs this tractor, going on and on and then I look over at over Mom, and I can see she's not buying it. She's looking at him with this straight face and it was pretty clear she's not happy, but she didn't say a word.

Well, by God, if it wasn't the next day that Louie Plueger (Erlene's dad) was out at the farm going to work on some renovation for the house. At that time Mom was still fetching water from a pump jack and I think Mom and Dad had previously agreed that once Dad sold those cattle, they would put in a sink with some hot and cold water, a few changes like that. Dad had changed course without thinking and by God, Mom realigned his thinking pretty quickly.

EYDIE: Mom did have the looks; I remember the time an electrician came out to the house. Mom wasn't home. The worker told us he had been called out to put an outlet on the wall of our bedroom and asked us where we wanted it. I said, "Right here, in the middle of the wall, close to the top of the dresser." When Mom came home and saw where we had it, I knew she was horrified. I could just see in her blue eyes that very distinct look of disapproval. But she didn't say a word.

MARK: Mom wasn't one to let things bother her and her advice to us never changed—from the first born to the last, "No, no, no, that's not the way it is, you have to go out and earn it, you have to go out and fix it. If the teacher's mad at you, well guess what, there will be other people that will be mad at you too, and you need to learn how to deal with it." Mom didn't believe in feeling sorry for yourself. She'd say, "Now don't come in here and tell me you've got a headache, or you got this, or you got that; if you just go outside and go to work, everything will be just fine." That was her solution for everything. I couldn't come up with a story she hadn't heard before.

Our parents didn't believe in hand outs, and that went for all of us. They treated us all the same. That was a big thing to Mom and Dad. "Don't expect any special treatment," that was the bottom line. If we asked Dad for money, he was very consistent with all of us, he said, "No." They didn't just buy us stuff and let me tell you, if they didn't buy it for one, they didn't buy it for the other. We had to get out there and earn it, that way we found out how much sweat it took to make a buck and we really valued that dollar. Looking back, I really appreciate this, because we learned how to "want" things and we learned how to take responsibility for ourselves.

DENNY: One of my favorite sayings of Mom's was, "All that glitters, is not gold." She wanted us to stop, think through our decisions, and make sure we were making them for the right reasons.

EYDIE: Our mom was loving, supportive, devoted and giving and she gave to many more out there other than her own children. She was faithful and she lived it. She co-chaired the annual church bizarre and made hundreds of meatballs, she delivered meals on wheels for many years and answered the call whenever she was needed.

We also appreciated how Edith and Chester supported our marriages as we moved on in our lives. They welcomed each of our wives and husbands into the family with open arms. Once

Edythe and Mabel (middle) with their mom, Edith, in the kitchen.

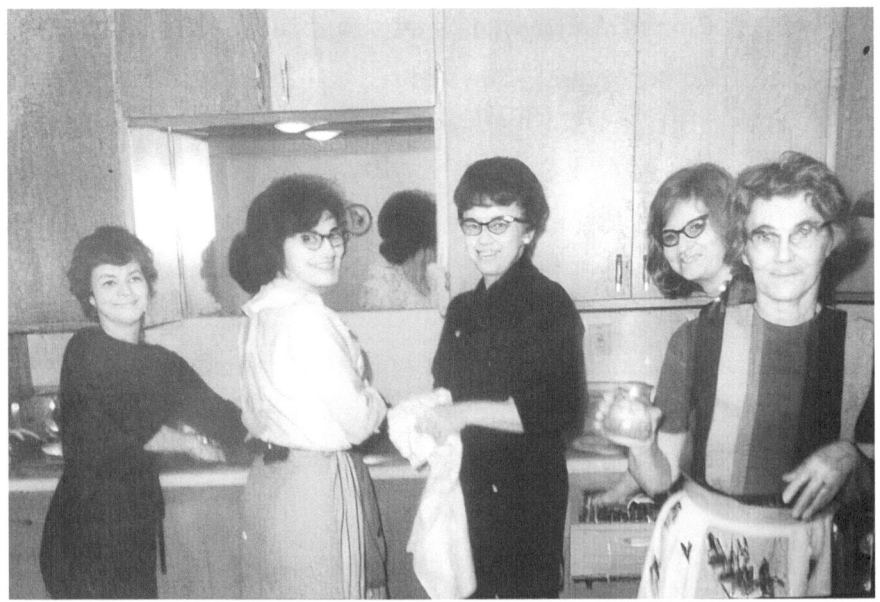
Edith in the kitchen with her daughter and daughters in law. From left, Von, Mabel, Erlene, Lynn and Edith.

we got married, Mom took a very hands-off approach. She was not a meddling mother-in-law and never told us how to raise our kids. Every one of her daughters-in-law and sons-in-law, loved her dearly.

It seemed retirement was good for Dad. This is a continuation of Janice's eulogy at Dad's funeral:

> *As age has its way with all things on this earth, so it had its mellowing effect on our dad. Only then, with many of the cares and responsibilities removed, did we see the humorous fun-loving side of his character emerge. We watched with amazement and joy his enthusiasm for the trips abroad and the people he met. We saw his involvement and compassion for the ever-increasing circle of grandchildren. We enjoyed with him his retirement years of gardening, tinkering, woodworking and travel. Now there was time for a cup of coffee and a chat around the table, and perhaps some reminiscing of days gone by.*

All our children received love and attention from their grandparents. They'd sit outside with their grandpa on warm summer evenings, listening to the cicadas and watching the bugs fly around the big streetlight. Their grandpa had a couple of chairs on his front sidewalk, where he liked to sit and talk to his visitors. They would talk about things like his tomatoes and his roses. He liked to play checkers with his grandsons and if he had bet on a game and won it, you better believe he'd take that dollar. He taught them how to win and how to lose. He had a deck of cards he'd played with so often, there was a thumb print worn in each one. The lucky ones grew up nearby and stopped by for cookies after school or rolls on weekend mornings. Grandpa would fix their bikes when they were broken. He'd spit on the tires looking for leaks. Others had to wait until Christmas or a summer break to visit, but whether they were nearby or further away, every single one of his grandchildren treasured their grandpa and the time he spent with them.

Absolutely nothing could compare to the love and belonging the grandchildren felt when they sat around their grandma's

Grandpa McDougall holding some of his tomatoes. Passing on his love of the land to his grandchildren.

kitchen table. A slow steady stream of aunts and uncles and cousins stopping by. It was the place everyone wanted to be, to check in and see how everyone was doing, share a roll and coffee, a piece of cake, or sit down for a big meal.

Edith loved her grandchildren and thought each one was precious. "There's not a dud in the bunch," she used to say. She was a doting grandmother and won the heart of every grandchild. She had a gift of making each one feel like they were her favorite. When they talked to her, she paid attention and remembered what they told her. She always wanted to hear the news from the source, she didn't like hearing about something important through other people. Her kids and grandkids loved spending time with her in the kitchen, around her table, playing Uno, having some iced tea, or sharing a meal.

She liked to make homemade clover leaf rolls for dinner. We'd all watch her fingers, rolling the dough into little balls, talking as she worked. If you ask her how to make something, she'd go to the kitchen and show you while she explained it: how to make a pie crust, a chocolate cake or how to "spin a hair" when she made frosting. Her house was neat and tidy and it always smelled so good. It was a warm, welcoming place to be and everyone wanted to be there.

Chester died on January 21, 1974; he was 80 years old. He spent 50 of those years as a husband, dad and grandpa. Edith lived to be 94. She was a wife, mother and grandmother for 75 years. Before Edith died on April 1st, 1999, she would not only say good-bye to her husband, but she would bare the devastating loss of her firstborn daughter and very close friend Mabel, who died of cancer

The Road to Love

Standing in back: Doug, Mabel, Bill, Jim, Dick. In front: Nick, Janice, Mark on Chester's lap, Edith, Edythe, Denny.

Back row: Jim, Bill, Mabel, Doug, Dick. In front: Edythe, Nick, Chester, Edith, Denny, Janice, Mark on floor.

The McDougalls and the Nicholsons

Back row: Doug, Dick, Bill. Middle row: Denny, Edythe, Jim, Mabel, Mark. Front row: Nick, Chester, Edith, Janice.

Back row: Doug, Bill, Nick, Dick, Denny, Jim. Middle row: Mark, Edith. Front row: Edythe, Janice, Mabel.

Edith and Chester 50th wedding anniversary.

on August 15, 1982. She would be there for strength, support and comfort when her loved ones buried their wives and mothers and children. Her daughter-in-law Erlene died of leukemia on September 24, 1983, her grandson Zachary died of cancer on October 19, 1987, her little granddaughter Quinn Marie died on March 6, 1967 and her little great grandson Daniel Neal died on July 25, 1986. On the day Edith died, she had 40 grandchildren, 62 great grandchildren and a great-great grandson.

The McDougalls and the Nicholsons

Edith McDougall.

CATTLE

Growing up, we spent most of our time on the farm with each other. We didn't have all the friends and activities kids have today. For the most part our friends were our brothers and sisters and cousins. Each member of our family was very important to us and each member was given a lot of attention.

In our family we got the message that "that's the way the family did it, and maybe that's the way they are expecting us to do it." This was a time when people took a lot of pride in their accomplishments: the growth and improvement of their farm, increasing their ownership of land and animals, how successful they were in life and the kind of kids they were raising. I think my dad was constantly looking for compliments, so to speak, other people reassuring him he was doing a good job. I think success was very important to him. He didn't want to be that guy people were making fun of, he wanted to be the guy that was doing it right, and he passed that down to us, the importance of doing things right.

He was certainly a big influence on all of us boys. We were always watching what he was doing and listening when he talked. In our house there was always talk about cattle and when we were young, we would sit and listen, with wide eyes and open ears, absorbing those conversations. We grew up out in the cattle yard with our dad, learning about buying, feeding, raising and selling cattle. Dad taught us how to take care of the cattle yard, what kind of yards you could use and you couldn't use, what to look for when buying animals and how to feed and care for them. We learned that there was a lot to consider when taking care of cattle and a lot of labor involved. We learned how to process feed, how to cut silage, how to handle forage, where and how to store it. On our farm, for storing sileage, we dug a valley or a "slit trench" into the side of the hill. After cutting and gathering the silage, we would dump it in the trench for storage. Dad knew how to pack it properly, so it wouldn't spoil.

We learned to keep our animals healthy with the proper vaccinations, how to treat them, and what to do for them when they were sick or injured. Dad never wanted to lose an animal.

We also learned which cattle were and weren't desirable for the job at hand. This is a big factor in the cattle business because if you wind up with cattle that nobody wants, you have wasted a lot of time and money. Some of this our dad learned the hard way but being part of those hard times also provided us with the opportunity to learn how to avoid some of those same mistakes.

As we grew older, we found ourselves becoming a bigger and bigger part of the cattle world. We would go with Dad to the stock yards and the sale barns. We were with him at auctions, bidding on cattle. We met different people that were associated with the world of cattle, and with time, as we sat around that table, we found ourselves taking a more and more active and important part in those discussions.

It certainly isn't surprising that every one of Chester's boys found themselves in the cattle business in one way or another. As for being prepared for a career, I don't believe our education came from sitting in a classroom. I think our real education came from our dad and each other, our daily experiences, being out in the field with farmers, making contacts and getting to know

The Road to Love

Talking cattle. Doug laying down on left, Chester, Jim, Dick are sitting. Denny and Nick are laying down in front.

other people in this cattle community. This is what shaped our thinking, gave us real-life experience and a solid base for success.

JIM: After my naval service, I married my sweetheart, Yvonne Welch, and we both went to school on the GI bill. Von and I first went to Yankton College at Yankton, South Dakota where Dana was born. I received a BA in Biology with a minor in Education. Then we went to South Dakota State in Brookings, where I received a BS in agriculture education, while Von studied journalism. After graduating from SDSU I taught vocational agriculture in three different high schools in northwest Iowa for four years. In June of 1955, I was hired by Cargill as a Product Manager in the Nutrena Feeds Division and moved up to Minneapolis, Minnesota. Cargill had been looking for someone to come in and train their people about what this cattle world was all about. They determined I had a solid cattle background and that's how I started my 33-year career with Cargill. I worked in a variety of capacities including Beef Feed Product Manager, Northern Regional Sales Manager, plus Beef Nutrition Consultant. I was also responsible for the nutritional needs of the Cap Rock Division of Cargill. I retired in 1988. I really enjoyed my time with this company, particularly the travel it allowed Von and I to do together.

BILL: I graduated from high school, then joined the Merchant Marines. After my service, I went back to the farm to help my dad and went back to work at the packing house. I also rented a small 80-acre farm for a couple of years, not far from my parents (four miles west and ½ mile south). I grew corn and soybeans, and my dad fed some cattle in a little pasture near the creek. After I married Erlene, her people were out in California and we wanted to try things out there, so I went out to the Los Angeles stock yards for a bit. It just wasn't where I wanted to be so that next fall, we came back, and I went back to the yards in Iowa. I got a job with Swanson Gilmore and Carroll, a commission company and then I bought cattle for Sioux City Dressed Beef, a packing company. From there I went to Luverne, Mn to run the buy for the beef division of Sioux City Dressed Beef. When Iowa Beef Packers bought them out, I spent most of my time buying in the country. At the end of my career, I bought feeder cattle on my own (1979–2008). I worked most of my career as a cattle buyer.

DICK: When I got out of the army in 1956, my brother Bill helped me out. He took me to the stock yards—he was working for Sioux City Dressed Beef at that time. I met a guy named Lloyd Needham who hired me as a runner for the cattle buyers. I did that for two months and then they started me buying cattle in the stock yards. I bought cattle until 1962, at that point I left the yards and went into country buying direct for Mid-Pack in Luverne, Minnesota. When I was country buying, I would go out to the farms and bid on the cattle. I had to figure out how many pounds of edible meat would be hanging on the rail after the steer was butchered. I would go check out the cattle in their yards, decide if they looked good and what I thought of them and then bid accordingly. Sometimes it took a bit of arguing with the farmers. I started that in 1962 and retired in 1988.

DOUG: I graduated from high school and went to college for two years. Then I stayed home and helped Dad for two years, and then I went to the military for two years. I returned from the military in May of 1958, I moved in with the folks and went back to farming. This was the last year Dad farmed. They had started social security for farmers and Dad was eligible, so he decided to retire. I got married and lived in town a short time. So, Mom and Dad were retired and Vonice and I were living in town. Mom and Dad decided if anyone was going to live in town it should be them, so in 1960, they moved to town and Vonice and I moved out to the farm.

NICK: After graduating from high school in 1961, I began working for Sioux City Dressed Beef as a cattle driver in the Sioux City Stockyards. Some of the cattle I attended to, were purchased by Bill and Dick. I went to college at Wayne State for a year and a half, then I married Donna Deegan and began our family of three children, Clif, Amy and Sara. At age 25, I started buying cattle in the Sioux City Stockyards for Blue Ribbon Beef. From there I went to Hampton, Iowa for six years mostly buying for Iowa Beef Packers (IBP). In 1974, I went to Canyon, Texas buying for American Beef Packers (ABP). I went from Canyon to Red Oak and Treynor, Iowa buying for Kane Miller and Missouri Beef Packers (MBP). From Treynor, I moved to Dumas, Texas buying for MBP which turned into Cargill. In 1987, after a total of 10 years of buying in Texas, we moved to Greeley, Colorado with the same company, Cargill (Excel). After 2 years in Greeley, we moved a short hop over to Fort Collins which was home for 24 years.

After 40 years of buying cattle, I put the whip away and retired. After 5 years of this, we decided to move into the Kansas City area to be closer to family. As of

2021, we have been in Olathe, Kansas (southwest corner of KC) for 8 years. Donna and I, are very thankful for all the blessings and great families we are a part of in this great country!

DENNY: I got out of high school in 1962 and worked at Peck's Electric until October, then I cleaned furnaces till the end of December. Then brother Bill gave me an opportunity of a lifetime and hired me to work in the cattle pens at MID Pack in Luverne, MN. In May of 1965, I moved into an office job there and worked with the cattle buyers in the buying and scheduling of cattle. March of 1968, I started as a cattle buyer in the country around the Luverne area. In October of 1972, I took a transfer to Pampa, Texas and bought cattle direct there until May 1986.

I started with a new company in Wichita, Kansas, Val-Agra Beef. Our corporate office was moved to Dallas, Texas the following March. Then in October of 1987, the cattle procurement department was transferred to Amarillo, Texas. In the spring of 1989, I was transferred to our plant in Cactus, Texas, which was 63 miles from Amarillo, so I drove each day to Cactus. I received a promotion to the Corporate office of the new company, Swift/Monfort that had bought us out and that was located in Greeley, Colorado. We lived in Colorado until the spring of 1999 when I went to work for a Kansas City based company, National Beef Packers whom I still work for. It has been extremely enjoyable and I haven't felt like I have had to work one single day since January of 1963.

MARK: In 1964, I graduated from Le Mars high school and entered Westmar. In 1966 I married Jeanie. I graduated from Westmar with a B.S. degree in 1968 and started right off working for Allied Mills until 1971. From 1971 to 2009, I worked for Cargill as a Territory Manager and Beef Feedlot Consultant. My responsibilities were to help establish and retain feed dealers, grow their feed business and bottom line, do more business with Cargill. To accomplish this, I worked with farmer cattle feeders and small commercial feed lots.

I frequently benefitted from my brother's excellent reputation with how they did business (Bill and Dick). If that wasn't enough, I also benefitted from my mentor, my older brother Jim, who helped me immensely during my time with Cargill. Living up to the McDougall reputation was tough but was well worth it to me. Working with and in the shadow of my older brothers is a gift I will always treasure. I guess it all started on the farm.

All of us brothers had similar careers and we remained very connected. We all spoke the same language, cattle. We were well acquainted with what we were all doing in our various jobs, whether that was working at corporate headquarters, feeding cattle, advising feeders, buying cattle in the stock yards, or heading into the country to bid on a farmer's cattle. What this brother was doing in his field, well, another brother might give him some good advice. We helped each other and looked out for each other in that big cattle world.

Bill had contacts in the stockyards and helped several of us get our starts. He played a role in my landing the job with Cargill and he helped Dick, Nick and Denny get their start in cattle buying.

After Mark worked a while with Allied Mills, he moved over to Cargill, he liked how Cargill was feeding cattle and that company was only too happy to hire him as a territory manager and consultant.

While Mark was out in the field with the farmers, he gave us at corporate headquarters a lot of valuable information on what was going on out there and the problems farmers were having, what they were needing and how we might attack the business. It helped Cargill headquarters develop healthy ways to feed cattle. We developed prescription feeding which was especially useful for our guys working with the farmers out in the fields. In return I could help Mark out by listening to the problems he was conveying and help develop solutions to get tools and recommendations out so we could help solve those problems. It was mutually beneficial, I had someone in the field I could trust, and he had influence with the direction the home office needed to take.

Doug was a large cattle feeder. He fed at least two hundred head per year. Mark and I (through Cargill) helped Doug develop a feeding program using his own feed ingredients and gave him some advice on what additional feed ingredients to purchase and help him keep his cattle healthy with the right vaccination and health management program. Doug owned a feed and seed dealership. He was a speaker a couple of times at some special cattle management programs that we helped put together for the farmers.

The McDougalls and the Nicholsons

In 1984, I was featured in an article with Cargill and this was the first paragraph:

> *There are four McDougall brothers working for Cargill. One is a cattle buyer for Excel. One is a Feed Division Territory manager, another operates a Cargill feed and seed dealership in Le Mars, Iowa and the fourth, Jim McDougall works here in Minneapolis as a Feed Division product manager. To round out the picture, there are a couple more McDougall brothers "working for the competition" as cattle buyers for Iowa Beef.*

Bill, Dick, Denny and Nick were all cattle buyers.

NICK: For a short time, Bill, Dick, Denny and I were all buying for IBP, because IBP bought out Luverne, Minnesota in '67 or '68. In '69 we were all together, but this was a short-lived deal, because I quit IBP, I wanted to get into Texas, so I left there in 1974. Most of the time we were competitors, but we never ever competed against each other. We never bid on the same cattle.

Now as far as Denny and I, we both started buying cattle in 1968, we had similar experiences in the stock yards trying to work up to being a buyer. Denny was buying in Minnesota and I was buying in Le Mars and we visited each other a lot with our kids. We just loved talking shop; we couldn't get enough of that cattle buying.

A Peek at Our Families in the World Today

To take a look at the Nicholson and the McDougall families is to witness the appreciation each one has for the other. We share a deep love of each individual, each family, each clan. I wonder if it's those Scottish roots that creates those strong bonds of brotherhood or sistership that helps make us think as one? Who knows?

As I step back and observe our family history, I see more vividly that these bonds are influenced by the underlying force of a similarity of life's values that glue us together. We tend to think much alike, to find the good things in life, appreciate each other, celebrate our successes, and share life's trials and tribulations. Although there are hidden reasons behind these similarities, some are clearly evident and will remain evident forever.

What our forefathers set into place is worthy of honor and recognition. They did many things to create a strong family unit and better the communities they lived in. They came during a time when the backbone of this country was being developed, they worked hard, sacrificed, and played a positive role in its growth. They invested their time and energy, persevered risks and setbacks, and did what they could to set the foundation for a better life for their children, their grandchildren, and ultimately all of us.

We are proud and thankful to them for everything they have done for us, but on the other hand, I believe they would be exceedingly proud of you and all you are doing to better the world and carry on their legacy in this family as well.

Jack Nicholson, in his write-up *The Nicholson Family's Contribution to America*, recognized the depth of accomplishments and contributions of this family:

> *Beginning with farming this family has branched out, and contributed in many career fields and professions. Dozens served and several continue to serve in the United States Armed Forces. Others wrapped their arms around the livestock industry from the feed lots to the marketplace. Similarly, our grain farmers comprise the underpinning to America's "Breadbasket of the World" acclaim. Many others contributed to commerce in banking, real estate development and entrepreneurial pursuits. Some became doctors and nurses, lawyers, and social workers, firemen and paramedics. There are teachers and trades men and women and Olympic athletes.*
>
> *The most common and binding traits running through these families, now comprising six generations in America,*

are the strong family foundations and loyalties that are trademarks of each branch and root of these family trees. What stronger fundament could a nation hope to have than this tradition of large and strong families, families that help each other and each individual as needed and as a matter of course.

As I come back to that large family photo in this book and look at all those smiling faces, I can assure you that this family is full of amazing accomplishments, sacrifices, risks, and victories. Some are big, and create riveting narratives; others tell the simpler story of a consistent, unselfish commitment to good and love and bringing out the best in who and what is around them. If I had the time, I would love to fill a book with everything about this family that should be told. But at 98, I'm short of breath and time, so instead, in the spirit of our Scottish roots of brotherhood and clansman ship. I would like to share a couple stories of brothers that I think are quite remarkable. It is easy to see their impact, on each other, their communities, their country, and in both of these cases, the world. I believe our forefathers would admire many qualities in Kyle and Andrew Swanson from the McDougall side of the family, and Jack and Jim Nicholson from the Nicholson side.

I can just imagine James Alexander McDougall returning to the world today and seeing the love of his land and farming continue through the family. He would see his hard-earned homestead still in the family, his land being cared for by his great grandson Doug and his great-great grandsons Miles and Shayne.

He would also see the threads of his greater humanitarian sacrifice of going off to a war to help others that weren't in a position to help themselves. He would see that sacrifice in Kyle and Andrew Swanson, donating their time, talent and energy, all the way over to Africa, helping those in hopeless situations.

This is a piece of Kyle and Andrew's story.

KYLE AND ANDREW SWANSON

Kyle and Andrew, sons of Dr. Gene and Edythe (McDougall) Swanson were similar in many ways. Both were gifted, intelligent, motivated young men, who performed exceedingly well at Mankato West High School, both in their studies and in their extracurricular activities. They also had the unconditional love and support of their parents, and as a result, when the two set off on the path to explore orthopedic surgery, the doors were wide open. Kyle was ahead of Andrew by five years and was accepted to the University of Notre Dame in Indiana, where he received his Bachelor of Science degree. His younger brother, Andrew, still in high school, took his Academic Decathlon Team to the finals in the national competition. After high school, Andrew was accepted to Dartmouth University in New Hampshire, and graduated Summa Cum Laude.

Following graduation, both men took a year of time for themselves. Kyle with his love of farming, spent a year working with his Uncle Doug and his sons on the McDougall farm. Andrew with his passion for mountain climbing and hiking taught at Burke Mountain Academy. He loved teaching, and the commitment to helping others became a unifying theme in his life.

When it was time to get back to his studies, Kyle had received a personal invitation from the dean of the medical school to study at the University of Georgetown, in Washington D.C. Kyle earned his graduate degree and his medical degree from Georgetown in 1996. He then completed a five-year orthopedic residency at Mayo Clinic College of Medicine and Science in Rochester, Minnesota. Kyle also pursued an additional year of training in adult reconstructive joint surgery through a fellowship at the Hospital for Special Surgery in New York.

Andrew received his medical degree from the University of Chicago in 2000. He completed his orthopedic residency at the Hospital for Special Surgery in New York City in 2005, one year later, he completed his fellowship in spine surgery at the Twin Cities Spine Center in Minneapolis. In 2007, he completed a one year Traveling Fellowship in Europe, a prestigious honor given by the Cervical Spine Research Society.

At the end of their training, both men were offered staff positions at the world-renowned Hospital for Special Surgery in New York City and both strongly considered it. But the lure of family, cleaner air, independence and the opportunity to practice together, and with their father, at the "Orthopaedic and Fracture Clinic" in Mankato, brought them back to Minnesota.

Now, an orthopedic surgeon, trained in total hip and knee reconstruction, Kyle dove into his career in Mankato. He established a large total joint practice and conducted clinical research with two major joint manufacturers. He also developed a teaching

Kyle Swanson

center utilizing robotics in hip and knee joint replacements. But he also found the time and energy to pursue his lifelong dream to farm. Kyle has a farm just outside of Mankato and his joy and relaxation are to hop on the tractor and work the soil.

Andrew became an orthopedic spine specialist, who also found time for adventure and activity. He was a rower, cyclist, photographer, pilot, cook and mountain climber. But above all, Andrew was a humanitarian. As his mom Edythe commented, "Andrew was many things, but his humanity outshined them all."

In his last year as a resident at the Hospital for Special Surgery in New York, Andrew was fortunate to work with the world-renowned spine surgeon, Dr. Oheneba Boachie-Adjei. Dr. Boachie was a native of Kumasi, Ghana, in West Africa and had immi-

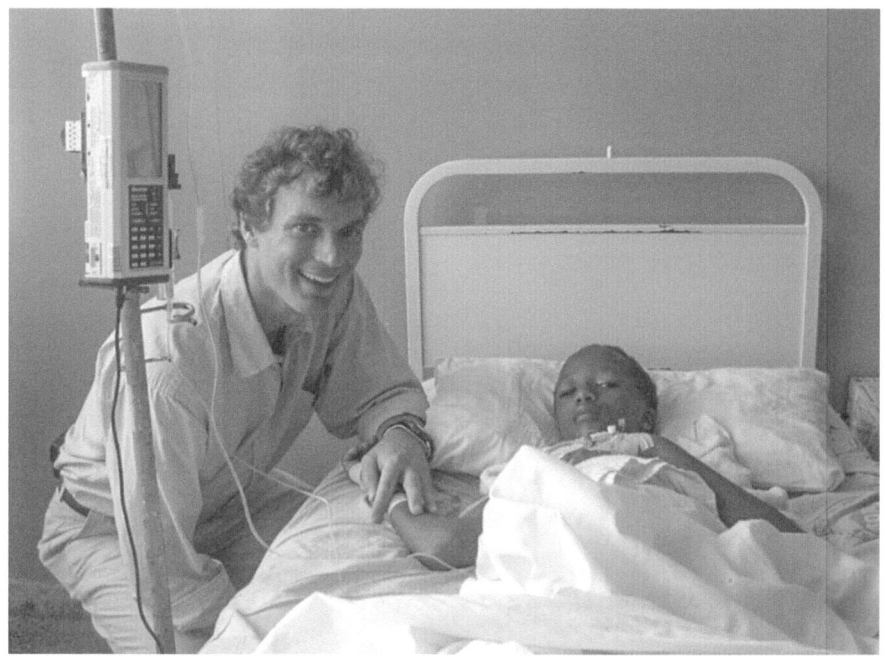

Andrew Swanson with one of his patients

grated to the United States in 1972. He earned his Doctor of Medicine Degree from Columbia University in 1980, and went on to become an expert spine surgeon, but he did not forget his roots and the dire healthcare needs of the people in his home country. He returned to Accra, Ghana, and established the Foundation of Orthopedics and Complex Spine (FOCOS), a non-profit organization, created in 1998 to provide comprehensive and affordable orthopedic care to people in desperately underserved communities throughout Africa. Working alongside Dr. Boachie, was Bettye Wright, a physician's assistant from Detroit, MI, who was a founding board member of FOCOS and a tireless organizer. She worked full time, 100%, for the operational aspects of the FOCOS Foundation's work in Africa. She organized everything.

When the clinics were going to be held and the surgical cases were scheduled, she would go to Ghana weeks before to make sure everything was in motion when the others arrived. Bettye was *the heart and soul of each Ghana mission. Before, during and after the missions, Bettye was in Ghana to ensure success for all involved.*

With the support of more than 250 international volunteers and through coordination with local hospitals, FOCOS is able to provide free evaluations and perform hundreds of complex spinal surgeries and joint reconstruction on adult and pediatric patients. The FOCOS surgeons are the best in their fields and come from all over the world to donate their time and talent.

Patients come from Ghana, and as far away as Ethiopia and Sierra Leone. Many are suffering from the consequences of diseases we don't often see in the United States. Tuberculosis, for example, can lead to twisted and deformed spines, even progressing to the point that the lungs collapse. Some are born with severe congenital conditions of the spine. Others have painful debilitating joint issues.

Decent health care is difficult to find and very hard to afford. An average agricultural worker in Ghana, Africa makes $180.00/year (in US dollars) They might make $800.00/year in Ethiopia. In Africa if you don't have the money, you don't get the care. So many problems are left untreated. Even small problems of the joints and bones, if not repaired, can lead to much more serious disabilities. Every patient the FOCOS surgeons work with are dealing with debilitating or even life-threatening conditions and come from hopeless situations.

When the surgeons arrive in Ghana for a mission trip, they hit the ground running. Spine cases are most complex and can take 10 to 12 hours each. Joint surgeries typically take two to three hours. Surgeons work in pairs, and they are in surgery all day, every day, for the duration of the mission.

Dr. Boachie had taken an interest in Andrew. Andrew was an unwavering humanitarian looking to enrich the lives of those who were less fortunate. He recognized this about Andrew, along with his talent and commitment. Dr. Boachie had never before taken a resident with him to Africa on a FOCOS mission, but he asked Andrew to come to Ghana with him on the next mission.

This was a life-changing experience for Andrew. He became a member of the FOCOS team, and a volunteer surgeon and he returned to Africa with Dr. Boachie, twice a year for the remainder of his life, spreading his talents and infectious smile to all those little ones under his care.

Andrew had an enormous heart for those kids. They were tough little guys.

> EDYTHE: When they signed into the hospital for surgery, they got a bag, and in that bag, they got a gown, some dressings and two doses of morphine, that was it. They were given only two doses of medication after having undergone a twelve-hour surgery, reconstructing their spine. But they never complained, they never cried, they were just little angels. It is an incredible thing to witness all this.

GENE: After one particularly complicated case, Andrew sat by this boy's bedside while he was recovering. He was having some difficulty. Now, these children are only allocated two units of blood, and you can imagine after 12 hours of surgery how much blood they might lose. Andrew was very concerned about his patient. Everybody was supposed to go back to the dormitory and other physicians were supposed to watch the patients, but Andrew didn't feel comfortable leaving this little one, so he stayed and sat by this child's bedside all night.

Tragically, on June 11, 2009, fourteen days after his last FOCOS mission, Andrew died in a mountaineering accident on the West Rib of Mt. Denali in Alaska. This was devasting to Andrew's family and friends, the FOCOS family, and the world. As one of Andrew's young patients wrote, "All of Africa cries today." After the accident, Bettye Wright wrote Edythe and Gene a letter reiterating how incredible Andrew was during their time in Africa:

> *When Dr. Boachie-Adjei asked for volunteers to accompany me to Sierra Leone to do clinics and identify potential surgical candidates, I was not the least surprised that Andrew volunteered. At that time, Sierra Leone was at the end of their ten-year civil war, peacekeepers were still there, I was scared to death, Andrew was fearless. Once we identified surgical candidates, if further medical investigations were needed, Andrew would provide the Sierra Leone FOCOS staff with funds to obtain the studies. It*

Andrew Swanson (11/9/1972–6/11/2009)

was during that trip that I realized that the kind, gentle and respectful manner that I had grown to love about him was "who he was." He treated all of our patients like this. Our circumstances for me were challenging and frightening, but Andrew was unaffected and acted as if these were his Park Avenue patients.

Only God and the angels know why Andrew was taken from us so early. He was a meticulously careful mountain climber. In fact, there is an award that Andrew and Andrew's climbing partner, John Mislow had received the highest honor the Denali Pro program gives: the "Denali Pro Award" and following their accident the award was renamed the "Mislow-Swanson Denali Pro Award."

> GENE: On Andrew and John's first attempt at climbing Mt. Denali, in 2000, they were within feet from reaching the summit. The weather was bad, and they were in a little tent, head to foot, laying there, waiting it out for three to five days. Finally, Andrew said, "You are too big for us Mt. Denali, you are too big for us." and they had to go home. Andrew and John took a day and helped a couple of Italian climbers build an igloo and also helped other climbers along the way. They received the Denali Pro Award that year.

The Mislow-Swanson Denali Pro Award honors members of the Denali climbing community who exhibit the highest standards in the sport for safety, self-sufficiency, Leave No Trace ethics and assisting fellow mountaineers. Throughout each climbing season, Denali mountaineering rangers recognize climbers with a Denali Pro lapel pin for exemplary expedition behavior, such as protecting the mountain environment, assisting fellow climbers and using good judgement to limit or eliminate injury.

Today, Andrew's brother Kyle, carries on Andrew's legacy with the FOCOS program in Ghana. As the older brother, Kyle had been the one to set the tone of hard work, determination, and a desire to pursue medicine. But now it was Kyle's turn to follow in Andrew's footsteps. Andrew had brought Kyle (as well as other family members) to these Special Clinics in the past. Now Kyle provides total joint reconstruction through FOCOS. He has a strong relationship with implant and equipment manufacturers and has been able to secure an immense amount of donations to FOCOS, which has become essential to the stability of the program. Kyle, his assistant Gerald Berberick, and Sara Campbell, his equipment specialist, travel to Ghana at least yearly to reconstruct severely deformed hips and knees, and follow those done previously, to determine the outcomes. They have done over 250 operations since they started accompanying Andrew. This wonderful program continues and grows each year.

Kyle's ability to maintain a successful profession, a sizable farming operation, a stable and loving family, and continue his brother's legacy, as an honored participant in a major humanitarian foundation is something, I believe, our forefathers would be extremely proud of.

JACK AND JIM NICHOLSON

Benjamin Nicholson chose this country as a place for his sons to prosper. This came at a very large sacrifice. He took a rough journey on a ship, thousands of miles, explored the American countryside, as far as California, searching for the best land available.

The sign on C-12, as you enter Struble, Iowa honoring Jack and Jim Nicholson.

He found it in Struble, Iowa. He then sent his young sons to settle there. His boys would take this same long journey and Benjamin knew he would rarely, if ever, see them.

If he returned today, I believe he would be very proud of the Nicholson contribution to this country. If he took a walk through Struble, he would quickly see the pride this town has in two of his great grandsons, John William (Jack) and Robert James (Jim) Nicholson. There is a sign erected in the center of that little town, on C-12, with a light shining on it honoring these two men.

As with Kyle and Andrew, Jack and Jim's stories are similar in many ways, but also of course, very different. Both Jack and Jim had a challenging upbringing around the Struble area, both were student leaders and athletes at Le Mars High school, and both went to the United States Military Academy at West Point.

> JIM: The early post World War II years were really difficult times for us in our family. My dad struggled to find and keep permanent employment. Housing was a very difficult issue, and for three years we lived in an abandoned house on a farm four miles east of Struble that had neither electricity nor plumbing. We did not have a car either, so often food was a real issue as well as contact with the outside world. It was our mother who kept us going as we often prayed at night huddled around a kerosene lantern. "You kids must keep your chin up, maintain your dignity," and she would add, "You must pray hard, study hard and work hard, and if you do, somehow we will get through this." She would often add her feelings that in America there would be great opportunity for us if we could get a good education. It sounded like a pipe dream at the time to us hungry ragamuffins, but she was right, and all seven of us attended college and America did provide us with great opportunities for which we are grateful.

When Jack was 15 and Jim was 11, the family moved into the town of Struble.

> JACK: When we moved to Struble in 1949, I thought we'd died and went to heaven. Here we now were, in a town,

in our own house. We had neighbors—nice neighbors. Our house had six rooms "and a path;" no running water. It was heated by a fuel oil stove in the center of the living room. But here, Jim and I had opportunities to work and earn money, and we were always on the lookout for work.

JIM: Although Struble had a small population, 90 people, it had amenities we lacked in the remote tenant farmhouse where we had been living. Our family appreciated the proximity to our St. Joseph Catholic Church, which had been built on land donated from our great grandfather, Peter Moran. We attended Mass every Sunday and Holy day. We were in the church choir. We liked the church socials which always featured delicious home cooked food. Our house was right across the street from the two-room schoolhouse where our dad and his ten siblings got their primary education a few decades earlier, and I would attend from the 5th through the 8th grade.

As Jack was approaching graduation from high school, his parents, Don and Helen Nicholson, recognized Jack's intelligence, determination and work ethic. They wanted to help Jack find a way to get to college, but money was still very tight, and they knew that financing an education would be an overwhelming hurdle. When Jack started expressing an interest in West Point, Helen went to work. Jack met the high academic standards, physical fitness standards and he certainly had the leadership potential, but acceptance into this elite academy also required a letter from a US Representative or a Senator. To meet this requirement would be no easy task, but Helen visited around and found a Congressman from Alton, that was willing to meet with Jack. It was no surprise that he was impressed with Jack and agreed he would be an excellent candidate for West Point. Representatives are allowed very few candidates to endorse, and they take care to choose only the best.

Following the recommendation from Congressman Hoeven, and Jack's acceptance, Jack was bound and determined to show his appreciation and make the Congressman, his mom and his family proud. Jack made an excellent showing at West Point. He was Captain of the varsity wrestling team and the second ranking Cadet in the Class of 1956.

In 1956, while Jack was a Cadet, Jim visited his brother at West Point. Jack introduced him to some of the faculty. The faculty was impressed with Jim and when Jack graduated in June as a 2nd Lt., they asked about him, "Where is Jim?"

Jack said, "He doesn't have an appointment." They said, "We can take care of that." That same month Jim flew in, passed all the exams, as well as the physical and leadership requirements, and was unanimously accepted. Ten days later he reported to West Point as a new Cadet.

> JACK: He went from being nominated, to being a full-fledged, dressed Cadet in less than four weeks. I believe that is a record. He earned his way in, passed the tests, did well and he continued to do well throughout his four years as a Cadet.

When Jim entered West Point, he knew he had some very big shoes to fill. Both Jack and Jim finished West Point, then went on to become Airborne Ranger, Infantry officers, serving in combat in Vietnam. Jim served one tour, and Jack served three.

I will now summarize a letter, written by former Major General Tran Ba Di, a man who fought in the trenches alongside Captain Jack Nicholson in Vietnam, which I feel demonstrates the kind of soldier and man Jack Nicholson truly is. The letter was submitted by LTG John Cushman who recommended Captain Nicholson for a Silver Star for his actions in December of 1963:

> *At this time, US Army Captain John W. Nicholson served as the Advisor to the Phong Dinh Province Civil Guard and Self Defense Corps (CG/SDC), a combined force of about 4,000. Captain Nicholson's main responsibility was to accompany and advise the CG/SDC on field operations aimed at protecting the rural population of Phong Dinh Province from enemy attacks. Captain Nicholson accompanied these missions on a routine basis, weekly, if not more frequently.*
>
> *At mid-day on December 27th, 1963, Captain Nicholson was accompanying Captain Phat, when his force engaged the VC in the Song Hau Farm area. Two VC were killed, and a home-made hand grenade manufacturing facility was discovered and destroyed. At about 4 pm, the lead elements were nearing a major canal where more VC engaged Captain Phat's forces. Return fire from concealed enemy positions on the canal bank caused many more*

friendly casualties. Captain Phat reported the action and a gun boat was dispatched down the canal toward the site of the firefight. Captain Phat's force met the boat and began loading friendly casualties. Suddenly, VC attacked from three sides, chaos ensued and Captain Phat and his troops and the gun boat hastily withdrew. Friendly casualties were abandoned on the canal bank and darkness crept in. But Captain Nicholson had stayed with the wounded. He managed to catch up with Captain Phat and told him, "We can't abandon those casualties." It took a lot of persuasion and convincing from Captain Nicholson, but Captain Phat reluctantly returned to the wounded. Captain Phat's force had now been reduced from the original number of 240 to a mere 39 men.

These 39 men picked up 13 wounded fellows and carried them up the canal where they were finally welcomed by the perimeter guard.

Four of the wounded died while being carried back, but the remainder survived and were medevacked at daybreak by helicopters called in by Captain Nicholson.

Those wounded who were rescued were especially thankful for Captain Nicholson's leadership in braving the enemy fire to save their lives.

For his brave deeds on the battlefield during this fight Captain Nicholson was awarded the Army of the Republic of Vietnam Cross of Gallantry with Gold Palm, the highest level of this type of military decoration.

Captain Nicholson served in this role for eight more

months and when he accompanied a mission he was always welcomed and even cheered. There were situations where the militia forces were unhappy or not confident in going on patrols and operations if Captain Nicholson did not accompany them. They said with Captain Nicholson along they knew they would never be abandoned. This meant a lot to them.

In 1986, Jack Nicholson retired, as a U.S. Army Brigadier General, who served our country in many capacities over 50 years. He spent 30 of those years on active duty as an airborne ranger combat infantryman. He served in Vietnam, Korea, Lebanon, Germany, Switzerland and the United States. His last active-duty assignment was as Commanding General of the Army Training Support Center at Fort Eustis, VA. His awards include the Silver Star, Bronze Stars for valor, Air Medals for valor, and three awards of Gallantry with Gold Palm. He also received the Distinguished Service Medal, two Legions of Merit, and several more awards for service. He was on the faculty at the Military Academy at West Point. He was on the Department of the Army Staff, the Staff of the Chairman of the Joint Chiefs, and was appointed by President Reagan to negotiate bi-laterally with the Soviets on nuclear weapons compliance issues. He is an Army War College graduate. He earned a master's degree in public administration at the University of Pennsylvania, and he was a Federal Executive Fellow at the Brookings Institute in Washington, DC, studying foreign policy. Following his retirement, he served as Under Secretary for Memorial Affairs, where he directed the National Cemetery Administration and in January 2005, Jack was appointed Secretary of the American Battle Monuments Commission (ABMC) by President George W. Bush. He also served on the Board of Advisors of the Code of Support Foundation, a nonprofit military service organization.

Jack and Jim both served on the staff and faculty at West Point at the same time during the late 1960's. It was during this period Jim met and married Suzanne Marie Ferrell from Highland Falls, New York. While on the staff at West Point, Jim pursued a master's degree in public policy at Columbia University in New York City, which piqued his interest in law. He decided he would like to become an Army lawyer, so he asked the Army to send him to law school, ironically, at about the same time, he got promoted to Major, and was therefore no longer eligible for the Army's law school program as he had become a field grade officer. Jim and Suzanne then had a very big decision to make: should he resign from the Army as a Major with a good career ahead, with all of that security, and having a family of two children? It was a very big decision to pursue a new career in law at the age of 32, versus staying in the Army with its job security, camaraderie and considerable opportunity. Jim chose to leave the Army and move to Denver to study law. He and Suzanne and their babies moved to Denver where they had no place to live, no job and no friends. The only thing they had was his admission to law school at the University of Denver in the fall of 1970. That was the beginning of a new career and a real divergence from Jack's career.

Jim went to law school while working full-time for the mayor of Denver and he also remained in the Army Reserves for 22 years, and retired as a Full Colonel.

After law school Jim started practicing law in Denver, and after two years of practice, his law firm made him a full partner. This led to his becoming the General Counsel of the Colorado Home Builders Association. Colorado was at that time gripped in a big controversy over whether it should pursue more growth or resist growth, and Jim became the spokesman and pointman for the pro-growth interest. His law school advisor, Gov. Dick Lamb, was the principal advocate for limited growth. This is how Jim became involved in Republican politics in Colorado, which led to his getting elected as the National Republican Committeeman from Colorado in 1986. This brought him into national politics, and in 1997 he was elected Chairman of the Republican National Committee. His principal objective in this job was to help take back the White House for the Republicans. After four years as Chairman of the RNC they won back the White House in 2000 with George W. Bush, and they also won a majority of governorships and state legislative chambers.

Jim was then chosen by President Bush to be the Ambassador of the United States to the Holy See. He served in this position from 2001 to 2005.

Pope John Paul II, knighted Jim while he was the US ambassador to the Holy See, for his work and leadership on human rights in Europe and Africa, especially in the areas of trafficking in human beings, and malnutrition and starvation. The latter work was aided greatly by his growing up in the Corn Belt and knowing the advantages of using modern agricultural practices. Jim convened two large international conferences in Rome to discuss the advantages of using GMOs (genetically modified organisms) to increase food production in Africa. Nobel prize winning laureate, Dr. Norman Borlaug, came to Rome twice at Jim's request to keynote these conferences. Borlaug himself an Iowan and college wrestler, like Jim, was the father of the "Green Revolution."

"My life experiences, including being hungry when I was growing up, and being from a hard-working productive family culture, as farm people, was very useful to me in working to improve conditions in Africa," Jim related, and this was acknowledged by Pope John Paul II at the ceremonies where he was knighted.

After serving for nearly 4 years in Rome, President Bush asked Jim Nicholson to come home and join his cabinet as Secretary of Veterans Affairs. "This was the biggest challenge yet in my life," Jim relates, "As we were in the thick of two wars—Afghanistan and Iraq—and we had hundreds of thousands of young veterans, injured physically and mentally, returning home for our care, and we needed to work very hard and very smart to give them the medical attention and benefits that they had earned. It was a great job with a great mission, and I was very proud that our over 40,000 doctors, and 85,000 nurses worked so hard, each and every day, as professionals serving our veterans." President Bush would often say to me, "Take good care of these veterans, Jim, they are our country's most precious citizens." He was right, and we did a great job.

Brigadier General John W. Nicholson, United States Army (Retired).

A Peek at Our Families in the World Today

Colonel R. James Nicholson.

Jim was Secretary of the VA for three years before returning to the private sector as a senior counsel in a major Washington DC law firm, a position which he still holds.

Jim also has received honorary degrees from eleven American and two Italian universities. He says he reflects a lot on his family heritage and his growing up in Northwest Iowa with its values of faith, family, community and country. Like Jack, he also credits his parents with the attributes he possesses and that were needed to make it through the many challenges during his life.

Along the way, Jim received many honors and much recognition. He says the honor that he is most proud of is being named a "Distinguished Graduate of the US Military Academy" which was bestowed upon him in 2005. In the Attachments at the end of the book are two letters, among the many, that were written to West Point in support of Jim's nomination to receive the Distinguished Graduate Award.

In the case of the Nicholson and McDougall families, Jim states:

> *Growing up in Northwest Iowa, it has become clear that our relationships with our relatives, our friends, our pastors, and our mentors made up a fabric of strong support, such that when combined with our faith and our inherited work ethic, we became not only equipped for success, but felt a commitment for success. Of all these attributes, faith and family are the most essential. We have been lucky in so many ways to have had both. The*

love, concern and mutual support of our families, our cousins and our friends were vital to our lives, our accomplishments and the many other things for which we are so grateful. We won the lottery to be Nicholsons and McDougalls, and Americans.

In Closing

As I close my version of our family history, I am hoping that this serves as just a start. There is much, much more to this family that can be written. In fact, there are even additional love stories from this same family along this very same road. John Deegan married Rose Mary Groetken and raised their family on C-12. Two of Rose Mary and John Deegan's daughters, Donna and Lynne, married two of my brothers, Nick and Denny. Denny and Lynne's son Jeff came out with a beautiful book called *The Good Life—the Remarkable Story of an American Farm Wife*. A full color book about this family growing up on their farmstead right on the Road to Love.

    It is my hope that this book is just the beginning of an increasingly comprehensive documentation of our family, that this will one day be considered just the "First Edition" as the story continues to be recorded. Further research can be done, more chapters can be added, and errors can be corrected. A bigger and bigger picture can be painted of the very brave souls that crossed thousands of miles of ocean, some with no more than the shirt on their backs, then traveled, by train or by horse and wagon, to set down roots in the small northwestern Iowa town of Struble. There are fascinating and entertaining stories of the people that followed. My hope is that this book isn't simply set aside, but that there is continued research, interviews, and exploration into the stories of the people that became and remain and continue to be the heartbeat of our family.

Appendices

A visit to the Road to Love

If you want to visit the Road to Love as it stands today, begin at Bob's Drive-in in Le Mars and head north on Hwy 75 about 7 miles. You meet up with C-12. This is the Road to Love. A majority of the tour takes you west on C-12.

Follow the map I have included here for you. Many of the landmarks on the map are now just fields. But take yourself back over 100 years when Chester and Edith's grandparents and parents were settling here and note the proximity of their farmsteads. Then imagine yourself in the time Chester and Edith married and began raising their family. Struble was a thriving town, and there were the farmsteads we lived on and the one or two room schoolhouses we attended.

The two houses Chester and Edith lived in when the first five children were born were hardly a mile from each other. Edith's family lived very close by. We could walk to our school and to the town of Struble. That was our world, and it was populated by a small number of people that we knew very well, our teachers,

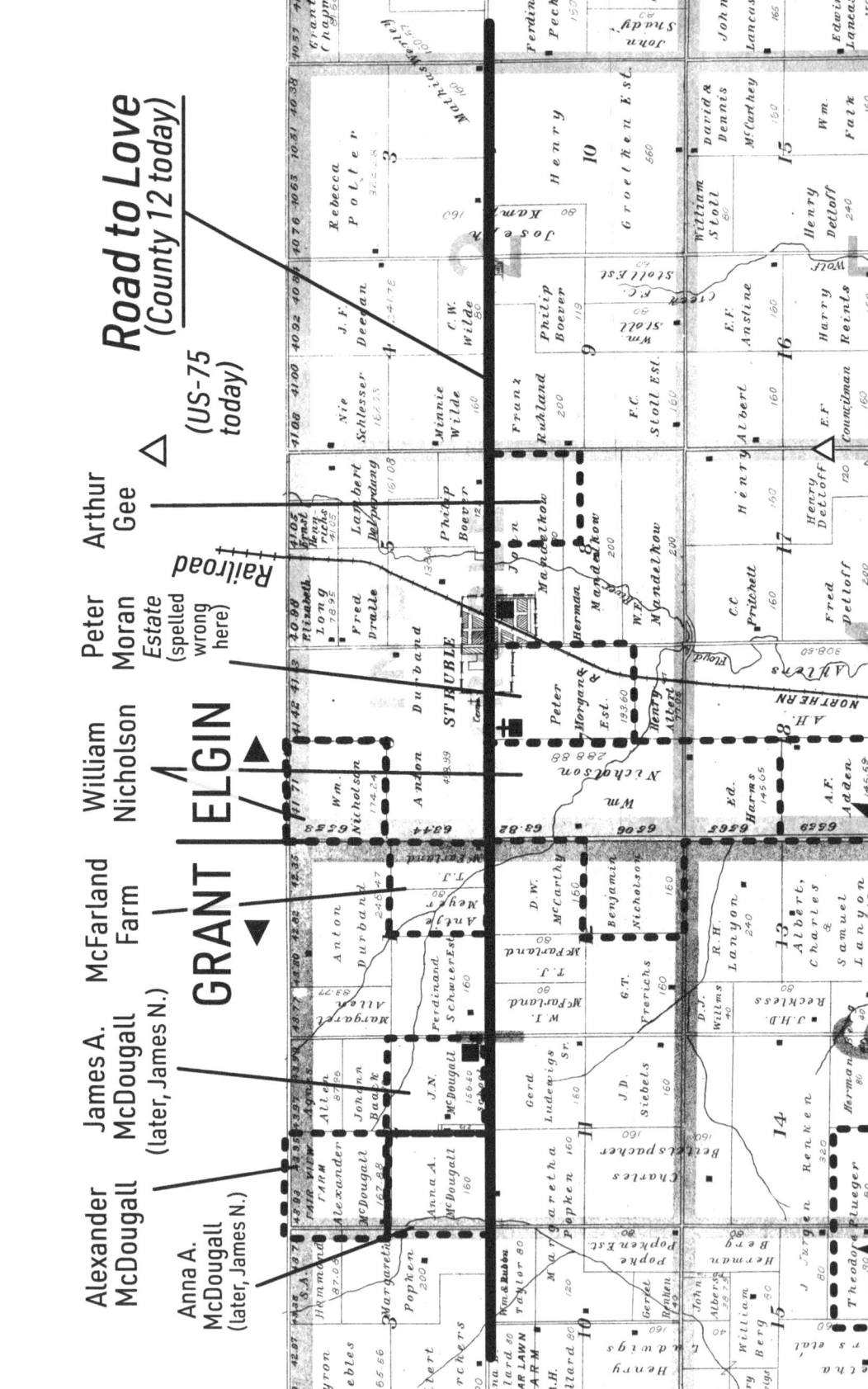

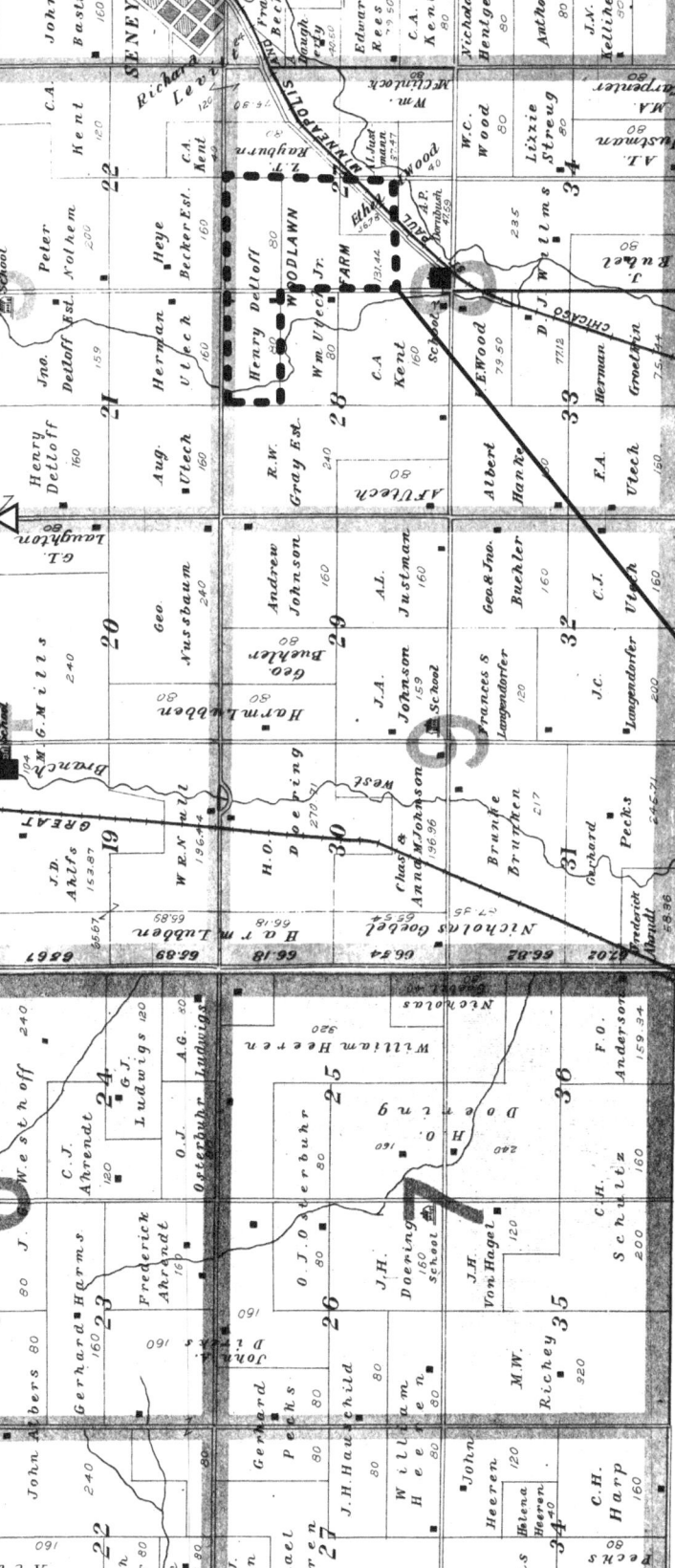

our family and our neighbors down the road. These were the people we lived with and near, the people that impacted us, the people we gave ideas to and took ideas from. It was a small world made up of a very friendly group, each wanting to help the other.

There are some excellent guides in Le Mars, and they are mentioned in this book. They grew up in this area and I would recommend you ask one of them to come along with you, because otherwise you will miss out on a lot of the color of what this world was like.

The Timeline

1746 (May 24) Jonah Nicholson born in Mouswald, Scotland (great-great-great-great-grandfather)

1746 Ann Carruthers born in Mouswald, Scotland (great-great-great-great-grandmother)

1775 Jonah Nicholson and Ann Carruthers marry

1776 Benjamin Nicholson born (great-great-great-grandfather)

1776 (July 4) Declaration of Independence signed

1789–1797 George Washington president

1800 (circa) Benjamin Nicholson and Jean Clark marry

1801 (Dec. 21) John Nicholson born (great-great-grandfather)

1801 Elizabeth Johnstone Lowther born (great-great-grandmother)

1809 Pete Moran born in Leitrim, Ireland (great-great-grandfather)

1809 Katherine Tafferty born (great-great-grandmother)

1815 War of 1812 ends—peace between England and America

1818 James Alexander McDougall born in Bowmore Scotland (great-grandfather)

1818 Benjamin Nicholson and family move from Mouswald to Annan Scotland

1820 Michael Neylan born in County Clare, Ireland (great-great-grandfather)

1822 (August 25) Anna Adeline Howard (great-grandmother) born in New York

1829 (October 5) John Nicholson marries Elizabeth Johnston Lowther

1830 Steam locomotive debuts in America

1830 Ann (Carruthers) Nicholson dies

1830 Pete Moran marries Katherine Tafferty (great-great-grandfather)

1830 (circa) Mary Glenn born County Clare (great-great-grandmother)

1831 Sarah Janet Birrell (great grandmother) born in Gretna, Scotland.

1832 James Alexander runs away and immigrates to Canada

1833 Benjamin E Nicholson born in Annan, Scotland (great-grandfather)

1833 Jonah Nicholson dies in Scotland

1834 (April 25) Joseph Warren born in Newsell, Hertfordshire, England (great-grandfather)

1834 (April 20) Emma Dodkins (Joseph Warren's wife) born in Berkway, Hertfordshire, England (great-grandmother)

1837 James Alexander immigrates to Cincinnati, OH from Canada

1840 (June 8) James Alexander and Anna Adeline Howard marry

The Timeline

1842 Alexander McDougall (1st son of James Alexander) born

1845–1850 potato famine—Ireland

1846–1851 Irish immigrants came through the Port of New York, New York

1846 Michael Neylan (father of Ellen Neylan) immigrates to United States from County Clare, Ireland (great-great grandfather)

1846 Mary Glenn (mother of Ellen Neylan) immigrates to United States from County Clare, Ireland

1846 (circa) Pete Moran (Sr.) immigrates to United States from Leitrim, Ireland

1847 (Nov. 29) James Alexander signs Affidavit of Rejection of Allegiance

1848 (Oct. 30) James Nelson McDougall born (Grandfather)

1849 (early) California Gold Rush

1850 (June 26) British Parliament repeals Navigation Act

1850 (December 3) First American Clipper delivers tea to English shores

1850 (Jan. 9) Peter Moran born in New Castle, Pennsylvania (Grandfather)

1850 Michael Neylan and Mary Glenn marry

1850 (Aug. 15) Martha Ann Warren born in Cambridgeshire, England (Grandmother)

1851 Beginning of the British clipper ship era in Scotland

1851 (June 25) John Nicholson dies (great-great-grandfather)

1852 Ellen Neylan (Peter Moran's wife) born in Rochester, New York (Great Grandmother)

1852 Nicholson and Company launch ship—Burns

1854 Joseph Warren and Emma Dodkins marry at Barkway Hertfordshire, England

1854 Nicholson and Co launched clipper ship Annandale

1855–1892 Castle Garden, New York, welcome 8,280,917 of the total 10,956,910 immigrants to arrive in this country during that period.

1855 Neylan family moves to Clayton County, Iowa

1856 Clipper ship Queensbury launched

1857 Clipper ship Shakspere launched

1857 Spirit Lake massacre

1858 Clipper ship Mansfield launched

1859 Clipper ship John Nicholson launched

1859 (Jan. 25) Benjamin Nicholson and Sarah Janet Birrell marry

1860 (Jan.) Benjamin Nicholson's first son John Nicholson born

1861–1865 Abraham Lincoln president

1861 American Civil War begins

1861 Clipper ship Mansfield launched

1861 (Aug. 21) Benjamin's second son James Birrell Nicholson born

1862 Clipper ship Brunswick launched

1862 (May 20) "Homestead Act of 1862" signed

1862 (Aug. 21) James and Alexander McDougall enlist for Civil War

1862 (October) James Alexander and his son Alexander muster into Civil War

1863 (January 1) Fire in James Alexander and Alexander barracks

The Timeline

1863 (March 27) James Alexander receives honorable discharge from injuries due to fire
1863 Clipper ship Elizabeth Nicholson launched
1865 (June 2) Civil war ends
1865 Alex musters out of Civil War
1865 Clipper ship Sarah Nicholson launched
1865 Benjamin closes shipping yard
1865 Pete Moran and family move to Elkader, Iowa
1866 (April 7) Pete Moran dies in Clayton County, Iowa
1869–1877 Ulysses Grant president
1869 (Sept. 12) Benjamin's third son Benjamin Jr. born
1869 Last British clipper, Cutty Sark (Jock Willis shipping) launched; official end of the clipper ship era
1869 Suez Canal opens
1869 Founding and naming of Le Mars
1869/67 Railway to Le Mars completed
1870 (spring) James Alexander receives letter with permission to homestead from General Grant
1870 (October 1) James Alexander and family settled on C-12
1870 Struble school held in a sod structure with a volunteer teacher
1871 (April 22) William Nicholson born (Grandfather) (Benjamin Nicholson fourth son)
1872 first school building erected in Struble with a paid teacher
1873 (Sept.) Richard Nicholson born (Benjamin's fifth son)
1875 (March 7) Peter Moran and Ellen Neylan marry in Elkader, Iowa

1875 (Nov.) Mary Elizabeth (Mollie) Moran (Grandmother) born

1873–1879 Grasshopper plague in northwest Iowa

1876 (Nov. 16) James Alexander and Alex receive official deed for homestead land

1877 Peter and Ellen Moran settled on C-12 bringing Mary Elizabeth

1879 Major fire at Peter Moran's farm

1880 Joseph and Emma Warren and family immigrate to Iowa, arrive at the Gee farmstead (bringing Martha)

1880 Peter Moran's son Frank Moran born

1880 (circa) Benjamin Nicholson buys land on C-12

1881 James Nelson McDougall (32) and Martha Warren (31) marry in Struble, Iowa

1881 (Nov. 5) Joseph Warren and family file for citizenship

1882 (Jan. 2) Mary Matilda born (James Nelson and Martha McDougall 1st child)

1882 James Birrell Nicholson (son of Benjamin) immigrates to Iowa

1883 (Dec. 11) Laura Isabell born (James N and Martha McDougall 2nd child)

1885 (Sept. 22) Hattie Mae born (James N and Martha McDougall 3rd child)

1886 Sarah Janet (Birrell) Nicholson dies

1887 (Aug. 6) Anna Pearl born (James N and Martha McDougall 4th child)

1888 William Nicholson (son of Benjamin) immigrates to Plymouth county, Iowa, from Annan, Scotland

The Timeline

1888 Completion of Sioux City and Northern Railway to Struble

1889 (June 27) John James (Jack) born (James N and Martha McDougall 5th child)

1890 Struble platted, train station and post office established

1890 (Oct. 27) Joseph and family receive official citizenship to United States

1890 Final sod home removed from the northwest Iowa prairie

1892 (January 1) First immigrants land in Ellis Island

1892 William Nicholson moves to Elgin township on C-12

1893 James Alexander McDougall dies in Struble, Iowa

1893 (Oct. 7) Chester Nelson born (James N and Martha McDougall 6th child)

1894 (Dec. 12) William Nicholson and Mary Elizabeth (Mollie) Moran marry on Peter Moran farm

1895 Richard Nicholson (son of Benjamin) immigrates to Iowa

1895 Struble is incorporated

1896 (Jan. 11) Jenny born (William and Mollie Nicholson 1st child)

1888 Katherine (Tafferty) Moran dies, buried in Sioux City, Iowa

1898 Peter's son, Frank Moran succumbs to tuberculosis

1898 (April 28) Benjamin (Buzz) born (William and Mollie Nicholson 2nd child)

1900 (Oct. 20) William Nicholson naturalized

1900 (March 17) Nell born (William and Mollie Nicholson 3rd child)

1901–1909 Theodore Roosevelt president

1902 (March 6) Molly born (William and Mollie Nicholson 4th child)

1903 Peter Moran dies

1903 (April 2) Mabel born (William and Mollie Nicholson 5th child)

1903 (later) St. Joseph church and Parish Hall in Struble erected on Peter Moran's donated land

1904 (Aug. 6) Edith Rose born (William and Mollie Nicholson's 6th child)

1904 Cemetery in Struble established

1904 Town Hall built in Struble includes a fire station and a jail in back

1905 (Sept. 20) William (Buck) born (William and Mollie Nicholson 7th child)

1906 (Nov. 23) Emma (Dodkins) Warren dies

1907 Anna Adeline (Howard) McDougall dies

1908 (Jan. 4) Dorothy born (William and Mollie Nicholson 8th child)

1908 Henry Ford introduced the Model T

1909 (Oct. 31) Richard (Dick) born (William and Mollie Nicholson 9th child)

1911 (Jan. 7) Joseph Warren dies

1912 (June 2) Don born (William and Mollie Nicholson 10th child)

1913 Benjamin Nicholson dies in Scotland

1913 (Aug. 18) Evelyn born (William and Mollie Nicholson 11th child)

1914–1918 World War l

The Timeline

1920–1933 Prohibition

1920 James Nelson McDougall retires, buys the Mullen house and moves to town with Martha and Mary

1922 (July 7) James Nelson McDougall dies

1922 Chester McDougall and Edith Nicholson marry

1923 (May 12) Jim born (Chester and Edith McDougall's 1st child)

1923 (March 1) Chester and Edith rent Adden place

1923 (circa) Martha and Mary move to Collin's house near foundry

1925 Ellen (Neylan) Moran dies in Struble, Iowa

1925 (April 23) Mabel born (Chester and Edith McDougall's 2nd child)

1927 (Aug. 4) William (Bill) born (Chester and Edith McDougall's 3rd child)

1929 (Oct.) Stock market crashed

1929–1938 Great Depression

1930 Big Struble fire (responsible for the destruction of the city's records)

1931 (Aug. 11) Richard (Dick) born (Chester and Edith McDougall's 4th child)

1931–1939 drought and dust bowl era

1932 (March 1) Chester and Edith McDougall move to the McFarland farm with Martha and Mary

1933–1945 Franklin D Roosevelt president

1934 (Jan. 26) Douglas (Doug) born (Chester and Edith McDougall's 5th child)

1934 (Aug. 11) Dorothy (Nicholson) Bertram dies

1936 (Nov. 1) Mary Elizabeth (Mollie) Nicholson dies

1937 (March 1) thru 1938 (March 1st)—Chester rents land on Buck Nicholson's

farm—Edith, family, Martha and Mary rent 12th St SW, Le Mars

1938 (March 1) Chester and Edith begin renting Utech farm. Martha and Mary stay at 12th St. SW, Le Mars

1938 (December 21) Janice born (Chester and Edith McDougall's 6th child)

1940 William Nicholson moves from his farm to Mabel Mueller's house in Le Mars

1941 (Dec. 7) Pearl Harbor Day

1941–1945 World War II

1941 near normal rainfall returns

1941 (Feb. 16) Edythe born (Chester and Edith McDougall's 7th child)

1942 Chester and Edith McDougall purchase Utech farm

1942 Martha and Mary McDougall move to Prest house

1942 (Oct.) Jim leaves for Naval Duty

1942 Martha McDougall (Grandma) dies

1942 (May 13) Nick born (Chester and Edith McDougall's 8th child)

1944 (March 18) Dennis (Denny) born (Chester and Edith McDougall's 9th child)

1945 Harry Truman president

1945 (June 19) William Nicholson dies

1945 (Oct. 20) Mark born (Chester and Edith McDougall's 10th child)

The Timeline

1945 (May) Bill enlists with Merchants Marines

1945 (Dec) World War II ends

1946 (Jan. 1) Jim returns from service

1946 (Dec 1) Bill returns from Merchant Marines

1947 (March 5) Dana McDougall—first grandchild of Chester and Edith born

1954 (Sept) Dick enlists in the Army

1956 (Sept) Dick returns from the Army

1956 (Sept) Doug enlists in the Army

1958 (May) Doug returns from the Army

1958 Chester retires from farming

1960 (Jan. 1) Chester and Edith move to 901 2nd Ave SW in Le Mars

1960–1973 American involvement in Vietnam war

1961 John F Kennedy president

1961 (April 23) Aunt Mary dies

1967 (Sept)–1973 Mark serves in US Army Reserves

1974 (Jan. 21) Chester Nelson McDougall dies

1979 (June 29) Tiffani McDougall—last grandchild of Chester and Edith born

1999 (April 1) Edith Rose Nicholson McDougall dies

Obituaries

Included below are some obituaries of our forefathers.

James Alexander McDougall....................302
Anna Adeline McDougall 303
Joseph Warren 305
Emma Dodkins (Mrs. Joseph Warren) 306
Michael Neylan 307
Mary (Glenn) Neylan 308
Peter Moran 308
Ellen (Neylan) Moran.......................309
Benjamin E Nicholson 311
James Nelson McDougall......................318
Martha Ann (Warren) McDougall...............320
William Nicholson.......................... 321
Mary Elizabeth (Moran) Nicholson............323
Chester Nelson McDougall....................325
Edith Rose (Nicholson) McDougall............326

JAMES ALEXANDER MCDOUGALL[1]

James A McDougall, Farmer, PO Struble, was born in Scotland, March 2, 1818, a son of Alexander and Margaret (Graham) McDougall. He was reared in Scotland and received his education in the public schools of that place. He learned the carpenter's trade early in life, but never made it his permanent occupation. He has been engaged in various lines of business and has met with financial success. In 1832 he came to Canada, and in 1837 he went to Cincinnati, Ohio and the same year to St. Louis, Mo. and engaged in railroading. In 1839 he went to La Salle county, Ill. And purchased eighty acres of land near Troy Grove, and remained there until 1846, when he went to Iowa county, Wisc. and engaged in farming.

In 1870, he came to Iowa, where he now owns 160 acres of land in section two, Grant township, ten miles from Le Mars. Beside owning a good farm in Grant township, he owns one of the best building in Le Mars, which is now occupied by the Security bank. In 1840, he married Annie Adeline Howard of American birth, and they are parents of six children, Alexander, Matilda, Mary, James Nelson, Sarah and John. Politically he was a republican.

1—From the book *History of the Counties of Woodbury and Plymouth, Iowa*.

Obituaries

ANNA ADELINE MCDOUGALL [2]

Death of Old Resident

Mrs. Anna Adeline McDougall, one of the pioneer residents of this vicinity, died at her home west of Struble, yesterday morning, her death being due to cancer and old age. Mrs. McDougall was nearly eighty-five years of age at the time of her death, having been born in New York, on August 25, 1822. With her husband she came to Plymouth county nearly forty years ago and was one of the brave women who helped the early settlers in their hardships in the days of drought, blizzard and grasshoppers. She was widely and affectionately known by the name of Grandma McDougall for many years, and her cheery help and neighborliness has won her a place in the hearts of many, especially those who have lived here for a number of years.

Her husband died about eight years ago. She leaves to mourn her death several sons and daughters and grandchildren. Two of her sons James and Alexander McDougall and two daughter, Mrs. Thos. Edwards and Mrs. James Andrews live in his neighborhood and another son Hohm lives at Ogden, Iowa. The funeral will be held today at the Methodist church in Struble, and the remains brough to Le Mars for interment beside those of her husband.

2—Le Mars Sentinel (August 6, 1907).

A second obit.

> After months of suffering Mrs. Anna McDougall passed peacefully away Monday morning at an early hour. A week before her death she sank into a stupor from which she did not regain consciousness. She was 85 years old. She was a devoted wife—her husband passed on some years ago—a loving tender mother striving earnestly to train her sons and daughters for useful men and women. She is survived by three sons and two daughters, namely, Alex, James and John. Mrs. Andrews and Mrs. Edwards, the latter has made her home with the deceased and tenderly cared for her the past few years. She was a dearly loved member of the M. E. and church was liberal in its support. She has fallen sleep to awake in the land of eternal bliss. Everything was done to make her declining days as comfortable as possible. Grandma was certainly a useful member of the community. She with her husband passed through the pioneer days and homesteaded the farm on which she spent her last days. The funeral service was conducted in the M.E. church of Struble which was beautifully decorated with flowers. The remains were laid to rest in Le Mars by the side of her husband and daughter Mrs. Craig who preceded her some years ago. The family have the sympathy of a large number of kind friends and neighbors in their bereavement.

JOSEPH WARREN[3]

Death of Joseph Warren
Deceased Had Lived in This Vicinity Thirty Years

Friends in Le Mars have received word of the death of Joseph Warren which occurred last week near Elk Point. Mr. Warren came to Le Mars in 1880 and was employed by Close bros. On their ranch near Kingsley and subsequently lived on a farm ten miles north of Le Mars. From there he moved to Westfield where he lived the rest of his life. The Westfield correspondence of the Akron Register Tribune contains the following obituary:

Thomas Warren received the sad news Saturday of the death of his father near Elk Point.

Joseph Warren was born at Newsells, Hertfordshire, England, April 25, 1834, where he spent the early part of his life. He was married to Emma Dodkins at Barkway, Hertfordshire, in 1854. To them were born twelve children, three of whom died in England. Mr. and Mrs. Warren came to Le Mars in 1880, where they lived about two years and then settled on a farm near Westfield, where they continued to reside until Mrs. Warren's death., November 26th, 1906. Since her death he had been living with his sons, George and Jonas, going with them last spring to Dakota, where they had claims. They had lately returned and were living on a farm ear Elk Point, where

---
3—Akron Register-Tribune.

he died January 7, 1911, aged nearly 77 years. The remains were brought to Westfield Tuesday and funeral services were held in the Congregational church. Reverend John Nickerson preaching the sermon. A large number of old-time friends and acquaintances gathered in respect to the one whom they had known in former years. The floral offerings were very appropriate. Interment in Riverside cemetery. Akron, beside his wife.

Joseph Warren leaves to mourn his departure, five sons and four daughters, Thomas of Westfield, George and Jonas near Elk Point, James of Canton, John near Alcester, Mrs. Mary Thompson of Le Mars, Mrs. Martha McDougall of Struble, Mrs. Sarah Hinchcliff and Mrs. Ama Perkins of Fergus Falls, Minn.

EMMA DODKINS (MRS. JOSEPH WARREN)[4]

Miss Emma Dodkins was born in Berkway, Hertfordshire, England, April 20, 1834, where she grew to womanhood. In December 1853, she was united in marriage to Joseph Warren. To this union was born twelve children, three of whom died in England. Mrs. Warren after a long illness, died November 23, 1906, at the Jonas Warren home south of Westfield. In 1880, Mr. and Mrs. Warren and family came to the United States. Coming direct to Le

---

4—Akron Register-Tribune.

Mars, where they stayed several years, but have lived near Westfield for twenty-six years. Nine children and an aged husband survive her. Five boys and two daughters were with her at the time of her death. She also leaves forty-nine grandchildren, six great grandchildren. Funeral services were held Sunday at 2 pm at the Congregational church. Reverend Brantneil preaching the sermon. A large number of people followed the remains to Akron where they were interred.

MICHAEL NEYLAN[5]

On Monday last at the home of his son, John in this township, Mr. Neylon passed away in the sleep that knows no awakening in this life. Mr. Neylon was born in County Clare, Ireland in 1820 and at the time of his death reached the advanced age of 85 years. He came to America about 1846 and after visiting almost every part of the country settled down in Highland township where he purchased forty acres of land. Later he bought more land in Boardman township. He was a quiet unassuming man, respected by all, having been a resident of this township for over fifty years.

Deceased is survived by his aged wife, his son John and two daughters, Mrs. Peter Moran of Struble, Iowa and

---

5—Elkader Register Thursday March 16, 1905 (Neylan is spelled as Neylon in this obituary).

Mrs. John Keleher of Boardman township and a number of grandchildren. The funeral was held yesterday at St. Joseph's church and was attended by a large number of friends and neighbors.

MARY (GLENN) NEYLAN[6]

On Friday occurred the death of Mrs. Mary Neylan at the home of her daughter, Mrs. J.L. Keleher of old age, she being about 84 years old. The funeral services were held Monday in St. Joseph's church, Rev. J.F. Reilly officiating.

PETER MORAN[7]

Moran, Peter, born 1850, died 1903, on same headstone with Frank buried in St. Mary's cemetery, Maurice, Iowa.
Peter Moran passed away at his home just south of town, Tuesday morning at 9 o'clock. He was born in New Castle, Pennsylvania and was 53 years old at the time of his death. He came to Plymouth county over 28 years ago and in the early days taught school. He finally bought land and has been a successful farmer to the time of his demise. Mr. Moran was back and forth to his Pennsylvania home

---

6—Register and Argus, Elkader, Iowa Thursday, January 4th, 1911.
7—Le Mars Globe Post Saturday April 4th, 1903.

and the mountains of the west several times. But because of his disease consumption could find no relief anywhere so returned to his family here last fall and had not been out of the house since, but said he came home to die.

Peter Moran was a man of strong convictions, earnest, honest, kindly and thrifty and a man who always made good on his word. He was an earnest member of the Catholic church and the new church will be built on his land.

Besides his wife, he leaves to mourn two sons Robert and John and two daughters Miss Jennie and Mrs. William Nicholson, all who were at his bedside in his last days.

The funeral took place Thursday at 9 o'clock from the house and the remains were followed by a large number of friends to the church in Maurice. Reverend Father Grady preached an eloquent sermon speaking most consoling works to the bereaved ones. The family has the sympathy of the community in their hour of grief.

ELLEN (NEYLAN) MORAN[8]

Elgin Pioneer

Mrs. Ellen Moran, a pioneer resident of Plymouth county, died at her home near Struble Friday following an illness caused by an internal malady at the age of

---

8—Le Mars Sentinel Tuesday, October 20, 1925.

73 years. Mrs. Moran was born at Rochester, New York, January 29, 1852 and when a child came to Iowa with her parents, who settled in Clayton county. She was united in marriage at Elkader to Peter Moran, March 7th, 1875, and soon after their marriage came to Plymouth county and settled on an eighty in Elgin township. Here they prospered and became owners of a fine farm increasing their land holdings. Mr. Moran died a number of years ago and Mrs. Moran made her home some of the time with her children.

Mrs. Moran leaves four children who are, Mrs. William Nicholson, of Elgin township, John Moran, of Ellsworth, Minn., P.J. Moran, of Elgin township, and Mrs. Hugh McDonald of Harington, Neb., one son, Frank, preceding her in death.

The funeral services were held yesterday at St. Joseph's church in Struble. Rev. J. Greteman conducting the services and the interment was made beside the remains of her husband in the cemetery in Maurice.

Mrs. Moran was well known in a large circle of acquaintances, especially among the older residents, and was respected and esteemed by all who knew her.

Obituaries

BENJAMIN E NICHOLSON[9]

The late Mr. Benjamin Nicholson
May 30, 1913
We regret to announce the death of Mr. Benjamin Nicholson of Cotton Lodge, Annan, Scotland, which occurred on Monday evening at the age of 80. Mr. Nicholson's end came peacefully after the gradual decline of his physical powers. Those that knew him were aware that his strength had been failing during the last few months, but he continued his customary habits with his usual regularity and punctuality, and he was actually confined to the house for only about a fortnight.

Mr. Nicholson was born in the house in which he lived throughout practically the whole of his long life and in which he finally died. He was the eldest son of the late Mr. John Nicholson, shipbuilder, and was born in 1833. He was educated at Annan Academy where he distinguished himself in mathematics and penmanship. He afterward spent a short time in the office of the late Mr. James Little, writer. He then went to Liverpool to gain an insight into shipping, and at the age of 18, returned home to enter his father's business. This was in 1851, and for the following 62 years, he gave an almost unremitting attention to his affairs here, although in late years much of the responsibilities of management fell upon his eldest son, Mr. John

---

9—A full-page article in the newspaper, the Annandale Observer that followed his death.

Nicholson. The record of the Nicholson family and its association with this district is one of considerable historical interest because it is possible to read through it with the general movement of social and industrial developments which have from time-to-time materially affected the channel in which the activities of the townsmen were directed. The founder of the Nicholson business was a former of that name who came from the outer neighborhood and engaged in the sale and transport of merchandise. The beginning of the firm takes us back to the end of the 18th century when Annan was a town relatively more important than it is today. It was then, and indeed remained, until the introduction of the railways, a gathering place for the sale and exchange of much of the agricultural produce on the whole of Annandale and even of districts beyond the vale. The Nicholson's were far seeing men, full of decision and purpose, and from merchants they passed not by an abrupt cleavage but by a natural process to be ship builders and shippers. Annan was a real maritime town, not merely in the geographical sense but in the sense that its interests were largely bound up with the proximity of the open sea. It occupied much of the same position that an important railway terminus does today. The sea was not merely an important international highway, the accessibility of inland towns for goods traffic was calculated not by the nearness of a railway station, for there were of course no railways, but by the distance from the sea. There were many thriving little ports along the shores of these islands, which the advent of the railways displaced from a proud provincial splendor. Annan was one of these. The Nicholson's began to build ships of their own and sail the ships frequently with their own merchandise. They were famed builders and exporters in those days. Their ships sailed the Atlantic Ocean. Trafficked with Far East and established periodical communication between the port of Annan and various ports along the coast of these shores. When Mr. Nicholson entered the business in 1851, the ship building yards were busy and the launching of a boat was a kind of general holiday because these were sights that few cared to miss. In the time of Mr. Benjamin Nicholson, the ship building reached its highest success, his grandfather and father had been increasing the size of the ships they turned out, but the greatest advance was the launching of the Sarah Nicholson of 1500 tons.

The Sarah Nicholson was also the last of big ships although to work up the wood in the yard a number of coasters were afterward built. Of course, the larger ships did not come up to Annan with cargo. They called at Liverpool, Glasgow and other important ports, but their local character was preserved by her being manned to a great extent by Annan men. This was, however, direct service between Annan and America and the European ports. The community of Annan was thus mixed with a seafaring as distant from a fishing population, so that the thoughts of the inhabitants were always more or less turned seaward. It was not at once nor immediately that the railways began to make themselves felt. Trade does not run easily along new channels, and for nearly another 20 years Annan was still a shipbuilding town. But Mr. Nicholson was born to face an industrial revolution, a revolution which at once changed the character of his business and the character of the town. While the mechanical inventions that were quickly following one another were pushing the world into little space, strangely enough they were in another sense widening—between Annan and many other small towns similarly situated and foreign countries . . . sense of personal intercourse was being lost and the thoughts of the people were being diverted no other directions. The day of the sailing ships began to pass. Steamships began to multiply, but they were built where there was a density of population and proximity of coal and iron. The carrying trade too, was diverted to the large centers, and a great readjustment of industry generally went on. Forces were at work, which no amount of skill or energy could counteract. And the crisis which affected Mr. Nicholson was equally felt by the town of Annan. His interest in shipping remained to the end and he generally make a point of seeing any new ship, which marked a development inbuilding launched on the Clyde. Indeed, he went to Glasgow to see the huge Aquitania launched a few days before he lay down, and at a time when prudence would have dictated caution. After giving up shipbuilding, Mr. Nicholson devoted his energies to the timber trade and built up a large section, which the firm maintains to this day and they also do an extensive business as slate merchants. Mr. Nicholson is succeeded by his son, Mr. John Nicholson, who for many ears now has been associated with the firm.

Mr. Nicholson was never particularly attracted toward public life. He sat on the town council from 1861 to 1872 and was appointed a bailie in 1863. He found a more lasting interest in the work of the parochial board and when the board was superseded, he joined the parish council and was a member at the time of his death.

In 1871, he was made a director of the Glasgow and Southwestern Railway company. To this work he gave a large amount of painstaking and detailed attention. He went into the working of the line with great minuteness and personally knew almost every agent on the line. For many years, he devoted two days a week to this work. About ten years ago he retired feeling the time was right for younger men and Mr. B. J. Brook of Hoddam was elected to fill his vacant place on the board. He had about forty years connection with Annan Savings Bank as a director and he was also a director of Annan gas company. He was a member of Annon Harbour trust since its incorporation. To religion, he gave much time and substance, and particularly to missionary enterprises. He was strongly evangelical and a strict and uncompromising Sabbatarian. Sunday was to him a day to be wholly consecrated and the modern tendency were a source of great anxiety to him. He was caught up in the famous revival in Annan in 1861 and the influence of that movement remained vivid and fresh with him to the end.

There was much in Mr. Nicholson's character that separated him from the conventional. His outlook on life was not certainly that of the average man. His ideas of order and punctuality he no doubt in a measure, inherited from his father, but there was a great deal that he added as a result of his own independent thought. His life was governed by a rigid self-discipline, his will was strong and virile. It brooked no interference. It formed his own habits with unquestioned authority. To every hour of the day Mr. Nicholson allotted its portion, and the daily calendar was observed with a religious constancy throughout the greater part of his life. He knew nothing of that easy trifling that most men seek as a relief from graver things. His purpose was too serious for that. Idleness to him an indulgence and his economy of life did not allow for it. In any case he had made up his mine how he would dispose of himself. Had taken his decision upon the result of his deliberation; and as far as he was concerned the decision could not be reopened or even argued. He could not be judged by popular standards. He was an exceptional nature, and it could bear lightly a discipline which few men would think of applying to themselves. The discipline under which he laid himself loosed its bonds and became his happiness. He loved to think that each hour was provided for. The thought of a blank diary or day or hour even for which nothing was arranged would have been a nightmare to him. The standard he set for himself, he expected of other men. He expected more from human nature than it was prepared to give. He was punctilious in fulfilling his own obligations and he looked for the same perfection all around. An obligation was always associated in his mind with a particular date. He never approved of anyone undertaking obligation when they did not see their way clearly to the end. He forgot nothing and overlooked nothing, and here also his experience disappointed him often. He set before him his ideals and he found them to be in conflict with the ways of men. He found human nature on the average too rebellious to be systematised. He was a strong man and as he never bargained with himself, so he would never kneel to the conventions of society. He might provoke criticism, but he was unmoved by it and certainly in it all the faintest shadow never fell on his honor or integrity.

In 1880, Mr. Nicholson bought a large tract of land in Iowa, in the United States, it is now being farmed by four of his sons, James, Benjamin, William and Richard. He paid several visits to America and to Canada and went as far west as the Pacific. He had also three daughters, one of whom is married to Mr. Murray Little, town clerk, Annan. Mr. Nicholson's wife, who died in 1886, was a daughter of the late Mr. Jas. Birrell, Gretna. Mr. W.L. Nicholson, Kent Lodge, is a brother of Mr. Nicholson, and another brother was the late ex-provost, John Nicholson, who died in 1900. Mrs. James Saunders, Seaforth, was the only sister,

The funeral took place yesterday in Annan Cemetery and was of a private nature, the undertaking being in the hands of Messrs., Chalmers and Co.

From an August 26, 1913 article in The Scotsman following Benjamin's death: "Benjamin Nicholson's personal estate was valued at 49,275 pounds." Converted to today's dollar that would be approximately $6,600,000.

JAMES NELSON MCDOUGALL

Death of an Old Resident
JAS. Nelson McDougall, Farmed here for Fifty years:
Was one of the First Settlers in Grant

Came to Le Mars with his father the year after the railroad was built through Le Mars. Traveling from Wisconsin with wagon and horses.

James Nelson, one of the well-known and highly respected pioneer citizens of Plymouth County, passed away at his residence in Le Mars on Friday evening, July 7. Mr. McDougall had been in failing health for the past two years.

James N McDougall was born at Mineral Point, Wisconsin in October 1848, being a son of James and Adeline McDougall. He received his early education in the schools in Wisconsin. On reaching manhood he worked in the lead mines and assisted his father on the farm. In 1870 he came with his father to Iowa. They made the trip across the state with horses and wagons. This journey covering a period of thirteen days and being fraught with hazards and adventure. There was only one log cabin between Cherokee and Le Mars in those days. On Mr. McDougall's arrival in Plymouth County, he preempted 160 acres of land in Grant township. And his holding was alone increased to 240 acres. His first residence was a cabin twelve by twelve feet in which he lived for some years. Since that time, he expanded many thousand dollars in improvements and created the place of one of the most beautiful farms in Plymouth county. He resided on the place over fifty years. John (Jack) McDougall now resides on the home farm.

In 1881, James N McDougall was united in marriage to Martha Warren in Le Mars. To this union were born nine children, two girls died in infancy. One daughter, Mrs. Laura Edwards, died eight years ago. Those left to mourn are his sorrowing wife, his children Edward McDougall at Westfield, Mrs. Frank Glaser of Le Mars, Mrs. Pearl Barkl of Sioux City, Mary and Chester McDougall of Le Mars and John McDougall at Struble, all being at his bedside when he passed away.

He is (unreadable words) two brothers, Alexander McDougall of Le Mars, and John McDougall of Ogden, Utah and one sister, Mrs. Mary Edwards of Ireton, besides a host of friends and acquaintances.

The funeral was held at two o'clock from the home residence at North Main street Monday afternoon and services were held at the First Methodist church, Rev. C.H. Seward, the pastor, officiating. The body was laid to rest in the city cemetery. The pallbearers were E.A Dalton, M.A. Cass, F.K. Veale, A.M. Duus, John Bogen and John Edwards.

MARTHA ANN (WARREN) MCDOUGALL

*Aged Pioneer is Called by Death
(Last Rites Held Today for
Mrs. James N. McDougall)*

Mrs. James N. McDougall passed away Monday at her home at 36 2nd Ave. SW after being sick with pneumonia for the past ten days.

Martha Ann McDougall was born on August 15th, 1850, in Cambridgeshire, England, and had reached the age of 92 years and 2 months. She was the daughter of Mr. And Mrs. Joseph Warren, Deceased, lived in England until 1880 and then came to Plymouth county. She was married in March 1881, to James McDougall and they lived on the homestead farm in Grant township until 1920. At that time, they moved to Le Mars. Mrs. McDougall was a devoted member of the First Methodist church and also belonged to the Happy Hour club.

Survivors are the children, Edward J. McDougall of Westfield, Mary McDougall, at home, Mrs. Frank

Glaser of Le Mars, Mrs. Henry Barkl of Sioux City, John J. McDougall of Struble, Chester N. McDougall of Le Mars; 20 grandchildren, six great grandchildren: brothers, Thomas Warren of Westfield, James Warren of Long Beach, California, John Warren of Atchinson, Kansas, Jonas Warren of Elk Point, S.D, George Warren of Sioux City, and sisters, Mrs. Alex Thompson of Gary, S.D., and Mrs. Sarah Henchcliff of Park Rapids, Minn. She is preceded in death by her husband, a daughter, Mrs. Le Roy Edwards and two infant daughters.

WILLIAM NICHOLSON[10]

William Nicholson, one of the well-known farmers and stockmen of Elgin township, Plymouth county, was born in Annan, Dumfrieshire, Scotland, April 22, 1871, the son of Benjamin and Sarah (Birrell) Nicholson, both natives of that shire. Benjamin Nicholson was a man of distinction in his home country and was engaged in the lumber business. He was for forty years a director of the Glasgow & Southwestern Railroad and a joint director of the Midland Railroad and was successful in his business ventures. In 1880 he came to Iowa and purchased three thousand two hundred acres of valuable land around Le Mars and in Grant and Elgin townships, this county, as

---

10—History of Plymouth County, Iowa.

an investment for the use of his sons. Benjamin Nicholson died at his home in Scotland in 1913. His wife died in the year 1886. They were members of the Congregational church and were prominent in the social life of the community in which they lived. They were the parents of eight children, four of whom came to this country, those besides the subject of this sketch being J. B. and Benjamin, residents of Le Mars, and Richard, a farmer of Elgin township.

William Nicholson received his primary education in the public schools of Annan and finished his schooling at Morningside College, Edinburgh, which he attended for three years. In 1887 he came to Plymouth county, locating on a farm south of Le Mars, where he remained for five years. In September 1892, he began the improvement of his magnificent farm in section 7 of Elgin township, and today has one of the most pleasant and substantial country homes in the county.

In December 1894, in Elgin township, William Nicholson was united in marriage to Mollie Moran, who was born in Clayton county, Iowa, and to this union the following children have been born: Janet, Benjamin, Nell, Mollie, Mabel, Edith, William J., Dorothy, Richard, Donald and Evelyn, all of whom are at home save Janet, who married L. E. Becker, of Sioux county. The home life of the Nicholson's is ideal, and they are held in the highest regard by their many friends throughout the county.

Mr. Nicholson's farm of four hundred and fifty acres, located in Plymouth and Sioux counties is all under high cultivation and well improved. He practices mixed farming, handles much stock and has for many years successfully engaged in the buying and feeding of cattle and hogs. He is identified with the Republican party and has always taken an active interest in local affairs but has never aspired to office. He is a prominent member of the Elks lodge at Le Mars and takes much interest in the growth and success of that order. Mr. Nicholson's personality has won for him many friends throughout the county and his home is noted for its hospitality.

MARY ELIZABETH (MORAN) NICHOLSON

Mrs. Nicholson, Widely Known Resident, Dies
Came to Plymouth county when a child and lived-in community since.

Mrs. Nicholson, wife of William Nicholson, well known farmer of Elgin township, died at the Sacred Heart Hospital in the city, Sunday morning. Mrs. Nicholson had been failing in health for a year and a half and, ten days ago, her condition became critical.

Mary E. Moran was born at Elkader, Iowa, November 26, 1875, and came to Le Mars when two years old with her parents, Mr. And Mrs. Peter Moran, who settled in Sioux County. Mrs. Nicholson lived in this vicinity the rest of her life. She was untied in marriage, with William Nicholson, December 12, 1894.

Her death is mourned by her husband, four sons and six daughters, Mrs. Le Becker, Ireton; Mrs. J.C. Rosburg, Hinton; Mrs. Verne Keough, Le Mars; Mrs. Emil Mueller, Mrs. Chester McDougall, and Miss Evelyn Nicholson, Benjamin, William, and Don, of Struble and Richard, of Le Mars. Two daughters preceded her in death, Elizabeth at the age of three and Mrs. Lorenze Bertram who died two years ago. She is survived by her two brothers, P.J. Moran, Struble, John Moran, Ellsworth, Minn. And a sister, Mrs. Hugh McDonald, Pueblo Colorado.

The funeral will be held Wednesday morning at St. James Church at 9:30 with Rev. L. J. Cooper officiating, and interment made in St. James Cemetery, Le Mars.

Mrs. Nicholson was widely known in the community, where she lived all her life and was held in the highest esteem by all who knew her.

CHESTER NELSON MCDOUGALL[11]

Chester Nelson McDougall, 80, died Monday January 21, 1974 at Floyd Valley hospital after an illness of several months. He had been at the hospital the last six weeks.

Mr. McDougall was a retired farmer and resided at 901 Second Ave SW. Le Mars. He was a lifelong resident

---

11—Le Mars Daily Sentinel, Monday January 21, 1974.

of Plymouth county and farmed until retiring to Le Le Mars in 1960.

He was born October 7, 1893 in Plymouth county and was the son of James N and Martha Warren McDougall. His marriage to Edith R. Nicholson took place November 23, 1922 in Sioux City.

Funeral services will be held Wednesday, January 23 at 2 PM at First United Methodist church, Le Mars. Rev Everett Staats will officiate, and burial will be in Le Mars Memorial cemetery under direction of Mauer funeral home in Le Mars.

Mr. McDougall was a member of the First United Methodist church in Le Mars.

Survivors are his wife, Edith, Le Mars, seven sons, James McDougall, Minneapolis; William, Richard, Douglas, and Mark, all of Le Mars, and Nick McDougall, Hampton, and Dennis McDougall, Pampa, Texas; three daughters, Mrs. Eugene (Mabel) Scholer, Le Mars; Mrs. David (Janice) Petry, Clinton, Iowa; and Mrs. Gene (Edythe) Swanson M.D. Rochester, Minn.; one brother, John McDougall, Le Mars. There are 39 grandchildren and two great grandchildren. He was preceded in death by a brother and four sisters.

EDITH ROSE (NICHOLSON) MCDOUGALL[12]

Edith R. Nicholson

Le Mars, Iowa—Edith Rose Nicholson, 94, of Le Mars died Thursday, April 1, 1999, at her residence.

Services will be 1:30 pm Tuesday at First United Methodist Church of Le Mars with burial in Memorial Cemetery, Le Mars. Visitation will be 2 to 9 pm today with a prayer service at Mauer Johnson Funeral Home.

Mrs. McDougall was born August 6, 1904 in Elgin township, Plymouth County to William and Mary Nicholson of Struble, Iowa. She was educated in the Struble and Le Mars schools. She married Chester N. McDougall in 1922. They farmed near Struble for several years. They moved in 1938 to a farm north of Le Mars. They retired in 1960 and moved into town.

She was a member of First United Methodist Church in Le Mars and enjoyed playing bridge.

Survivors include two daughters and their husbands, Janice and David Petry of Hudson, Iowa, and Edythe and Gene Swanson of Mankato, Minn.; seven sons and their wives James and Yvonne of Minnetonka, Minn.; William and Dee, Douglas and Vonice, Mark and Jeanie all of Le Mars, Richard and Patricia of Okoboji, Iowa, Nick and Donna of Ft. Collins, CO., Dennis and Lynne of Kansas City, Mo; a son-in-law Eugene Scholer of Le Mars; a

---

12—Sioux City Journal April 5, 1999.

sister-in-law Ida Nicholson of Omaha, Neb.; 40 grandchildren; 62 great-grandchildren; a great-great grandchild; and many nieces and nephews.

She was preceded in death by her husband, Chester; a daughter, Mabel; a daughter-in-law Erlene; four brothers; six sisters; a granddaughter; and two great grandsons.

Pallbearers will be several of her grandsons. A memorial has been established with Hospice.

Attachments

WWII Connection. 330
Benjamin's "Flying Heart Clippers" 330
A letter written by Jack Nicholson about his life in
Struble. 332
letter of Jack Nicholson in Vietnam 335
Jim Nicholson letters 340
Andrew Swanson—the complete letter from Bettye
Wright 342
Written by Janice and read at our dad, Chester
McDougall's, funeral. 343
Written by Amanda McDougall Diercksmeier for
Grandma at her funeral 346
A fun story that was told in the newspaper 347
The full interview between Janice (McDougall) Petry
and Edith McDougall 348
McDougall Coat of Arms. 371
Nicholson Coat of Arms 372

WWII CONNECTION

During World War II, a Catalina flying boat sea plane base existed in Bowmore, a shallow protected spot of the Isle of Islay. Sunderland and Catalina flying boats operated from Loch Indaal. These were the same planes Jim flew in during his years as an ordinance man/bombardier throughout WWII.

BENJAMIN'S "FLYING HEART CLIPPERS"

From a paper titled "Annan Tea Clippers"—The Nicholson Ships and Flags by Boyd Cable. (Boyd Cable states that "Most of this article is from The Moffat News and Times, February 15, 1934. On the other side of the newspaper, it reads "The Annandale Observer, February 16, 1934.")

> *From some time, I have been endeavoring to collect as many as possible of the old House Flags of Sail, especially those which although once famous have now passed into the limbo of forgetfulness and can only be found again with considerable research—as in the case of the Nicholson flag. Amongst all the authorities I consulted, not one had the slightest idea of what the flag was, although one of these authorities has a collection of over 6,000 House of Flags recorded. I found it—or rather them because there were two flags—thanks mainly to the kind efforts of Mr. John Nicholson of Annan, a son of the owner of the tea clipper fleet.*

The first flag had on a while field two dark blue slender wigs, curving sharply upward from the ends of a baton or "roll" of alternate red, white and blue twist, and between the wings, a red heart. This is to be seen clearly on a contemporary picture and print of the clipper "Queensberry," and it is evident that the "Bloody Heart" of the Douglas and the name of "Queensberry" was adopted in compliment to the Marquis of Queensberry branch of the Douglas family whose seat at that time was at Kinmount, near Annan and whose estate ran practically up to the boundaries of the Royal Burgh. This is the estate sold in the '80's to the late Mr. Edward Brook of Huddersfield and still owned by that family.

I find some branches of the Douglas family—of Mulderg and Kilteam for example—had for crest the heart "between two doves' wings, proper," which may account for the "Flying" Heart. The flag's Red Heart design was apparently used from 1855 to 1860, but a picture of another ship of 1861 shows a change to a yellow spur instead of the Red Heart. Here again, in the crest of the Johnstones of Annandale and the name of one clipper, was a friendly gesture to a local family of note, with the additional reason that the oak of which the "Annandale" was built was bought off the Annandale Estate in Upper Annandale, this flag is "worn" by a model owned in Annan by a relative of one of the "Sarah Nicholson's" crew.

A LETTER WRITTEN BY JACK NICHOLSON ABOUT HIS LIFE IN STRUBLE

MY LIFE IN STRUBLE
(J. W. Nicholson)

When we moved to Struble in 1949, I thought we'd died and went to heaven. Here we now were, in a town, in our own house. We had neighbors—nice neighbors.

Although Struble had a small population, 90 people, it had amenities we lacked in the remote tenant farmhouse where we'd been living for three years just 4 miles east of Struble, the Hinde's farm.

Struble had several families with kids about the ages of our six Nicholsons, which ranged from 2 to 15. There were the Ohms, the Brunkens, the Harms, the Millers, the Dobberts, and the Whitakers, and Joanne Dominick only half a mile away. Struble formed a boy's baseball team a couple years later—the Struble Canaries.

Struble had a church, St Joseph's Catholic Church which had been built on land donated by our great grandfather, Peter Moran. There was a small grocery store that sold the essentials, bread, lunch meat, canned soup, milk, eggs, and butter. This store, run by Vincy Lewis, also comprised a post office. There was a grain elevator run by our neighbor, Henry Groetken, who also was the town mayor.

A Great Northern Railroad depot served the many trains that ran thru the town. The depot agent, who lived above the depot, was Jim Roach with his wife Ann. His son, Jim Jr., returned from World War II service about the time we moved to Struble which was the winter of 1948–49. Jim Roach was replaced by Jack Whalen in 1952.

And, last but not least, Struble had three beer joints, all doing a booming business. These saloons were the social focus of many of the near-by farmers as well as the adult men who lived in town. Remember, there were very few recreational outlets and no TVs at that time.

But times were good, relatively speaking, and they were noticeably getting better as far as opportunities to find work and earn money were concerned. That is what I liked the opportunities to work and earn money. Brother Jim, four years younger than I, also was on the lookout for work.

Our family appreciated the proximity to our St Joseph Catholic Church. We attended Mass every Sunday and Holy day. We were in the church choir. And we liked the church socials which always featured delicious home cooked food.

Our house was right across the street from the two-room schoolhouse where our Dad and his 10 siblings got their primary school education a few decades earlier. Our house had six rooms "and a path;" no running water. It was heated by a fuel oil stove in the center of the living room. The combination kitchen stove used propane gas and cobs. Mom made it work and turned out some very tasty meals and pastries.

Fortunately, our property also had a small two stock barn and a small hog house. This was fortuitous because I had joined the Future Farmers of America and had to have a livestock project. I chose to raise pigs and had two sows and 20 pigs each year that I lived in Struble (from 1948–51). I bought an adjoining acre and a half from John Moltke in 1949, fenced it in, with the help of Pussy Lendt, and created a super pasture for the pigs. This pasture endured for decades after my project, as a pasture for Dad's horses. That fence I bought and installed lasted until 2009, until brother Tim, with the help of Ron Kallsen, tore it out. Sixty years was not bad!

We were poor. No question about that, but throughout the 1960's Dad's job got better and better. He owned a car. He remodeled the house by enlarging the kitchen and installing a bathroom and a separate shower in the newly created basement. He installed central heat and air conditioning. Wow! What a difference. For over 15 years, Mom and the family lived in a place that had no running water, no refrigerator, and an outdoor toilet.

Also, the rations got better as I noticed during my visits home while on furlough and leave from my military duties in Europe, Asia, the Middle East, and various places in the USA.

Mom was the pillar of strength that kept us kids inspired, motivated, hopeful, and guided by Christian principles. She not only performed the miracle of the loaves and fishes more times than I care to count, but she also used her many talents to provide for our physical and psychological needs. She sewed. She made dresses, shirts, trousers coats, and almost anything else we needed. But, most of all, she provided hope, encouragement, motivation and confidence that we should "go for it," if it was an honorable goal!

Attachments

LETTER OF JACK NICHOLSON IN VIETNAM

STATEMENT

US Army Captain John W. Nicholson, or "Dai Uy Nick", as we called him, was the Advisor to the Phong Dinh Province Civil Guard and Self Defense Corps (CG/SDC), a combined force of about 4,000. Captain Nicholson's main responsibility was to accompany and advise the CG/SDC on field operations aimed at protecting the rural population of Phong Dinh Province from enemy attacks. Captain Nicholson did that on a routine basis, weekly, if not more frequently.

In December 1963, Phong Dinh Sector/Province conducted a coordinated search and destroy operation in the North-Western remote rural area of the province, with the participation of regional forces-Civil Guard and Self Defense Corps of 3 neighboring districts. Captain Nicholson accompanied CG Captain Phat, commander of the Phong Dinh Province Self Defense Corps Training Center, who commanded O Mon district forces totaling about 240 troops, including the 807 CG Company and 3 SDC platoons. The Province Chief/Sector commander, Major Tran BA Di of the ARVN, controlled the operation at a field Command Post with one 4.2-inch mortar and a canal gun boat providing fire support to Captain Phat's forces.

At mid-day on December 27, 1963, Captain Phat's force engaged VC in the Song Hau Farm area. Two VC were killed, and a home-made hand grenade manufacturing facility was discovered and destroyed. At about 4 pm, the lead elements were nearing a major canal where more VC engaged Captain

Phat's forces. Captain Phat attacked on a wide front through rice paddies towards the canal. Return fire from concealed enemy positions on canal bank caused many friendly casualties. Phat reported the action by radio to Major Di at his field Command Post (CP) who dispatched the gun boat from the CP down the canal toward the site of the firefight. Phat's force met the boat and began loading friendly casualties.

Suddenly, VC attacked from three sides with automatic weapons and mortar fires. The initial mortar rounds landed on the boat and the nearby shore. A machine gunner on the boat was decapitated by a round that also bent the 30 cal. barrel upward. The gun boat began to reverse its engines and retreated. Chaos followed as the enemy kept up their fires. Capt Phat and his troops hastily withdrew along the canal in the direction the boat had retreated. Friendly casualties were abandoned on the canal bank. Darkness crept in.

At this time, Captain Nicholson, who had been helping with the wounded, caught up with Captain Phat. Through the interpreter, Khiem, Dai Uy Nick told Capt Phat: "We couldn't abandon those casualties", and he urged Phat to recover them. Friendly troops were hesitant and reluctant to follow the advice. Dai Uy Nick then told Khiem that he better be more persuasive and convincing in his translation. Finally, Capt Phat agreed with Capt Nick who then used Capt Phat's radio to request supporting fire from the 4.2-inch mortar located at the CP about 3 kilometers up the canal. By then it was very dark.

The initial 4.2-inch mortar round landed on the opposite side of the canal. The range was correct, but the direction was not.

Dai Uy Nick adjusted the mortar fire via radio thru Captain Lake, a US Artillery Advisor who was with Major Di at the CP. Subsequent mortar rounds bracketed the diminished CG/SDC forces as Capt Phat and Capt Nick went back down the canal to retrieve the wounded.

Meanwhile, the VC still fired on Capt Phat's force from three directions but with little effect because the friendly mortar rounds were keeping them from closing in. Capt Phat's force had been reduced to 39 men from the original number of 240. These 39 men picked up 13 wounded fellows and began carrying them up the canal toward the CP. Suffering more casualties, Capt Phat's forces returned fire to its flanks and rear but kept going until about 2 a.m. next day when they reached the CP where they were welcomed by the perimeter guards.

Four of the wounded died while being carried back. The remainder survived and were med-evaced at daybreak by helicopters called in by Capt Nick. Interpreter Khiem lost no time in relating his poignant experience of surviving both the VC attacks and the admonishment of his Co Van My (American advisor), Captain Nick.

Captain Nicholson was credited by me and others as the leader who saved the friendly wounded despite heavy enemy fire and fear of the friendlies to re-enter the fighting area. The dutiful actions of Capt Phat and his remaining forces redeemed what would have been a total and shameful rout in the face of enemy action. The friendly wounded who were rescued were especially thankful for Dai Uy Nick's leadership in braving the enemy fires to save their lives.

For his brave deeds on the battlefield during this fight, Captain Nicholson was awarded by the Army of the Republic of Vietnam Cross of Gallantry, with Gold Palm, the highest level of this type of military decorations.

In the remaining eight months as the combat advisor in Phong Dinh Province,"Dai Uy Nick" continued to accompany the CG and SDC troops on combat missions. He was always welcomed and even cheered! There were situations where the poor little under paid and under trained CG and SDC militia forces were unhappy or not confident in going on patrols and operations if "Dai Uy Nick" did not accompany them. They said with Dai Uy Nick along they knew they would never be abandoned. This meant a lot to them.

These same CG/SDC troops participated in three attempts to rescue American Captain Rocky Versace who had been captured by the VC in Chong Thien Province in October 1963. On an operation near Xa No Canal in August 1964, these CG/SDC troops with Dai Uy Nick as the senior advisor, suffered 120 casualties one night in an attempt to rescue Capt. Versace. Capt. Nicholson managed to successfully guide fighter bombers in defense of this beleaguered force during darkness so they we not overrun.

It was about this time that Col Jim Kiersey, the Senior US Advisor to the 21st ARVN Division, and Captain Nicholson's boss, ordered Capt Nicholson not to go out on any more combat operations unless he was accompanied by at least one additional US Advisor.

May I also add that in the spring of 1964 during a fierce firefight during which I was wounded, my Vietnamese deputy was wounded, and Captain Nicholson's accompanying US Advisor was killed, Capt Nick helped me personally by applying a tourniquet to my leg and by helping direct friendly artillery fire point blank at the attacking enemy on both flanks. After forcing an enemy retreat, Capt Nick then ensured our successful medical evacuation by helicopter. By this time, the Vietnamese forces regarded Captain Nicholson so highly that he became a legend in the Mekong Delta.

"Dai Uy Nick" is a gallant soldier and a true friend of his Vietnamese Allies.

This narration is submitted at the request of LTG John Cushman, US Army-Retired, who recommended Captain Nicholson for a Silver Star in December of 1963 and recently learned that the award had never been made. General Cushman was Senior US Advisor (then Lt Colonel) to the ARVN 21st Division controlling the 42nd Tactical Area including the Phong Dinh Province when this action occurred in 1963.

Respectfully submitted by,

TRAN BA DI 12 Sept 08
   Formerly, Major Di, Phong Dinh Province Chief/Sector Commander, 21st ARVN Division/42nd Tactical Area of Operations.
   Former Major General, 9th ARVN Division Commander
   Former captive of NVA in a Hard Labor Camp for 17 years (1975–1992)
   And currently, an American Citizen since 2003, living and working in Orlando, Florida

The Road to Love

JIM NICHOLSON LETTERS

GEORGE BUSH

October 15, 2004

To the Members of the Distinguished Graduate Committee:

Having just recently written a letter endorsing Dick Trefrey's nomination to be a 2005 Distinguished Graduate of the Military Academy, I now learn that my long time friend, Ambassador Jim Nicholson also is a candidate.

I have been told that, since more than one graduate is presented this distinguished award each year, it is not inappropriate to endorse more than one candidate.

So, at the risk of overloading the Committee with letters of endorsement, I write now on behalf of Jim Nicholson.

When I think of Jim Nicholson, I think about one of the finest public servants I have ever known. I think about honor, decency, and integrity. In addition to his distinguished military career, he has served in some very important posts at home and abroad, always with distinction, always making his country proud.

Ambassador Nicholson's dedication and commitment to excellence is well documented and rightly acclaimed, and the Distinguished Graduate Award would be fitting tribute to his accomplishments.

Respectfully submitted,

[signature: G Bush]

P. O. BOX 79798 · HOUSTON, TEXAS 77279-9798
PHONE (713) 686-1188 · FAX (713) 683-0801

Attachments

THE VICE PRESIDENT
WASHINGTON

October 12, 2004

Dear Colonel Hudgins:

I understand the United States Military Academy Class of 1961 is nominating Ambassador R. James Nicholson for the 2005 USMA Association of Graduates Distinguished Graduate Award. I am pleased to endorse this most deserving nomination.

My association with Jim goes back many years, and I know him to be a man who has dedicated his life to upholding the West Point motto of "Duty, Honor, Country." Throughout his career -- as a combat veteran of Vietnam, as a businessman, as Chairman of the Republican National Committee, and now as U.S. Ambassador to the Holy See -- Jim has demonstrated the leadership, integrity and conviction expected of a West Point Graduate. He does his alma mater, his uniform, and our country proud.

I am honored to call Jim Nicholson my friend, and I am happy to join the Class of 1961 in recommending him for selection as a Distinguished Graduate of the United States Military Academy.

Sincerely,

Dick Cheney

Colonel Seth F. Hudgins, Jr.
President and COO
Association of Graduates
United States Military Academy
698 Mills Road
West Point, New York 10996-1611

ANDREW SWANSON—THE COMPLETE LETTER FROM BETTYE WRIGHT

Dr. Andrew Swanson

God did not make many like this young man. When we initially met, he was doing a spine fellowship at Hospital for Special Surgery in Manhattan, New York with Dr. Oheneba Boachie-Adjei, who was also the founder of FOCOS, Foundation of Orthopedics and Complex Spine and I was a board member of FOCOS. We were at a social event and Andrew treated me like a precious antique. when I shared that with him, he casually said, "You are."

Andrew later became a member of the FOCOS surgical team, traveling to Ghana several times a year to perform complex spine procedures on patients from Ethiopia, Sierra Leone and Ghana. These life-threatening surgeries were performed on patients from economically devastated countries.

When Dr. Boachie-Adjei asked for volunteers to accompany me to Sierra Leone to do clinics and identify potential surgical candidates, I was not the least bit surprised that Andrew volunteered. At that time, Sierra Leone was at the end of the ten-year civil war, peacekeepers were still there, I was scared to death, Andrew was fearless. Once we identified surgical candidates, if further medical investigations were needed Andrew would provide the Sierra Leone FOCOS staff with funds to obtain the studies. It was during this trip that I realized that the kind, gentle and respectful manner that I had grown to love about him was "who he was", he treated all of our patients like this. Our circumstances for me were challenging and frightening but Andrew was unaffected and acted as if these were his Park Avenue patients.

His commitment was contagious and commendable. If you did not embrace that it was impossible for you to be a part of Andrew's team. In his non-confrontational way, he convinced you that you were really needed in another location. His last Ghana trip was very demanding, he did a record number of cases, one case was extremely challenging, and he had concerns with how the patient would do immediately post-op, so he instructed the driver to not let me know that he was staying at the hospital until we were driving. When I called him, he refused to leave the patient. When he left Ghana, he was so excited because he was going mountain climbing with one of his college and medical school buddies that he had not seen for a long time. The two of them taught safety climbing classes. His death left such a void not only to his family, adopted family, but to the spine community, medical community, and the world. He was incredible and I miss him so much.

(Bettye Wright)

WRITTEN BY JANICE AND READ AT OUR DAD, CHESTER MCDOUGALL'S, FUNERAL

A Tribute to Our Dad
by Janice (McDougall) Petry

Long forceful steps leading across the barnyard, a broad, erect figure seated behind a team of horses or a tractor, a lift of the hat and running of fingers through the hair; these are among the first recollections for many of us of this grand fellow who was our dad. For more than three-quarters of his life we think of him always in connection with his ambitions, his dreams and his land. Surely his vision of success for himself and his family lay in the soil, and it became his challenge and his reward. We all know what strength and fortitude this challenge took; we saw this strength demonstrated many times down through the years.

The glimpses of our dad in those years tended to be more of the rougher side of the diamond, a stern discipline to his work, with little time for fun or play. With so much responsibility and so many dependent on him, we don't but wonder why he was not less cheerful but cheer he did have and cheer he gave to us, many, many times. We cannot bring our thoughts to our dad in a cheerful, happy mood, and not think of Christmas, for this was most certainly his favorite season of the year. So many times, over and over, we were to see his love and generosity, given so freely, with "no strings attached." To those of us he loved. Especially we felt this spirit at Christmas. We cannot say or think enough of our dad's wonderful generosity, for we all know it in great measure at one time or another in our lives; whether it was the gift of our education, furniture to begin married life, or the down payment on a house.

As are birds to the Spring, and water to the rivers, so was the correlation between our dad and unbounding energy. From the moment his feet touched the floor in the morning, we saw this tireless energy in every movement, be it lifting a bale of hay or building a doll chest. We watched this force sustain him through long, arduous tasks about the farm and through the tortures of his last illness. It was always there, almost seeing to make him leap at any task, we just had to say, "Fix my bike, plant this tree, put us the shelf and he was there, tool in hand.

His great energy, pride, and ambition enabled our dad to accomplish a great deal while he lived. These achievements, being far too numerous to mention; let us simply say that they were enough to have done justice to the lifetime of two lesser men.

And as age has its way with all things on this earth, so it had its mellowing effect on our dad. Only then, with many of the cares and responsibilities removed, did we see the humorous fun-loving side of his character emerge. We watched with amazement and joy his enthusiasm for the trips abroad and the people he met. We saw his involvement and compassion for the ever-increasing circle of grandchildren. We enjoyed with him his retirement years of gardening, tinkering, woodworking, and travel. Now there was time for a cup of coffee and a chat around the table, and perhaps some reminiscences of days gone by. Would that this time could have lasted forever, but as for all of us, this is not to be.

The Lord blessed our dad with eighty fine years and for this we are most thankful, but the Lord's greatest blessing was to each of us for having given us our wonderful parents. The ways that their love has affected our lives is immeasurable and we may not know the full extent of its impact for generations. We only know that because of them, we are among the lucky ones, for we learned by their examples what is love.

WRITTEN BY AMANDA MCDOUGALL DIERCKSMEIER FOR GRANDMA AT HER FUNERAL

I was Grandma's Favorite.
I was Grandma's favorite,
it was plain to see.
All the cookies and the rolls,
I'm sure they were meant just for me.
She'd bake all my favorites,
because they were always ready, when I went over there.
I was Grandma's favorite,
though I was grandchild 39.
With all those other birthdays,
she never forgot mine.
Sending cards and money -
it was obvious I was so dear.
I know I was her favorite,
because she gave me extra every year.
I was Grandma's favorite,
she treated me so well.
She knew my news and latest moods,
she thought I was special, I could tell.
Everyone mattered to Grandma,
but when we talked, I was the only one.
I know I was her favorite,
because we had so much laughter and fun.
And I was Grandma's favorite,

for another special reason—
Which my Dad has told me of,
season after season.
He said, Amanda, my dear, of all the grandkids,
you must be a favored one.
Because you are the daughter,
of Grandma's favorite son.
Please don't be mad at Grandma,
now that the truth's come out.
You all know how she never liked,
for anyone to pout.
Grandma you were our favorite,
all our love we send.
We were all Grandma's favorites,
her love knew no end.

A FUN STORY THAT WAS TOLD IN THE NEWSPAPER

"In 1914, Struble raised the speed limit in town from 8 mph to 10 mph. Chester and his brother Jack were each in a different car and they came down the hill that went into the town of Struble. They didn't want to slow down, so they raced each other through Struble. They were going about 30 mph and they both got arrested. After their arrest, the two 'swore revenge.'"

As told by Doug McDougall

THE FULL INTERVIEW BETWEEN JANICE (MCDOUGALL) PETRY AND EDITH MCDOUGALL

JANICE: This is Edith McDougall and her daughter Janice McDougall Petry on Monday February 19, 1996.

EDITH: Then you'll translate it on to something??

JANICE: Probably

EDITH: That's what Mabel did you know . . .

JANICE: She made a recording . . .

EDITH: And then Jack's stenographer or somebody put it down.

JANICE: Who were your parents?

EDITH: Will Nicholson and Mollie Moran

JANICE: Can you tell me about them? Where they came from?

EDITH: Well, my dad came from Scotland when he was quite a young man and he farmed for a while with his brother down by Le Mars because he was supposed to teach him how to farm and that didn't go very good with my dad.

JANICE: They didn't get along?

EDITH: No but then he came up to Elgin township and started farming and my mother was already living there. Her folks had come up from Elkader. I think her dad came out in a covered wagon with a team of horses. Her dad came in the fall and the other two came out later, I think. Mollie was their only child then. I think they all came with a team of horses. I don't think there were trains out there yet. I think that was about 1890, but I don't know for sure.

I think my dad came out a year or two later, but Grandpa Moran came out here and homesteaded. I don't know who came first, my mother or my dad, but I kind of think my mother came first.

JANICE: How did grandpa (Nicholson) get his land to farm?

EDITH: His father came out here and bought up a lot of land.

JANICE: So, he had money to do that?

EDITH: Well, I think he had money he wanted to invest, and I guess they claimed it was a good investment to come out here. He bought land down south of Le Mars and he bought land out in Elgin township. Several sections, I think.

JANICE: How many brothers came?

EDITH: Uncle Jim was the older one, he was here farming, then Uncle Ben and Uncle Dick and my dad came, but I don't think Uncle Ben ever went for the farming part of it, but he was supposed to teach my dad and Uncle Dick how to farm but they didn't care for Aunt Georgie, that didn't work very well. Uncle Dick was younger than my dad.

JANICE: What age would he have been when he got married?

EDITH: My dad?? I think he was about 21, he was quite young when he came out there. You see his mother died when he was real young and I think he was kind of wild and I think grandpa sent him out here because he was kind of a handful for him.

JANICE: But he was a long way away from Scotland.

EDITH: I think as soon as he got done with school in Edenborough, his dad sent him out here.

JANICE: Did he go to high school or college or what?

EDITH: I think it was some kind of college, I don't think they had a regular high school in those days.

JANICE: What about your mother?

EDITH: She came out here for some kind of normal training or something for college. I don't know how many years she went. She was four years younger than my dad I think he was 23 and she was 19 when they got married.

JANICE: Where were you born?

EDITH: Out in the farm in Elgin Township, we were all born out there. A mile west of Struble and a half a mile south. The house is still there, but it doesn't look anything like it did when we lived there. The front porch and a balcony that came out onto it is gone. The house was kind of changed around from how we had it. Mabel and her girls went out there one time and Betty told her that was where her grandparents lived and she offered to show them the house, so they went in and saw the house. The dining room they were using for the kitchen and the kitchen is now a utility room.

JANICE: Did the farm have a lot of buildings?

EDITH: Yes quite a few, but ohhhh, last time I was out there they had a truck right up beside the house and the grove was mostly gone. It didn't look like it did when we lived there. He always had a lot of hogs and fed cattle, if he had a hundred head that would be a lot in those days. But they raised quite a few hogs. Buzz was a good hog man, he used to do the hogs. They would drive them into Struble and load them on the train. They would take them to market in Sioux City. Once in a while they would ship to Chicago. They could ride on the caboose with their freight free, but they would have to pay their way back. He and Ed Durband were in a partnership with the cattle, they were kind of scalpers is what they were called. Some fellow out in the country would have seven or eight head of cattle and that wasn't enough, they'd have to have a load to ship them. They'd buy them up and then once they had a load, they would pay the freight and ship them.

JANICE: Did you ride the train a lot??

EDITH: When we went to Sioux City we did. Our mother used to go to Sioux City to shop a lot and one of us always went with her. There was a train down in the morning and another one back at night. It didn't go through Le Mars; it went west of Le Mars. That railroad is still there, it goes from Sioux City to Struble, its out at West Le Mars, it was Dalton in those days now they call it West Le Mars. It doesn't come through here. The Illinois Central and the Great Northern, I don't know. This long pull train that goes through here, that doesn't go through Struble, that goes through Le Mars and up through Seney, up that way, it goes to Minneapolis. But there was a train that went to Sioux City in the morning and came back at night.

JANICE: What was a typical day when you were a little girl? In the wintertime?

EDITH: You mean when I was going to school?? We got up in the morning and we all had our hair in braids and that was quite a deal to get all that hair braided and our dad was always going to cut it off and our mother said, "If you do, I'll go cut your horses tails off." Then of course when we all got old enough to take care of ourselves, we cut it off anyway. But nobody wore bobbed hair in those days. If we had something at home to pack, we had to pack our lunch, if we didn't, we went up to the store and bought something at noon. We went a mile and a half to school, but we didn't walk. For a long time, we went in a surrey and then our dad came down here one time and bought something with two long seats facing each other in the back with a horse pulling it. It was kind of enclosed and it had curtains on it. Dad never wanted us to go to school on a real cold day because when we got to school the schoolhouse wouldn't be warm. They had a furnace that never worked right and an old guy that didn't know much about it, took care of it. And some days the room would be full of smoke instead of heat. We never wanted to miss. We wanted to go. One day him and Uncle Dick went down to hot springs and he bought a thermometer and if it was below a certain temperature, we weren't to go to school. And if we didn't eat breakfast, we weren't to go to school because he said if his horses didn't eat their oats in the morning, he wouldn't work them that day.

JANICE: He really compared everything to horses . . .

EDITH: Oh yeah, he thought a lot of his horses. They had a lot of horses, the barn held ten or twelve head and that would be full. They did all the work with horses there was no tractors. We had two buggies, beside the ones us kids had. We always had a surrey two seated buggy to go to school because see there was a bunch of us going. About five or six.

JANICE: Name your brothers and sisters and where you were in the order.

EDITH: Jenny was the oldest then Buzz then Nell then Mollie then Mabel and I and Buck and Dorothy and Dick and Don and Evelyn.

JANICE: Your nick name was Bitty how did you get that nick name?

EDITH: Well, they always said my dad looked at me when I was born and said she's a regular little bitty, an Irish bitty.

JANICE: What's an Irish bitty

EDITH: I think Bridgett is an Irish name with nickname Bitty. I always said I don't know why they didn't call me Bridgett. But I was named after some friend of my mother's. I was really called Rose Edith, but I didn't like Rose. When I went to school, I was Edith, I changed it.

JANICE: Your legal name was Rose Edith and you changed it?

EDITH: Well, I wasn't baptized as a kid and when we went to go to Europe and get our passport, I wasn't registered at all.

JANICE: Why weren't you baptized.

EDITH: Well, we never went to church. Our mother was Catholic and our dad I think was brought up Presbyterian and there was a Methodist Church in Struble. Our dad wouldn't let us go to the Catholic Church but he didn't take us to the other church, so we never went to church. I was born at home and I don't know why I wasn't registered. When I went to get my passport, there was no record of me. I said here I had ten kids and I wasn't there. Then I had to get my school records to get a birth certificate to get a passport. Then Mabel signed that I was born because she was older than I was. I think some of the rest of my brothers and sisters probably had that problem too. When kids were born in the hospital, they kept a record of them, but we were all born out there in the country and all Jenny's kids were born at home. People didn't go to the hospital then like they did later. Mabel's kids were born at home.

JANICE: How would you have been dressed when you went to school?

EDITH: Oh, we wore dresses, we never wore any kind of pants. And we wore long underwear and cotton socks. My daughter Mabel wore long underwear, she hated it. But they didn't have snow pants and no women wore slacks.

You see all those old women working in those long skirts in the covered wagons. How much simpler it would have been if they could have worn pants in those days.

Attachments

My mom's dresses were long, but not real long, they were around her ankles. We always had our dresses made. She had a dressmaker come out to the house and stay about a week and sew, probably twice a year. My mother had a sewing machine, the kind you would pump.

JANICE: What are some of the best memories of your childhood?

EDITH: We had a good childhood. Our dad was a pretty well-off man, but we never knew it. We always had plenty to eat, warm house and clothes to wear, but we never took trips or anything like that. One time when I was 14, they rented a place at Lake Okoboji and we all went up there, but that was about it. That is where I learned to swim. My dad had some friend who had a place up there, so my mother and Buzz and some of us kids went up there and we went to the place and there were weeds higher than us kids' heads and my mother said, "We're not staying here." So, there was a Detloff who was married to Hugh Daley and we went to see her, and they owned a house and beside their house was a house they rented out and we rented that house for a month, for $100 a month. Mom stayed there for the month and us kids took turns going up there, but before the month was up everyone had had their turn. But they never did anything like that again. That was 1918. Then I went to high school that fall. World War 1 was going on, and I remember that. I came down here to high school and stayed with Norma Becker.

Norma and Allan and I were all starting high school and what a jolt that was, to go from a country school to a high school. I'd never even been in a high school before.

JANICE: Were you scared?

EDITH: Well sure I was scared. I was green, dumb. Well, I wasn't so dumb but you know everything . . . it was different, I'll tell you that.

JANICE: Did you get homesick?

EDITH: No, not really because I stayed with Norma Becker and I knew her really well, because after Jenny got married, we got real well acquainted with them. When we were kids, they used to come down to the farm pretty near every Sunday, they had an old horse they rode, they called him Old Colonel and we'd play games outside. And the McFarland kids lived up the road a half mile and maybe they'd come down too, so we'd have a good gang. We'd play baseball and hide-and-seek. The girls and the boys would all play together.

JANICE: When you went to high school did Mabel come with you?

EDITH: She came about a month later. And then we went to stay with Elsie Cane. She was a cousin of ours. In those days nobody wanted to keep anybody in their house, but she was going to keep us. Well, she had just had a baby. She kept us maybe a month and then she said she just couldn't do it anymore. We had a room there and we'd have breakfast, and she'd fix us a nice evening meal. So, then we went to live upstairs in a room across the street from where Norma Becker lived. It was a bungalow and had a big closet that went way back. We would eat our supper and our breakfast and go to the restaurant for our dinner, for our noon meal. We did that through our freshman year but I didn't want to go back the next year. But Mabel went back and then she roomed with XXX crawly and she stayed with some old people. They weren't married. They were brother and sister and oh that was something else, I guess. They were real close people and their room was cold. They were always giving them this eggplant and we'd never ever had anything like that at home. Mabel didn't like it, but she stuck it out all year. I don't know why Mabel didn't go back then the next year.

JANICE: So, you or Mabel didn't go beyond your sophomore year?

EDITH: I only want my freshman year. I was telling Vonice that one day and she said, "Well how'd you get so smart?" I said, "I don't think I am very smart!"

JANICE: So, if you weren't in school what did you do at home?

EDITH: We had plenty to do at home. We had to do the housework, but I didn't do any more studying. I suppose we read books. But we had to work. Our mother wasn't very well you know. Molly and I were home that year. Jenny and Nell were gone.

JANICE: Did any of the younger kids go on up in high school?

EDITH: Evelyn and Dick did. Buck and Buzz used to go to Sioux City to the NBT school National Business Training in the winter. They went there a couple winters, when everything was done on the farm, and as soon as the field work started our dad had them come home. And my mother had a friend in Sioux City whose husband was a teacher at this school, his name was Barrett but her name was McGrane. And at one time the McGrane family lived in Struble, he was the head of the section crew in Struble. A section crew goes out and fixes the tracks for the trains. And our grandma Moran used to go out and stay with this woman's folks in Sioux City for a month in the wintertime, they were good friends. Grandma Moran lived with us when we were kids.

JANICE: What was she like?

EDITH: She was a big woman, nice looking, snow white hair and big brown eyes and could she ever roll those eyes. She was always with us kids. I really remember somethings about her more than my mother. She would come out and help us pick chickens and help us do dishes. Oh, she was a fast worker, she could make her hands go. She was kind of like an Aunt Mary, but she didn't do that much work. She was Catholic and some of us always had to take her into church. We always took her to church on Sunday so that was the only church we went to was when we went with grandma to the Catholic Church. There was a Methodist Church in Struble, but our dad never went to it and of course our mother didn't go. We never read the bible; we never had much religious training.

JANICE: Funny you all ended up being quite religious .... which of your sisters were you the closest to?

EDITH: Well, Mabel and I never ever had a fight, never and when we went to high school down here, the woman we stayed with had three daughters, it was a whole bunch of women who lived there. There was another lady that lived there with her two girls, she had kind of an apartment there. She did her own cooking, and then there was another lady that lived there, Bessy Trip, she worked downtown, I think she had a stepmother at home that didn't like her or something. Mabel and I and that lady with those three girls would walk down the street together and she never got over it, that we weren't fighting all the time, but Mabel, Mollie and I, we never had a fight. But Nell, that was a different story, you could fight with her. But Jenny was always easy to get along with.

JANICE: Nell was bossy?

EDITH: Well, she was different. Mabel and I shared everything and got along. Never to her dying day did we ever have any words.

JANICE: Who was your best friend when you were growing up?

EDITH: Well, I don't know, Margaret Durband was a good friend of mine, till I went ahead of her in school, then we weren't very friendly after that. Well, Molly, Mabel and I were all stuck in one room at home, and we'd go to bed at night, and they'd tell me everything they learned that day. They were ahead of me in school. Bob Edwards, Margaret Durband and I were in a grade and one day the teacher said I should come up and read with the next grade. I went up and read with them and she said, "Well you can stay in there." So, I really went two grades in one year and Margaret stayed behind, and she never liked me after that.

JANICE: You said you had to work around the house, what was the thing you did mostly?

EDITH: We always had to go upstairs and make all the beds in the morning, and make them, not just throw them together. Some woman came in one day to check my lifeline and for some reason my bed wasn't made. Sometimes I air that little thing I got, and I apologized for my bed not being made. "I never make my bed" she said. I pretty near died. "Oh," she said, "I never make my bed."

JANICE: Did you help with the cooking or the baking a lot?

EDITH: Oh, yeah, we had to do the cooking. Our mother tried to teach us to cook but she had a hard time.

JANICE: Did you have hired girls that cooked or cleaned?

EDITH: We did when we were kids in school, she always had help, that is if she could get it. Old Alice Tierman, she worked for us for years. She lived with us.

JANICE: You had a big house then?

EDITH: Oh yeah and we used to have a lot of people. The house had five bedrooms upstairs and one down and then there was what we called the storeroom where you went out to this balcony and you could get a bed in it, a single bed. We used to have a bed in there, but that room was pretty cold in the wintertime. It was way on the northwest corner of the house. We didn't use it much in the wintertime.

JANICE: How did you heat your house?

EDITH: We had a furnace.

JANICE: So, it was a pretty modern house?

EDITH: Yeah

JANICE: And how was the house arranged??

EDITH: It had a kitchen and a dining room, a sitting room and a living room and then a hall that went upstairs and an outside door, and then there was a downstairs bedroom. My mother generally bought furniture from Sioux City. My dad would always be mad when she got it. Like she bought a new davenport one time, and he about threw a fit, but it wasn't long before he was laying on it all the time.

JANICE: Describe your living room.

EDITH: We had an overstuffed davenport; I think we had a couch too. We had nice chairs and a piano. We all took Lessons, but Nell was a nice piano player. She got the piano. How was that though? I think the piano wound up in Jenny's house. And then I think the piano was over at Amy's house when Jenny's house burned down. I don't know whatever happened to that piano.

JANICE: You shared your room with Mabel and Molly??

EDITH: I shared a pretty good size room with Mabel and Molly, we had two beds in it. But see, if there had been a high school in Struble, we would have all gone to high school and my dad tried hard to get a consolidated school in Struble. You know they were really good in those days: they went out with busses and brought the kids in and I'm sure if there had been one in Struble we would have all gone. But it was really a problem to go to school down here. When Mabel and I were going to school down here, if we wanted to go home for the weekend, we would have to leave school early and take a train and go to Merrill and wait for the train to come up from Sioux City and take us to Struble. Or else get someone to take us over to Dalton and catch the train up from there. A few times Uncle Ben took us up there or there was an old guy who ran a taxi and he'd take us for a dollar.

JANICE: That was a lot of money in those days. Did you always have money in your pocketbook?

EDITH: Yes, and I always made mine go further than Mabel did.

JANICE: How did you meet dad?

EDITH: Well, he used to come to our place and Buzz kind of ran around with him. But I never had anything to do with him and then one time there was a parade in town, and he had his car all fixed up and he called and me asked me if I'd ride in the parade with him. I think I was about 16. Then we dated off and on after that.

JANICE: Were you stuck on him after that?

EDITH: Well, I don't know. Not really at first sight I don't think. I never had a lot of steady guys.

JANICE: Did your sisters date a lot??

EDITH: Mabel always had a lot of boyfriends.

JANICE: How about Mollie?

EDITH: Well Vern was always after her. He lived on a farm close to Beckers about four miles away.

JANICE: How did dad propose?

EDITH: We were at a celebration at Remsen.

JANICE: Remsen?? That was pretty far away.

EDITH: He always had a car so we could get there.

JANICE: When did your family get their first car?

EDITH: I don't remember what year that was. But it was a Cole. It was a big car, it had to be. My dad and Buzz were the first ones that drove it. My mom didn't drive right away, but she finally did. Who was it the other day that said the woman didn't drive a car . . .

JANICE: Sheila's grandma . . .

EDITH: Well, Von doesn't either.

JANICE: No, there are still some people that don't drive cars.

JANICE: Did you have a big wedding?

EDITH: No, we just went to Sioux City and got married.

JANICE: Who stood up for you?

EDITH: Aunt Pearl.

JANICE: And Henry?

EDITH: No, somebody Pearl worked with.

JANICE: Did your mom and dad like Dad?

EDITH: I don't know if they did or not.

JANICE: Then when you got married, you lived on a farm?

EDITH: Not right away. We lived in town for a while, in that funeral home down there. Well, it isn't a funeral home anymore but where Mabel was when she died. Lukens, but it isn't a funeral home anymore It's a nice house and I guess it's going to be a home. Those people that had Mabel's funeral, they split it up. It's in the 400 block on North Central Avenue. But I went there and played cards one day and oh it's a nice house, it's got real nice dark oak woodwork and she's got it furnished really nice. Well then, they made it into a funeral home, and they lived upstairs and then I guess they finished the attic and now it's not a funeral home. Their living quarters are on the first floor now.

JANICE: Now that was Grandma and Mary's house?

EDITH: Then they lost it.

JANICE: And Dad's Dad was dead then?

EDITH: Well, he was alive when they bought it.

JANICE: How long did he live?

EDITH: They moved in there in 1920 I think, and he died in '22. He died before we were married. He kind of lost his mind before he died.

JANICE: Oh, why was that?

EDITH: I don't know.

JANICE: Was that when times started to get bad?

EDITH: Well, that's what they claimed. They said there was a big debt there that they didn't seem to know about. But he was supposed to have all this corn and that was when corn went to two or three dollars a bushel and then everything dropped, and corn went down, and he couldn't pay for the house.

JANICE: But there was no depression then.

EDITH: Well things started going down then. But the great depression was supposed to be in 1929.

JANICE: The market crashed in '29.

EDITH: Well, that didn't affect them any.

JANICE: Yeah, but that's when the banks started going broke.

EDITH: Yeah, I think it was about the time my dad started going broke too. See, when land prices dropped, that's what broke him. He and Ed Durband had bought all this land over in Granville for like 400 or so, thinking they were going to sell it at a big profit and then the prices dropped, and they never sold it, they lost it. And then things just went from bad to worse and he mortgaged the land at home and lost everything.

In 1920 he took a trip back to Scotland and he thought he was worth quite a bit of money at that time. He owned a lot of land. So, it was after that, I think it was that fall that the grain prices dropped.

JANICE: That was quite a while before the depression hit though.

EDITH: Yeah, when they talk about the Great Depression in the east, I think it kind of came out here first.

JANICE: How many kids did you have when the depression was really bad?

EDITH: Mable was born in '25 Jim was born in '23. In '29 we were living on the first farm we farmed, we always called it the Adden place.

JANICE: Where was that farm?

EDITH: Well, it was two miles south of Struble and one-half mile west, then back in the field.
JANICE: Did that farm have a nice house?
EDITH: No, it wasn't modern. We lived there for seven years. We rented it from my dad.

My Uncle Dick had lived there for a long time. But he went back to Scotland. He just left the house the way it was. He married some woman there and he never came back. Then all his friends and everyone from Le Mars came out and took anything that was any good from the house, so it was just junk left when we moved out there. There were some beds upstairs we used, but we refurnished the downstairs. My mother and I bought a dining room set and a living room set, and I had bought some dressers before that from some woman that was selling them in town and Dad had a bed, so we had the downstairs furnished nice. But it wasn't modern at all. It had a heating stove and an outhouse. But it did have a bathtub in it, a great big bathtub. It had a pump that you could pump soft water in that bathtub, and I guess Uncle Dick used to pump that water in it every morning and get in there and take a bath in that cold water. It was in a little room off the dining room. The house had a summer kitchen and believe me it was a summer kitchen. It didn't have a foundation under it, and it wasn't plastered. It was okay in the summertime, but we couldn't live there in the wintertime, so we moved that bathtub out into that summer kitchen and then we used that little bathroom for kind of a kitchen. It wasn't very handy. We lived there seven years and then we moved up to the McFarland place which was a mile west of Struble just half a mile from my home. And that was a nice modern house for the time, but it isn't modern anymore. There was a bathroom there, but we had to haul hot water up to take a bath. We were there for five years, then we lived in town for a year and then we moved out to where Doug is.

JANICE: Where were you when I was born?

EDITH: Where Doug lives. We moved out there in the spring of '38 and you were born in December of '38.

JANICE: Where were you when Doug was born?

EDITH: Out on the McFarland place.

JANICE: Was Dick born there too?

EDITH: No, he was born in the hospital.

JANICE: Where were you living when he was born?

EDITH: On the McFarland place.

JANICE: And Bill?

EDITH: On that first farm we lived on, the Adden Place. We had Jim when we moved out there, Mabel was born the first spring we lived there, and Bill and Dick. Dick was a baby when we moved off there. He was born in August of '31 and we moved off there in March of '32. Then all the rest of the kids, the younger five, were born on Doug's place.

JANICE: What was the happiest time of your life?

EDITH: I wonder . . . Well, I never had any real sad part of my life. When I was a kid, I always thought about the day my mother died, but she'd been sick so long that it wasn't really as sad as I thought it would be.

JANICE: What would have been the hardest time of your life?

EDITH: Well, I think as far as finances go—when we lived on the McFarland place. See Grandmother and Mary lived with us and I think it would have been harder if they hadn't been there because Mary used to raise this great big garden in the summer and that sure helped out a lot. We always had enough to eat. Nobody had any money, so it wasn't so bad to be without money. But our kids will never remember a day they went to bed hungry. Jim will tell you that. There was always something there. We always had three meals a day. But that house was pretty cold. But dad would always cut a lot of wood and in the real cold weather we would burn coal at night.

JANICE: Where'd you get the money to buy coal?

EDITH: Well, that was it, you didn't have the money to buy it, so you couldn't buy very much but we could always go into Struble and buy coal.

JANICE: How'd you pay the rent?

EDITH: When we lived on the McFarland place, we had 240 acres. We paid our rent in shares. But we had 80 acres with the buildings on it and we'd pay cash rent of six dollars an acre for that part. It was $480 for 80 acres. It was hard scraping. We'd make it in two payments but up the road we gave a share rent for that and when we rented from my dad, we gave share rent. Except the last year we were there he went to cash rent and we never had a good crop down there as long as we lived there. It always dried out or hailed out or something. We never really started raising a crop till we came over on this farm out here.

JANICE: Did you get discouraged?

EDITH: Oh, I'm sure we got discouraged.

JANICE: What did you and dad do for fun?

EDITH: Oh, we used to have a lot of fun!

JANICE: Really?

EDITH: No. We never went any place. We did used to go to a movie though once in a while.

JANICE: Did you go to dances?

EDITH: No. We used to go to dances before we were married but not much after we were married.

JANICE: Was dad a good dancer?

EDITH: Yeah, pretty good, I don't think he really like it though.

JANICE: Didn't you tell me that Dad went to Detroit or somewhere looking for a job?

EDITH: No, he had a job. Him and Frank Glaser went out to show them how to run an oil drilling outfit from the foundry. They were gone about six weeks and while they were gone Bobby Glaser was born. Dad wanted me to go out there and live and I was thinking about going out and all of the sudden they came home. I think Frank really got more lonesome than Dad did because he had that new baby at home. I'm quite sure Bobby was born while they were out there. Yeah, because Bobby is in between Jim and Mabel and I only had Jim then.

JANICE: If you had your life to live over, would you do anything different?

EDITH: Don't know, I suppose I would. I probably would have gone to school and had some kind of trade or profession to do. I used to always think I wanted to be a nurse.

JANICE: When you were young what was your favorite thing to do as a pastime?

EDITH: We used to do a lot of embroidery work. We liked to do that. We always had another house on the farm where we grew up. Our dad kept a married man there and they boarded the other hired man, and the woman that lived over there was a good crocheter and she taught us kids how to crochet. We did a lot of crocheting when we were kids. Mom used to crochet those fuzzy bonnets for the kids, she could crochet but I suppose by that time she never had time to.

EDITH: Come on now, this is getting kind of long.

JANICE: Time to eat huh mom? We'll sign off for now, maybe we can get more later.

MCDOUGALL COAT OF ARMS

NICHOLSON COAT OF ARMS

Bibliography

BOOKS
The 1862 Sioux Uprising by Jeffry D. Wert
History of the Counties of Woodbury and Plymouth, Iowa,
    A Warner and Co. Publishers
The True Story of the Spirit Lake Massacre by David L. Bristow
Inkapaduta's Revenge by David L. Bristow
Struble Iowa Centennial, 1890-1990
Annan—From Queen Victoria to Queen Elizabeth by John
    A. Thomson
The Heritage of the Solway Firth by James Irving Hawkins
Annan Now and Then by A. Alex Baylock
Plymouth County History by Freeman (Volume I)
Frontierswomen—the Iowa Experience by Glenda Riley
The Dying Burying the Dead—The Great Famine of Leitrim by
    Gerard MacAtasney
Death Records of Plymouth County Iowa (Book 1 and 3)

ARTICLES AND SOURCES
State Historical Society of Iowa at Iowa City (Iowa land values, 1803-1967)
University of Illinois at Urbana-Champaign (Average value of farmland per acre by state and county, 1850-1982)
Annan's Maritime Connections
Annandale Observer (March 2, 1934)
Iowa Genealogy Trails/Plymouth County
Plymouth County History Book
State Historical Society of Iow—The Palimpset
Janice Alberts for the Northwest Iowa Genealogy Fair
The Iowa Experience, PBS

WEBSITES
www.annan.org/UK
www.teaepicure.com/tea harvest/dates
www.enidia.com/1900 education overview
www.Irelandstory
www.kingsleyia.com/Kingsley, Iowa, Official City website
www.hathitrust.org
www.in2013dollars.com/inflation calculator
www.history.com
www.islayinfo.com
www.marineinsight.com/clipper ships
www.worldhistory.us.com
www.si.edu/inside a sod house
www.worldhistory.us/sod houses/pioneers
www.uni.edu/keeping warm

Bibliography

www.ourdocuments.gov/homestead act of 1862
www.wisconsinhistory.org/Crawford County
www.iowadot.gov/abandoned roads
www.wordpress.com/pioneers/agriculture
www.historyplace.com/Irish potato famine
www.civilwartalks.com/river ferries
www.clydeships.co.uk/John Nicholson ships
www.southbaysail.com/clipper ships
www.sweetteajunkie.com/tea clippers
www.newenglandhistoricalsociety/Irish emigrants guide to surviving the famine ships
www.wyoming.com/Scotland traditional naming patterns
www.oxfordjctgenealogy.com/small towns in Iowa 1870
www.wisconsinhistory.org/early map of Pairie du Chien
www.davidrumsey.com/map of Plymouth county/historical map collection
www.livinghistoryfarms.com/farm life 1930s
www.loc.gov/railroad map of Iowa
www.iagenweb.org/Iowa genealogy
www.lemarsiowa.com/historical museum
www.antiquemapsandprints.com/annan/mouswald
www.uiowa.edu/crossing the Mississippi
www.archives.gov/covered wagon
www.archives.gov/Famine Irish Passenger Record Data File
www.ancestry.com/Warren/McDougall

NEWSPAPERS
Shipping Gazette

Harwarden Independent
Moffat News and Times
Alton Democrat
Le Mars Semi-Weekly Sentinel
Le Mars Sentinel
Dumfries and Galloway Standard
Le Mars Globe Post
Akron Register Tribune
The Ireton Ledger

FACEBOOK GROUP
Annan—Open for Business

This group brought us several valuable contacts from Annan, Scotland, including:
- a man whose father bought Cotton Lodge from Benjamin Nicholson's grandson in 1944. He now lives in the house the Nicholson's inhabited for many years. His great grandfather was a boatbuilder at the Nicholson's Welldale yard and was ship's carpenter for the maiden voyage of the Sarah Nicholson.
- a relative of the Nicholson, still living there and whom we never otherwise would have gotten to know.
- a daughter of John Thomson, who included a chapter on the Nicholson's shipbuilding, and information about Provost Nicholson in his book: Annan from Queen Victoria to Queen Elizabeth.
- several other people that were happy to share information about the Nicholson's in Annan.

Through this site we learned that the people of Annan recognize and appreciate the contribution of the Nicholson's to their town. They have not forgotten the role this family played in the development of the town of Annan. The Annan Harbour Action Group is in the process of securing funding to refurbish a building and create a museum. In it, they intend to feature John and Benjamin Nicholson and their ships.

Respectfully, I will refrain from printing names and contact information in a book, but if you are interested in talking with them, please let me know, and I will ask their permission before I give you their contact information.

FAMILY

We have also included information that was drawn from various collections within the Nicholson and the McDougall family